Emile Durkheim

ON INSTITUTIONAL ANALYSIS

THE HERITAGE OF SOCIOLOGY

A Series Edited by Morris Janowitz

Emile Durkheim

ON INSTITUTIONAL ANALYSIS

Edited, Translated,
and with an Introduction by

MARK TRAUGOTT

THE UNIVERSITY OF CHICAGO PRESS

CHICAGO AND LONDON

The University of Chicago Press, Chicago 60637
The University of Chicago Press, Ltd., London

© 1978 by The University of Chicago
All rights reserved. Published 1978
Paperback edition 1994
Printed in the United States of America
98 97 96 95 94   9 8 7 6 5 4 3 2

Library of Congress Cataloging in Publication Data

Main entry under title:

Emile Durkheim on institutional analysis

(Heritage of sociology)
Includes index.
1. Sociology—Methodology.   2. Durkheim, Emile,
1858–1917.   3. Solidarity.   4. Social institutions.
I. Traugott, Mark.
HM24.E49   301   77-25105
ISBN 0-226-17330-5 (cloth)
ISBN 0-226-17371-2 (paper)

Contents

Acknowledgments

I would like to recognize the assistance I have received from several quarters in the preparation of this work. My longest standing debt is owed to Robert N. Bellah, who encouraged me to undertake this project in the first place. Despite enduring differences in emphasis, the formative influence of his perspective on my own interpretation of Durkheim is readily apparent in the pages which follow. I would also like to thank John Kitsuse for his generous support of a junior colleague, often intimidated by the task at hand. My editor, Morris Janowitz, as well as Walter Goldfrank, Robert K. Merton, and Edward Tiryakian all read a draft of the introduction and provided helpful comments, which I hope I have incorporated to their satisfaction. The flaws which mar the finished product are surely many, but they are my own and would have been still more problematic without this aid.

A Note on the Translations

In general, the task of translating Durkheim's French is quite straightforward. His thought is thoroughly disciplined and arguments flow logically from one point to the next. Durkheim employs a rather standard vocabulary and phraseology, and his style remains consistent even over three decades of intellectual development. While it is quite true that the quality of his prose varies among the works collected in this volume—"The Conjugal Family," "Introduction to *Morality*," and the "Review of Schaeffle" are notably poor in this respect—the lapses occur primarily in texts which have been reconstructed from notes or from drafts never intended for publication.

More typically, Durkheim's style makes up in conciseness for what it lacks in flourish. The writing, like the man himself, exudes sobriety and intensity of purpose. The most common difficulty encountered in rendering Durkheim's prose into English is to temper its sometimes disconcerting stiffness.

Contributors of footnotes to the articles are identified by initials. Those marked "E.D." are Durkheim's own. I have left his elliptical references, often to sources now long out of print, as they appeared in the original, except to indicate those few cases where texts which Durkheim discusses at length now exist in English translation. Those initialed "M.M." are the comments which Marcel Mauss appended to the manuscripts that he edited and published after Durkheim's death. Footnotes initialed "M.T." are my own.

I have also adopted a convention used frequently by Durkheim himself, that of inserting in the text, enclosed within parentheses,

key foreign-language words or phrases. Especially where my translation is highly interpretive, where Durkheim gives to an expression an
idiosyncratic twist, and where no exact English equivalent exists or
quite conveys the full sense of the French, I have called the fact to
the reader's attention in this manner.

Two of the terms which received this treatment deserve further
clarification because each is central to the understanding of several
of the essays collected in this volume. The first is the phrase *la
science sociale*. When Durkheim employs the plural, *les sciences
sociales*, his meaning is nearly identical to the English cognate, "the
social sciences." In the singular, however, the term is usually
synonymous with *la sociologie*, and, indeed, Durkheim, at least in
his earliest publications, employs the two expressions interchangeably. This usage is more easily understood when we recall that
Durkheim's vision of sociology was of a synthetic academic enterprise which would ultimately span the full range of contemporary
social sciences by raising their findings to a higher level of generalization than was possible so long as they remained in isolation.
When applied in this way, the term bears the almost explicitly
Comtian implication that sociology is *the* social science.[1]

The second expression which merits special mention is the French
word *conscience*. The term figures prominently in his work, especially through the concept of *conscience collective* on which he relied
heavily in his earlier writings. It has long been a subject of debate
not merely because of the difficulty of translation but also because
its inherent ambiguity contributes to its pivotal significance in the
development of Durkheim's thought. Here I wish only to consider
the issue it has raised for me as translator and to explain and justify
the course I have adopted.[2]

The crux of the problem is that the French language makes do
with one word where English uses two. *Conscience* has been
rendered by Durkheim's English translators as either "conscience"
or "consciousness." It is true that the French word corresponds to
both these English equivalents. At the same time, it could be said
that the French term corresponds to neither of them, and that to
select one over the other deprives the translation of some of the
essential connotations of the original.

The English word "consciousness" properly conveys the cognitive element of *conscience*.[3] Given a forced choice between the two English equivalents, I believe "consciousness" to be more frequently the correct translation of Durkheim's meaning. But "consciousness" lacks the often equally important emphasis on the normative dimension of *conscience*.

"Conscience," in its current English usage, does convey this normative sense, but all too strongly. In this post-Freudian era, it immediately conjures up images of the constraining inner voice of the super-ego. Such an association, however, runs sharply counter to Durkheim's primary purpose. While Freud clearly recognized the social origins of the super-ego, and while Durkheim just as clearly acknowledged that society's moral order had to be thoroughly internalized by properly socialized individuals, the colloquial meaning of "conscience" has come to be largely psychologistic in its application. Durkheim, on the contrary, used *conscience* to underscore the sense in which a transcendent, externally imposed normative order is the precondition for the individual conscience as such.

The most satisfactory rendering of *conscience*, in almost all instances, would, I believe, be the phrase "moral consciousness." However, not wishing to add to the complexities and confusions which already surround its translation, and since neither simple term would be everywhere appropriate, I have chosen to be inconsistent, employing either "conscience" or "consciousness" as the context of Durkheim's thought seemed to demand.

Finally, a word of caution is in order because of the inclusion of several book reviews among the pieces collected here. Durkheim's style was didactic in the extreme. In composing reviews, it was his habit to provide a lengthy paraphrase of the book's main arguments before passing on to his own analytical comments. Unless this synopsis, which was often presented in the declarative voice of the person being reviewed, is clearly differentiated from Durkheim's own critical remarks (usually but not always or wholly confined to a brief concluding section), the reader risks the most serious misapprehension of Durkheim's true position. The possibility for error is heightened by the fact that Durkheim tended to develop in the early part of the review precisely those ideas he intended to attack most vigorously at the end. To help avoid this sort of confusion I have, where appropriate, inserted extra space at the point at which Durkheim changes voices and begins his personal commentary. *Caveat lector.*

Introduction

This volume presents translations of a selection of related Durkheim writings, most of them new to the English language. Read in conjunction with the fresh primary and secondary sources which have recently appeared, they underscore the continuing relevance of Durkheim's work. The remarks which follow are directed primarily to the distinctive strengths of the writings collected here, but a few unifying themes help place these selections in the larger context of Durkheim's total oeuvre. Chief among these are the vitality and clarity of Durkheim's conception of sociology, the coherence provided in his work by the study of social solidarity, the synthesis he effected of materialist and idealist analyses as elements of a structural-functionalist perspective, and the personal and political stance which characterized his research.

DURKHEIM'S VISION OF SOCIOLOGY

The logic of Durkheim's intellectual development can hardly be understood apart from his all-consuming commitment to the founding of a discipline which came in France to be so closely associated with his name. Durkheim was a crusader, from the beginning to the end of his career, for the acceptance of sociology in academic circles. Alpert aptly terms him a *Berufsmensch*, one called to speak and to spread his personal gospel.[1] There is ample indication that Durkheim conceived of himself in just this way. Bouglé, a friend, disciple, and fellow editor of *L'Année sociologique*, composed the following reminiscence some years after Durkheim's death. "Contained vehemence and controlled trepidation—these, it always seemed to me, were the principal characteristics of Durkheim's eloquence. One perceived in him the fire of a preacher. Once, as we were passing before Notre Dame, this son of a rabbi asked, with a smile: 'Is it from a rostrum like that that I should speak?' "[2]

Rarely has a personal campaign of this type been pursued with such success. Durkheim's own career defined the progress of sociology's early years in the French academy. In 1887 the university at Bordeaux offered the system's first class in "social science," one created expressly for Durkheim. His successful defense of his doctoral thesis in 1893 "was taken to indicate a victory for the new science of sociology over the traditionalists at the Sorbonne," who sought in vain to inject a measure of humility into the claims Durkheim made for the discipline's future.[3] In 1896 he was awarded France's first professorship in social science. Two years later he founded *L'Année sociologique*, which functioned until 1913 as an organ for the dissemination of his perspective, as a center for the recruitment of a circle of outstanding disciples, and as a research institute of recognized excellence. Durkheim's meteoric rise was capped by his appointment at the Sorbonne in 1902 and consolidated in 1913 when he was able to arrange to have his chair rededicated as a professorship in the "Science of Education and Sociology" and, thus, to achieve the official recognition for which he had long struggled. Together, Durkheim and the discipline of sociology had arrived, both in the intellectual community and in relation to a growing public audience.

Proposed Organization of the Field

The precocity and consistency of Durkheim's vision of sociology is highlighted by the first two essays of this collection, which sketch the field's compass and suggest the lines of its future development. The first is the "Opening Lecture" delivered in Durkheim's 1887 course on "Social Solidarity" which, in Terry Clark's words, "marked the beginning of a structural differentiation of sociology in the university from the established discipline of philosophy."[4] In the second, published more than two decades later, in 1909, Durkheim's position on the origins, proper organization, and objectives of sociology remained substantially the same.

It is hardly accidental that the five categories into which Durkheim divided the field of sociology in his early formulation roughly correspond to the rubrics used to organize this volume. They are social psychology, morality, law, criminology, and economic phenomena. The conception of the discipline he presents, less systematic than the position he had developed by the time of the 1909 essay, is still notable for its exposition of the author's working assumptions, including a brief summary of his structural-functional precepts. He spells out the nature of the interdependence of the form and content of social institutions and the advantages of a research strategy which seeks to establish the correspondences in the evolution of the two over time.[5] Despite his recognition of their gross equivalence, Durkheim insisted on the ultimate priority of function over structure, an assumption which consistently guided his own research. In his attempt to develop the subtleties of this relationship, Durkheim arrived at the following enunciation of the doctrine, which today would be termed unintended or unanticipated consequences.

> Among lower organisms there exists a narrow and rigid relationship between the organ and the function. A modification in the function is impossible unless it produces a corresponding change in the organ. The latter is set in its role because it is fixed in its structure. But it is not the same with the superior functions of superior beings. Here the structure is so flexible that it is no longer an obstacle to changes: it can happen that an organ or a part of an organ accomplishes different functions. We know that among living organisms different lobes of the brain can replace each other with great facility; but it is above all among societies that this phenomenon manifests itself most strikingly. Again and again, we find that social institutions, once created, serve ends which no one foresaw.[6]

In encountering such passages, the reader is torn between the pleasant twinge of recognition of what has become an everyday sociological concept and the sinking feeling that we are condemned to elaborate—with far greater sophistication, we are quick to reassure ourselves—the offhand remarks of sociology's classical exponents. His numerous anticipations of what we think of as contemporary tenets are at once a measure of the power of

Durkheim's thought and of its formative influence upon the modern discipline. Can we doubt that this 1887 artifact of sociology's past would, in its essentials, stand up remarkably well as an introductory lecture today?

Yet in any direct comparison, "Sociology and the Social Sciences" is the superior piece. It provides us with a more mature and finished statement of the internal organization of the field. In Durkheim's three-way division, Comte's distinction between social statics and dynamics has been superseded by the more promising dialectic of morphology and physiology, or structure and function. A third category, general sociology, reflects Durkheim's desire to distill from empirical study the principles and laws which rule the social world.[7] Here we also find those brief asides of mainly antiquarian interest: Durkheim's rather naive celebration of strict (natural) scientific objectivity; an elaboration of the extremely fecund notion of freedom as conformity to law and the product of constraint which he developed more fully in *Moral Education*; and the amusing contortions to which he is led by his desire to differentiate sociology from all related disciplines which might threaten its independence and at the same time to lay claim on its behalf, with a sort of rampant academic imperialism which is still very much with us, to an ultimately superordinate status. Durkheim tended to perceive himself and his discipline as embattled on many fronts. In his review of Schaeffle, for example, he rejects the wholesale appropriation of biological analogies as ultimately reductionist and destructive of the unique contribution which it was sociology's destiny to make. For similar reasons, he criticized the perspective of economists as varied as the liberals and utilitarians on the one hand and materialist socialists on the other. In "Sociology and the Social Sciences" he leveled much the same objections at the psychological perspective according to which the social world represented a mere summing of individual characteristics. And he attacked history for having failed to attain the high level of generalization of which, with the help of sociology, it was capable. But even as he defended his discipline against attempts to reduce its import, he kept in constant view the role which its distinctive outlook and methodology preordained it to fulfill in synthesizing the various strands of the social science tradition.

Methodological Orientation and the Sociological Use of History

The sociological literature has placed great stress on Durkheim's role as precursor of the quantitative tradition. "Divorce by Mutual Consent" further justifies this association. In it, Durkheim revives Bertillon's observation that in all Europe the rates of suicide and divorce covary despite the cultural and related differences represented by national boundaries. Durkheim's argument builds upon the determinitive effects of religious affiliation and national origin which he had established in *Suicide*. The article on divorce, in fact, parallels that earlier classic both in its general substantive focus and in its unerring anticipation of the logic of multivariate analysis.[8]

In order to discount the possibility of spuriousness in Bertillon's assertion, Durkheim makes use of the technique of internal replication. Dropping down to a unit of analysis, the Swiss canton, smaller and more homogenous than the nation-state, he is able to discriminate among and control for the known effects of a range of potentially confounding variables. This respecification of the unit analysis allowed him to set bounds upon what we would today call the ecology fallacy.[9] By instituting a series of ingenious controls, first by sex and then by marital status and urban or rural residence, Durkheim goes on to construct a convincing case that a certain moral climate, which is responsible for elevated rates of divorce, also underlies the increased tendency to self-destruction. With little more than descriptive statistics and his personal flair for causal argument, Durkheim has outlined the conceptual model of much modern quantitative analysis.

But statistical techniques were but one weapon in Durkheim's sociological arsenal. In America especially, the identification of his methodology with the quantitative tradition has sometimes fostered the false impression that his work was largely ahistorical.[10] Yet when Durkheim considers the problem of social science methodology, he thinks first, not in terms of statistical techniques, but in terms of comparative history, "the only instrument of which the sociologist disposes" to gain intellectual leverage in analyzing institutions. The student of societies, he argues, enjoys none of the privileges of the natural scientist in dealing with his chosen topic of inquiry. Only history can overcome the practical or ethical constraints inherent in social research and establish controls, both through time and across cultural boundaries. It does so by exploiting natural variations in social forms. History, then, becomes the social science equivalent of the experimental method.[11]

The type of history which Durkheim envisions is, of course, different in important respects from that practiced by the discipline of that name. The latter attempted to explain particular and idiosyncratic events. Durkheim, however, proposed to bend historical studies to his own purposes. Sociology, he tells us, is

> in large part a form of history which has been extended in a certain way. The historian also deals with social facts; but he considers, above all, the way in which they are peculiar to a determinate people and time. In general, he proposes to study the life of a given nation or a given collective individuality taken at a given moment in its evolution. His immediate task is to rediscover and to characterize the particular, individual physiognomy of each society and even of each of the periods which comprise the life of a single society. The sociologist sticks solely to discovering the general relationships and verifiable laws of different societies. He does not especially try to find out what religious life or property law was like in France or England, in Rome or in India, in a particular century; but these specialized studies, which are, moreover, indispensable to him, are but the means of arriving at the discovery of a few of the factors of religious life in general. We have only one way to demonstrate that a logical relationship (for example, a causal relationship) exists between two facts; we would have to compare cases in which they are simultaneously present or absent and to see if the variations which they present in these different combinations of circumstances bear witness to the dependence of one on the other.[12]

This program of historical study was no mere idealization posed in the abstract, but a concrete strategy of investigation of which Durkheim offers us several elegant applications.

Durkheim's sociology of the family presents a case in point. While this was a topic of lively interest to him, and while he made frequent reference to it in his major books and in many review essays, the three articles which comprise part five of this collection are the only substantial texts in which he deals primarily with the family. "Divorce by Mutual Consent," as we have seen, adopted a quantitative approach. But "Introduction to the Sociology of the Family," an outline of the strategy of inquiry which Durkheim employed in his 1888 course on that subject, highlighted the utility of historical study for placing in relief long-term developmental tendencies. "The Conjugal Family" is simply the faithful application of that method to the problem of the emergence of the modern nuclear family from its antecedent forms. These early articles offer glimpses of arguments Durkheim would later develop in his major books. "Introduction to the Sociology of the Family," for example, sketched the distinction between mechanical and organic solidarity and employed customary and legal practices as indicators of the state of social integration. In addition to its use of suicide rates to illustrate the diffuse integrative functions of the family unit, "The Conjugal Family" introduced the concept of the occupational group or "corporation" as a potential palliative of the moral crisis of modern societies. Here, as in "Introduction to *Morality*" and "Two Laws," Durkheim's generalizations were grounded in his extensive reading of the historical and ethnographic sources then available. These articles testify with eloquence to the prominent role Durkheim assigned to the comparative historical method.

The Possibility of Integrated Social Science

Durkheim's efforts to define the place of sociology within the social sciences had a dual thrust, the contradictions of which he managed only loosely to resolve. On the one hand, he struggled to differentiate his discipline from all others with which it shared substantive or methodological interests. His was, he believed, an age of specialization in which the advantages of an academic division of labor were not to be denied. Yet at the same time, he aspired to an eventual reconciliation of the social sciences in which sociology would assume its predestined role as orchestrator of a grand intellectual synthesis. Of future relations between sociology and history, for example, he declares himself convinced that they are destined to become ever more intimate and that a day will come when the historical spirit and the sociological spirit will differ only in nuances. In effect, the sociologist can proceed in his comparisons and inductions only on the condition of knowing well and from close up the particular facts which he relies upon, just like the historian; and, on the other hand, the concrete reality which the historian studies can be most directly clarified by the results of sociological inductions. If, then, in what precedes we have differentiated history and sociology, it was not in order to raise an impassable barrier between these two disciplines, since they are, on the contrary, called upon to become more and more closely integrated; it was only in order to characterize as exactly as possible what the sociological perspective possesses in its own right.[13]

The convergence of sociology with history would be duplicated not only with closely related disciplines like psychology and anthropology, but also in fields as diverse as geography, political economy, and demography.

Thus, Durkheim's crusade for the institutionalization of the discipline was fought on two fronts. The essays in part 1 are a record of his determination to rescue sociology from the confusing welter of what had previously been termed "philosophy." But it is also possible to see his efforts as aiming at the reintegration of the three component elements into which that primordial matter had, from the time of the Middle Ages, come to be divided. Stealing a page from "Natural Philosophy," he sought to establish the "organic" character of the social world. For if that world is simply another aspect of our ordered universe, then it, too, is subject to scientific scrutiny. The objective methods developed in the natural sciences could, therefore, be adapted to yield sociological laws.

From "Political Philosophy" Durkheim appropriated his unit of analysis. The idea that, viewed in their totality, social phenomena constitute a working system he traced back to the classical economists and utilitarians. Indeed, he criticized them, and by extension, all liberal political economy, for having left this insight undeveloped and accepted the limitations of an individualistic unit of analysis. They had dimly perceived the intimate relationship of parts but failed to recognize the emergent character of the social whole, which only sociological analysis could bring to the fore.

"Moral Philosophy" contributed the crowning element in this new synthesis. From it he borrowed sociology's ultimate objective, the creation of a reinvigorated normative order. Drawing upon its inspiration, sociology would teach us the benefits which accrue from life in a well-ordered social system and the basis for enlightened intervention in the crisis confronting modern society.

This fusion of elements yielded a vision of sociology from which Durkheim never allowed himself to be deflected. Each of his major books represents a renewed attack, conceived from some fresh angle, on an old problem. Even his less accessible work, as this collection tries to show, converges in the attempt to resolve what is, at bottom, a single issue. With only minor divergences but endless variation, Durkheim returns to what constitutes the core of his sociology, the explication of social solidarity.

SOCIAL SOLIDARITY

In the inaugural course in social science, Durkheim spoke of social solidarity as the "initial problem" which sociology must address. Its importance in Durkheim's conceptual scheme cannot be overstated. Sociology was for Durkheim not to be defined in terms of the substantive nature of its objects of study. Rather, it consisted in a distinctive analytical style or mode of inquiry which could be applied to the most diverse kinds of human behavior. The discipline's crucial distinguishing characteristic was its adoption of a group perspective. Though far from consistent in applying this tenet, Durkheim clearly stated that as a matter of principle, truly *social* behavior occurs only when an individual or group acts with a subjective sense, whether or not conscious or willing, of solidarity with others. The emergent phenomena which are sociology's special province result from a process of interaction. Social facts, precisely because they are exterior to and constraining upon the individual, presume the existence of integrating bonds. These bonds lift purely individual acts to a new level where qualitatively different principles of operation apply. It is undeniable that society acts only through individuals; yet sociology's distinctive task is to demonstrate how individual behavior is itself the product of social forces. These are principles which Durkheim never ceased to reiterate.

The existence of integrative bonds is the great *sine qua non* for the application of Durkheim's sociological method. It is also the necessary precondition of fruitful relations between individual and society. He is quick to elaborate the moral and philosophical implications of these axioms. While highly critical of "metaphysicians" who begin with an idealization of individual human nature to arrive at a complete explanation of the proper means and ends of social life, it is possible to discover the Durkheimian equivalent of such assumptions. For him the individual is innately endowed with an insatiable appetite for an elusive sense of satisfaction, yet capable of generating only finite energy in the pursuit of potentially infinite desires. Left to himself, this individual cannot distinguish between ends which are possible and healthy and those which lead only to ennui and exhaustion on the one hand or anxiety and anomie on the other. Durkheim's explanation of the salutary influence of marriage upon husbands is entirely in keeping with his general view of the moral influence of social regulation.

> Marriage, by subjecting the passions to regulation, gives the man a moral posture which increases his forces of resistance. By assigning a definite, determinate, and in principle invariable object to his desires, it prevents them from wearing themselves out in the pursuit of ends which are always new and always changing, which grow boring as soon as they are achieved and which leave only exhaustion and disenchantment in their wake. It prevents the heart from becoming excited and tormenting itself vainly in the search for impossible or deceptive happiness; it makes easier that peace of mind, that inner balance which are the essential conditions of moral health and happiness. But it only produces these effects because it implies a respected form of regulation which creates social bonds among individuals.[14]

Durkheim's conception of freedom follows logically from this perspective. The old minimalist conceptions, which defined freedom and constraint as polar opposites, are anathema to him. What could be more simplistic, he asks, than to believe that acts which violate limits imposed by our inner nature or by the nature of the physical or social worlds in which we live, could somehow enhance our lives? Of the person who loses all sense of self in a steadfast refusal to accept any given definition of self, as of the person who steps in front of an onrushing locomotive or fails to abide by elementary taboos, we say not that they are free but that they are insane. Durkheim's equation of freedom and constraint is a dialectic subtly attuned to the modern consciousness of the individual's place in an enveloping social fabric.

Out of both scientific and moral convictions, then, Durkheim turned in his earliest work to the study of social solidarity. His first assault on the problem, the formulation that led to *The Division of Labor in Society*, was more direct than the approach adopted in his later writing. From the delineation of mechanical and organic solidarity, Durkheim derived both a typology of forms of social integration and what he hesitantly believed to be an empirically observable developmental trend. Yet, as a review of some of the writings collected in this volume will quickly demonstrate, his position was never frozen in the form in which it appeared in his first book.

Mechanical and Organic Social Forms

In Durkheim's review of Schaeffle, the first writing which he published, he employed the terms "mechanical" and "organic." However, at that early point in the development of his thought, he was more intent on assessing the worth of organismic analogies, and the labels carried none of the specific meaning he later attached to them. It was only in 1888, with the publication of "Introduction to the Sociology of the Family," that he discussed the concepts of mechanical and organic integration which he had worked out in the course on social solidarity offered in the previous year. The first, of course, produces cohesion in the social group based on similarities among its members; the second achieves the same end through the interdependencies induced by individual differences. He treats these forms as ideal types, never fully realized in any specific instance, yet clearly recognizable as the principles of organization of primitive and modern societies, respectively. He is careful to point out that neither ever exists in the total absence of the other, but the reader is left with the unmistakable impression that organic solidarity has tended historically to gain ascendancy, almost to the point of exclusion of mechanical. He pauses only long enough to suggest the dynamic by which the former has achieved its dominion. As later elaborated in *The Division of Labor*, this process begins with an increase in "social volume" (sheer demographic mass) which leads in turn to a simultaneous increase in "social density" (the rate of social interaction), itself reinforced by such factors as the improved communications and concentration of population in urban areas which the growth of the social network makes possible. This denser social milieu engenders competition and its natural consequence, differentiation of function. Thus, for Durkheim the division of labor is not the ultimate cause but merely a mediating variable through which the change to modern social forms becomes both possible and necessary.

The timing of this published account leaves no doubt that Durkheim's ideas predate his exposure to Tönnies' *Gemeinschaft und Gesellschaft*, which appeared in 1887. This convergence in their thought is truly striking. But, as ever, it was to the fine distinctions which separate their positions that Durkheim devoted his attention when he reviewed Tönnies' work for the 1889 edition of *Revue philosophique*.[15] From it we receive an answer to a question with which undergraduate students of sociological theory have long plagued their instructors, namely, why Durkheim, contrary to common sense, assigned the term "mechanical" to simple social aggregates still closely tied to nature, while reserving the label "organic" for the complex industrialized nations of the present day. Durkheim explains his choice of terms by way of criticizing Tönnies for allegedly characterizing *Gesellschaft* as a derivative and artificial type of society which requires the aid of the state to guarantee its very existence.[16]

The notion that societies are manmade and artificial Durkheim considered to have been among the greatest obstacles to the founding of the sociological enterprise. For if society were no more than a human creation, it would be subject to change by direct intervention and could, in principle, be unmade just as it had been made. But an object thus the product of sheer will and whimsy would surely prove neither susceptible to nor worthy of scientific study.[17] Precisely to counter the imputation that contemporary society is any less natural than its antecedents, he labeled it "organic" and aptly likened its method of achieving cohesion through differentiation to the relationship which holds among the organs of a living body. He applied the term "mechanical" to a type of society still close enough to a state of nature for there to be no question of its organic quality. In this context, the label "mechanical" is used to suggest a purely physical juxtaposition of homogenous, self-sufficient, and therefore semi-independent units.[18] Only by thus deliberately controverting the usual associations of the terms could he first underscore his view that both forms of solidarity are natural phenomena and then go on to suggest the lines of continuity which linked the two.

Durkheim wavers between the opinion that the *conscience collective*, the fund of common beliefs and sentiments which makes possible mechanical integration on the basis of resemblances, is contracting and destined finally to disappear, and the alternative view that it continues to exist under organic solidarity by undergoing a transformation in its content and a redefinition of the scope of its jurisdiction to the smaller subunits where primary relations retain their vigor. It is true that even in the earliest presentation of the ideal types, Durkheim is careful to qualify the inference that a direct developmental relationship links the two by stating that, "... it might, strictly speaking, be possible to say that neither of these two types of solidarity has ever existed without the other ..."[19] But just as frequently, Durkheim treats mechanical and organic forms as sequential states of social development. In effect, we are forced to choose between what Durkheim says and what he does. On the one hand, Durkheim was intellectually committed to a variety of cultural relativism and strenuously objected to any linear ordering of social forms.

> Today it is manifestly impossible to maintain that there is a human evolution which is everywhere identical and that societies are all just different versions of a single and identical type ...

Zoology has already renounced the linear classification whose extreme simplicity once seduced scholars. It is increasingly accepted that the genealogical tree of organized beings, instead of having the form of a geometric line, resembles more nearly a very bushy tree whose branches, issuing haphazardly all along the trunk, shoot out capriciously in all directions. It is the same way with societies. Despite Pascal's famous formulation, which Comte wrongly revives, humanity cannot be compared to a solitary man who has lived all these past centuries and still survives. Rather it resembles an immense family, the various branches of which, as they diverge more and more from one another, gradually detach themselves from the common source to live their own lives.[20]

But at the same time, the adjectives "primitive," "inferior," and "lower," which were all part of Durkheim's working vocabulary, betray his view that modern European society represented the most advanced and therefore "perfect" institutional structure known. He tells us that it is "certain that, if the genealogical table of social types could be completely drawn up, it would resemble a tufted tree, with a single trunk, to be sure, but with diverging branches. However, in spite of this tendency, the distance between two branches is measurable; they are higher or lower. Surely we have the right to say of a type that it is above another when it began with the form of the latter and yet has gone above it."[21] It is impossible to ignore the implicit assumption of a slow developmental sequence which informs all his work or the use which he makes of the concept of social differentiation as a yardstick of its progress.

Durkheim's later work, in fact, demonstrates his desire to resolve these ambiguities. For example, in "Individualism and the Intellectuals," he contended, in a seemingly paradoxical inversion of his original argument, that the modern drive toward individualism, which began by apparently setting us apart, would end by constituting the principal shared value.[22] Individualism itself would become the sole remaining common ground on which to base a reinvigorated moral order. Thus, Durkheim's position on the character and causes of social solidarity continued to evolve. Nowhere is the dynamism of his conception more apparent than in his writings on legal and penal institutions.

Changes in the Durkheimian View of Penal Evolution

In *The Division of Labor* Durkheim used as indicator of diffuse states of social integration, inaccessable to direct measurement, the type of legal system to which they give rise. He delineated, to be precise, systems of law dominated by repressive and restitutive sanctions, corresponding to mechanical and organic solidarity, respectively. Or so he argues. For here, as in *Suicide* and *The Elementary Forms*, the power of his conceptualization survives despite the flaws of the data on which he based his generalizations. Modern evidence indicates that Durkheim's hypothesis regarding penal evolution is seriously deficient, and that no simple transition from one to the other type of punishment, such as he described, accompanies social differentiation and modernization.

The argument of *The Division of Labor* rests in part on an array of cases of societies in which repressive codes predominate. Many of these were drawn in a highly selective fashion from the category of nonindustrial societies and incorrectly labeled "primitive." The Hebraic and Roman systems, on which Durkheim relies most heavily, are particularly problematic, for while these societies did retain a tribal or clanic base, they already possessed the rudiments of central state organization and a not negligible degree of internal social differentiation.[23] Thus, the scheme of classification which Durkheim used to order his observations is immediately called into question.

This criticism would be devastating if the position it attacks represented Durkheim's final word on the subject. But only recently have sociologists begun to assimilate the important advances which he later made in his theory of legal sanctions, particularly in "Two Laws of Penal Evolution."[24] In that crucial reworking of his ideas, first published in the 1900 edition of *L'Année sociologique*, we find Durkheim groping toward a reformulation which answers some of the objections leveled by critics familiar only with *The Division of Labor*.

In "Two Laws of Penal Evolution" the simple opposition of repressive and restitutive sanctions is discarded in favor of a classification of crimes into those fundamentally "religious" in nature—that is, those which strike at the shared moral tenets which constitute the remnants of what Durkheim had earlier termed the collective consciousness—and those which are "individual" in the sense of involving the essentially private interests of increasingly autonomous individuals. Penal sanctions are seen as varying not only quantitatively in terms of intensity, but also qualitatively from corporal punishment toward the exclusive reliance upon privation of freedom. The latter development is intimately connected with the material changes which accompany social differentiation. On the one hand, more primitive social forms possess neither the resources for nor the physical means of incarcerating suspects and convicts. But they experience no need for prisons as a form of punishment, since their moral code permits the use of severely repressive measures which in modern societies are proscribed by the respect which is accorded the individual, criminal as well as victim. In stressing the causal impact of general social development on legal and penal institutions, Durkheim is in one sense extending the logic of *The Division of Labor*.[25] The thesis of "Two Laws," however, gains in sophistication from the introduction of a new constellation of independent variables.

The first law of penal evolution, that of quantitative variation, has two parts. On the one hand, Durkheim continues to assert that the mitigation of penal law accompanies the advance of social differentiation. But this underlying secular tendency is now seen as long-term and gradual in its elaboration, and he concedes that it may be opposed by and even submerged beneath the more immediate effects of variations in political institutions. To the extent that governmental power is absolute—that is, concentrated in an agency which encounters no countervailing limitation from other quarters in society—punishments themselves become more severe. Thus, Durkheim has introduced a second category of determinative forces, political in nature, the inclusion of which responds to the inadequacies of the original thesis.

Yet even as he came to acknowledge the importance of the political dimension, Durkheim perpetuated two errors which deprived his insight of much of its potential for clarification. The first is that Durkheim continued to insist that changes in his two explanatory variables, the level of social differentiation and of political centralization, are independent rather than systematically interactive.[26] He even asserted that the former are truly determinative, the latter derivative and almost epiphenomenal. Modern evidence, on the contrary, indicates that social and political differentiation are intimately related and that the influence of political factors directly affects the penal system.

This discrepancy is compounded by a second flaw in Durkheim's reasoning, really an extension of the sampling problem already encountered in *The Division of Labor*. While the range of Durkheim's examples in "Two Laws" is considerably broadened, he still employs an essentially dichotomous classification of social types, which fails to make certain distinctions crucial to the interpretation of patterns of penal evolution. The legal systems of "primitive" societies are not, as Durkheim argues, everywhere dominated by repressive sanctions; nor do religious crimes "comprise, almost to the exclusion of all others, the penal law of lower societies ..."[27] In fact, where kinship groups remain vital, the principle of collective responsibility makes even a crime such as homicide a civil wrong which can be rectified by compensating the relatives of the victim.[28] While important variations occur, truly primitive societies appear to rely disproportionately on the principle of restitution.[29]

Nor is a society's rise from the ranks of "lower" social forms uniformly accompanied by a moderation in its use of punishment. On the contrary, the emergence of centralized political authority which is, Durkheim notwithstanding, the natural concomitant of differentiation in other social spheres, is typically associated with an increase in the extent and intensity of repressive law. In its formative period, the state, whether the result of internal development or an imposition of imperial powers, defines new crimes and redefines as criminal many offenses which were previously treated as purely civil matters. It engages in this criminalization of the law both in order to assert hegemony in its struggle with traditional institutions and in order to exercise regulatory control over its new subjects, not yet accustomed to rendering it the proper respect and obedience. At the same time, because the growth of the state undermines the preexisting, local legal institutions oriented to restitutive justice, the shift toward repressive law is exaggerated. The colonial experience of the late nineteenth and the twentieth centuries has provided a far more complete basis for generalization concerning the dynamic of this transitional stage than was available to Durkheim.

At a further stage of development, when the authority of the state has been affirmed, further social differentiation makes possible a renewed reliance on more flexible restitutive sanctions.[30] The saliency of "human" crime and civil law increases. This pattern suggests that the course of penal evolution is not linear, as Durkheim contended, but curvilinear; and that it depends not solely on diffuse social development, but, more particularly, on the changes in the political sphere, which Durkheim had begun to recognize in "Two Laws."

The discrepancies in Durkheim's analysis can be largely reconciled by a trichotomous categorization of societies according to whether state organization is essentially absent, rudimentary, or advanced. This helps correct the error of *The Division of Labor*, where exceptions to the rule of penal moderation were seen as representing perturbations of an underlying trend, rather than a meaningful pattern in their own right. Where consensus and internal coherence are high—either in the case of homogeneous stateless social units or of complex societies with highly articulated political institutions—a moderate penal system predominates. In the transitional phase between these two extremes, where competing principles of social cohesion and antagonistic institutional forms are locked in combat, legal sanctions are fiercely repressive.

This reinterpretation of the evolution of penal systems casts a new light on Durkheim's line of reasoning. At first glance, it would seem plausible, according to the argument advanced in *The Division of Labor*, to expect precisely the development we have just outlined. For if repressive sanctions are exacted by mechanically organized societies in order to reaffirm the validity of core beliefs, then we would anticipate a peak of repression at that point when the collective consciousness is under sharpest attack, that is, in the transitional phase. This seems to suggest that Durkheim's hypothesis, muddled by improper use of fragmentary data, could yet be made compatible with the observed pattern of penal evolution.

However, closer examination reveals that when repressive sanctions are invoked in the intermediate stage, it is not in the name of traditional values and institutions but rather on behalf of the "modern" forces which seek the former's overthrow. Increasingly severe legal codes are a weapon employed by the emerging state to consolidate the position of both the organically organized social structure and of the differentiated individual over the formerly powerful community of primary relations. Durkheim's case for the symbolic role of penal sanctions in homogenous societies remains compelling, as far as it goes. However, it seems to ignore the equally significant instrumental and regulatory function which they may also provide, especially in those very periods when the existence of a social or moral consensus is most problematic.

Reprise of the Scientific Study of Morality in the "Later Period"

Durkheim's interest in the many-faceted problem of social solidarity never waned. It did, however, continually adopt new forms, the most significant of which was the increasingly central role which religious phenomena were to enjoy in his conceptual framework. Durkheim himself perceived this shift in emphasis as a turning point in the evolution of his perspective. "It was only in 1895 that I gained a clear sense of the capital role which religion plays in social life. It was in that year that I found for the first time the means of approaching in a sociological way the study of religion. This was a revelation for me. This course of 1895 establishes a line of demarcation in the development of my thought and to such a point that all my previous research had to be reworked all over again in order to be placed in harmony with these new views."[31] But this change was a matter of degree, not of kind, and *The Elementary Forms of the Religious Life*, the outstanding work of Durkheim's later years, hardly constitutes a departure from his earlier concerns. Indeed, as early as the period in which *The Division of Labor in Society* was composed, Durkheim appears to have developed in skeletal form his thesis on the origins of religion. In the latter book he criticized the theory of Fustel de Coulanges along lines which clearly foreshadow the arguments he was to elaborate twenty years later. "M. Fustel de Coulanges has discovered that the primitive organization of societies was of a familial nature and that, on the other hand, the constitution of the primitive family had religion for its basis. However, he has mistaken the cause for the effect. Having postulated the religious idea, without deriving it from anything, he has deduced from it the social arrangements he observed, while, on the contrary, it is these latter that explain the power and nature of the religious idea."[32] Thus, in *The Elementary Forms* Durkheim was engaged in completing an intellectual program he had sketched for himself at the very outset of his career and from which he never deviated in any lasting fashion. The keystone of this conceptual edifice, which Durkheim barely had time to begin, was to be the work entitled *Morality*.

Only the first two parts of the introductory volume of this study survive, and those in the form of an unpolished draft. Mauss has indicated the direction this work would have taken by reconstructing its general outline from the lecture notes of Durkheim's course on "The Physics of Mores," which Durkheim had set out to use as a guide in his writing. The remainder of the first volume would have raised criticisms of traditional conceptions of morality, in particular those of Tarde and Kant. It would have gone on to consider the role of values and ideals in the construction of a moral code and the importance of the notion of autonomy for reconciling the demands of modern individualism with the authority of a moral system imposed by society.[33] He would have stressed the superiority of the scientist's objective, empirical approach to the issues of morality over the value-laden introspective or metaphysical orientation of the philosophers.

In Durkheim's view, moral concepts are historically and culturally specific—that is, tied to the specific conditions in which men live. Yet they are not, for all that, fixed and unchanging within any given social setting. Those who see his work as a shallow exaltation of the status quo will perhaps be surprised to find him insisting that "all life is change and is refractory to static states," or be pleased to discover the warmth and enthusiasm with which he observes that "only eras morally divided are inventive in moral affairs." It is in dealing with morality that Durkheim comes closest to an explicit notion of sociological praxis.

Durkheim was critical of disciplines concerned solely with

normative considerations, with what *should be*.[34] The first task of any science must be to know and understand *what is*. Only upon this solid foundation can programs and ideals be constructed with assurance.[35] The realms of thought and action must, of course, eventually find their synthesis in a creative enterprise which employs both ethics and morality. The latter are, so to speak, the science and art of moral affairs, the one concerned with the investigation of past and present, the other with their projection into the future. The contribution of sociology in its formative period had, for the most part, been limited to the preliminary task of establishing empirical correspondences among patterns of social behavior. In sketching the role his discipline was to play in the rehabilitation of society's moral order, Durkheim resurrects the phrase "a science born yesterday," the very words he had used in his opening lecture some thirty years previous. But now, he suggests, the moment has arrived when sociology can do more than inventory observations of social behavior; it is at last prepared to emerge from the wings and fulfill its proper destiny as society's guide in the construction of new institutional forms which will meet the challenge of modern social conditions.

Precisely because sociology engages in the analysis of social facts, the external and constraining manifestation of social order, it cannot finally escape a normative orientation. There is reason to doubt that the several volumes which Durkheim projected for *Morality*, a work which he surely realized his health would prevent him from seeing to completion, would have broken this new ground and permitted sociology to transcend its more humble scientific role.[36] However, as an expression of hope and confidence in an intellectual venture he had done so much to nurture, this last statement on an issue of undying concern stands as Durkheim's testament to those sociologists who aspire through their work to transform society in its most fundamental aspect.

DURKHEIM'S ENCOUNTER WITH SOCIALISM AND TRANSCENDENCE OF THE MATERIALIST/IDEALIST DICHOTOMY

Durkheim's interpreters have tended to stress the idealist character of his thought, especially as evinced by his later writings. This judgment often seems based on no more profound reason than that he grew increasingly preoccupied with the integrative role of religion and morality. The fact remains that over the entire course of his career, Durkheim adopted a variety of tactics in confronting the problem of social order and solidarity; he focused attention on both the ideal and material determinants of the forces which bind the individual within the social context. Several of the writings collected in this volume demonstrate Durkheim's reliance on a materialist vein of analysis and permit us to strike a more judicious balance in the assessment of his work. From such a reexamination emerges not only an enlarged view of his conceptual repertory but also insight into the origins and synthetic power of his structural-functionalist position.

Of course, Durkheim employed materialist analysis as one among many approaches and never ascribed to it any ultimate superiority over alternative strategies of research. Furthermore, he practiced what we might call a "generic" materialism, which can be broadly defined as an explanatory framework wherein the more concrete and "objective" elements are seen as causes of those which are more abstract and conceptual. His approach remained utterly distinct from that of economic or historical materialism. For this reason, it is quite consistent to maintain that, although materialism played a role of the first order in his theories, Durkheim's personal reaction to and rejection of the Marxist perspective is an important point of reference in understanding his intellectual system.

Sociology and Socialism

Durkheim's relationship to socialism, and to the Marxist variant in particular, can be surmised from such fragments of his published writings as the reviews of Labriola and Richard which appear below. These constitute a necessary complement to *Socialism* which, to the surprise of the modern reader, deals almost exclusively with the so-called utopians of the French tradition. These reviews make clear that Durkheim's reservations were first intellectual and only secondarily political. Indeed, from the time of his matriculation at the Ecole Normale and his association with such figures as Jean Jaurès and Lucien Herr, and still more through his involvement in the Dreyfus affair, Durkheim grew toward a staunch Republicanism colored with strong socialist overtones. Yet he was always careful to maintain an attitude of skepticism toward the specifically intellectual pretensions of what remained for him an ideology. On this account he made his position quite clear. "Of socialism, viewed as a theory of social facts, sociology has only one statement to make: it must, as a point of methodology and in order to remain true to itself, refuse to view it as a scientific enterprise."[37] In this typically condescending assessment of the intellectual merits of socialist doctrines, Durkheim belies his true motives. It is sociology, the academic vocation for which he served as spokesman, which he wished to preserve from the taint of mere ideological controversy. Socialism was that much more dangerous a rival because it falsely purported to explain social facts in an objective manner.

This is not to say that socialist formulations are without interest to the sociologist. Quite the contrary, he argued, they constitute a social fact in their own right, and one deeply revealing of the character of modern social life. But their significance often lies concealed even from their most ardent advocates, and can be revealed only in the cold light of objective analysis. Socialism may surely provide grist for the analytical mill of sociology, but it will forever remain subservient. Behind the facade of a positive, empirical orientation, it conceals a partisan nature which relegates it to a separate and inferior status vis-à-vis the science of sociology.

What accounts for Durkheim's determination to treat socialism with such disparagement? As so often in the interpretation of his work, we must keep in mind the importance he attached to winning recognition for his chosen field. Socialism posed a serious threat to the sociological perspective precisely because as intellectual systems they share a number of basic assumptions and objectives.[38] Just because they appear to converge in a common enterprise, it became for Durkheim a matter of practical concern and almost a point of honor to hold them at a distance, in order that the reputation of the fledgling discipline not be sullied by this unfortunate association.

Durkheim is amply aware of the extent of this convergence. He seems to take up Richard's view of socialism as "a certain way of conceiving and explaining social facts," a definition posed in much the same terms he used to define the program of sociology itself. And in his review of Labriola, a turn-of-the-century exponent of the type of strict economic materialism which Durkheim found so distasteful, he specified several further points of contact between the two. First, they both adopt a group unit of analysis, and, as a consequence, seek to explain social facts in terms of social causes. Second, they assume the interrelationship of analytically distinct parts within a tightly integrated, wholistic social system. Finally, they join in the common recognition of the need for transcendence, through collective action, of the malintegrated social forms which are characteristic of the modern age.[39]

Yet, despite this awareness of the congruence which existed between the two frameworks—or precisely because of it—Durkheim the sociologist was not ready to embrace socialism as an intellectual perspective. Moreover, he was highly selective in his assessment of the strengths and weaknesses of its many strains, reserving his praise for one in particular and thus exaggerating quite out of proportion the tradition out of which his own work had in part developed. How many impartial analysts of our own or even Durkheim's day would make the following claim? "Personally, I believe the entire essence of socialist doctrine is to be found in the philosophy of Saint-Simon."[40] With respect to the work of Marx, on the other hand, Durkheim was just as excessively critical. In fact, it often seems that Durkheim eulogized Saint-Simon in an attempt to combat Marxist notions of irreconcilable class conflict and rigid economic determinism. While, as a rule, Durkheim steadfastly refused even to mention Marx's name, we find in the review of Labriola one of his few explicit references to this most influential social theory of modern times.

> We think it a fertile idea that social life must be explained not by the conception of it created by those who participate in it but by profound causes which escape awareness; and we also think that these causes must principally be sought in the way in which associated individuals are grouped ... We believe this proposition is self-evident. However, we see no reason to associate it ... with the socialist movement, of which it is totally independent. As for ourselves, we arrived at this proposition before we became

acquainted with Marx, to whose influence we have in no way been subjected.[41]

If we are to take Durkheim at his word, his exposure to Marx's work at the time of his stay in Leipzig in 1885-86 either postdated or had no lasting effect on the formation of his intellectual perspective. But more is in question than the precise extent of Durkheim's acquaintance with the Marxist oeuvre. The claim not to have been influenced seems either incredibly ungracious or incredibly naive on the part of one major social theorist, writing of another whose ideas were so much in the air in Europe of that day. Durkheim protests too much.

Once again, questions arise as to Durkheim's motives in rejecting with such vehemence the Marxist position in its entirety. And once again, we must look to his personal and intellectual history for an answer. The crucial fact is that when Durkheim composed his diatribes against Marxist materialism in 1896 and 1897, he was still smarting from certain reviews of *The Division of Labor in Society*. In them, Durkheim's thought was sharply criticized on grounds *that he was a materialist*, first for invoking the division of labor as the principle around which modern societies were organized and further for tracing the origin of that principle directly back to such considerations as the actual disposition of human beings in their physical environment and economic milieu.[42] Durkheim was aghast that his position had been so thoroughly misunderstood. For someone as self-conscious as he about achieving a balanced view, the mere suggestion that he had advanced a narrow and potentially reductionist perspective was sufficient cause to incite a vigorous reaction.

Thus, Durkheim's attempt to differentiate his own and his discipline's outlook from Marxist materialism can be viewed at least in part as a polemical counteroffensive against what he saw as attempts illegitimately to label his work. The edge to his response is apparent in the criticisms he directs at the Marxist theoretical position. He attacks it first at the level of its assumptions. He argues that its emphasis on the pervasive character of conflict in society obscures what is the more remarkable and significant fact in need of explanation, namely, that social systems cohere at all, that there exists a degree of consensus which permits the construction of a social order in the first place. In more concrete terms, the Marxist view that class is the natural expression and basis of social solidarity Durkheim believed to be a superficial interpretation which accepts as normal and desirable what is merely the artifact of a forced and unhealthy division of labor.

Furthermore, Durkheim objected to the reductionist tendency of the specifically economic variant of materialism, which to him appeared to run counter to its avowed reliance on a group unit of analysis. In assigning systematic priority to the realm of economics, it ended with a one-dimensional and simplistic portrayal of social behavior which Durkheim rejected in no uncertain terms. "Just as it seems true to us that the causes of social phenomena must be sought outside individual representations, it seems to that same degree false that they can be reduced, in the final analysis, to the state of industrial technology, and that the economic factor is the mainspring of progress."[43] Far from denying the interrelatedness between material and ideal factors, Durkheim asserted it and sought only to establish that causal connections run in both directions, that the latter have an independent, determinative impact all their own.

> While the different forms of collective activity also have their own substratum and while they derive from it in the last instance, once they exist they become in turn creative sources of action, they have an effectiveness all their own, and they react on the very causes on which they depend. We are, therefore, far from maintaining that the economic factor is only an epiphenomenon: once it exists, it has an influence which is special to it; it can partially modify the very substratum from which it results. But we have no reason to confuse it, in some way, with this substratum and to make of it something particularly fundamental.[44]

On the one hand, Durkheim wished the study of social structure to strike at the deeper "substratum" which underlies even economic forms, while on the other he reserved an independent role for the many varieties of social action, economic among them, once they had thus been derived.

Durkheim's criticisms, to this point measured and precise,

assumed a more acerbic character with respect to the claims which Marxist theory made to scientific status. He first disparaged the scope and quality of its empirical foundations, asserting that all its grandiose ramifications had been extrapolated from a few vague historical allusions and a single case study. He came, in fact, very close to suggesting that even this much had been rather shoddily researched.

> Even without opposing any definite fact to economic materialism, how could one help but notice the insufficiency of the proofs on which it rests? Here is a law which pretends to be the key to history! To demonstrate it a few sparse, disjointed facts are cited, facts which do not constitute any methodical series and the interpretation of which is far from being settled: primitive communism, the struggles of the patricians and the plebians, of the common people and the nobility, are advanced as having economic explanations. Even when a few examples borrowed from the industrial history of England are added to these rare documents, rapidly passed in review, they will not have succeeded in demonstrating a generalization of such magnitude.[45]

Thus, Durkheim found economic materialism not only derivative, reductionist, and polemical, but added to the list of its faults an unwillingness to submit itself to the test of meticulous research. The very ardor of Durkheim's reaction suggests that something vital was at stake, that he perhaps had his own sociological designs for the materialist perspective.

Durkheim's Use of a Generically Materialist Perspective

Durkheim believed the economic materialist thesis to be not only inadequately grounded in empirical evidence but actually to be contradicted by a factual record already accumulated through laborious sociological investigation. He expressed his skepticism as early as 1897, by which time he had already begun to move toward the focus on the primacy of religious phenomena which would come to dominate much of his later work.

> Not only is the Marxist hypothesis unproved but it is contrary to facts which seem well established. Sociologists and historians

tend more and more to meet in the common affirmation that religion is the most primitive of all social phenomena. From it, by successive transformations, have come all the other manifestations of collective activity: law, ethics, art, science, political forms, and so on. Everything is religious in principle. We know of no way to reduce religion to economics nor of any attempt truly to accomplish this reduction ... More generally, it is indisputable that in the beginning the economic factor is rudimentary while religious life is, on the contrary, rich and overwhelming. How then could the latter result from the former, and is it not probable, on the contrary, that the economy depends on religion much more than the second on the first?[46]

Durkheim would have wholeheartedly concurred in Max Weber's disclaimer of the intent "to substitute for a one-sided materialist an equally one-sided spiritualistic causal interpretation."[47] Rather, he sought to achieve a more balanced view of the determination of social facts. In his own work, he fully recognized the value of materialist analysis, once conceived in sufficiently broad and anti-reductionist terms, without ever according it a special and privileged status as a mode of explanation. The proof lies in a brief examination of a selection of examples drawn from the translations presented here and from the major books.

In the very first work which Durkheim published, the review of Schaeffle which appears below, we find him already in search of this synthetic position. On the one hand, Durkheim praised Schaeffle for having oriented the investigation of social solidarity in a new and more sophisticated direction by arguing that "the members of human societies are not attached to one another by a material link but by ideal bonds."[48] Schaeffle represented an advance over Espinas' earlier but more equivocal statement of this point because he resisted psychological reductionism and located the origin of these ideal bonds in rational human activity. Durkheim praised Schaeffle for avoiding the potential excesses of the mechanistic conception which had so often resulted from reliance on biological analogies. Yet at the same time, he remarked favorably on Schaeffle's openness to more materialist notions, for example, the idea that wealth might serve as a medium of exchange for a wide variety of social resources.[49] In short, Durkheim joins with Schaeffle in the belief that sociology can learn from the experience of the more mature natural sciences without yielding to the temptation to appropriate their models wholesale. It must guard against this impulse, for in losing sight of the very characteristics which set the social world apart, it would also lose its right to exist as an independent discipline. From the first, then, Durkheim sought to define a middle ground on which the interplay between material and ideal elements of the social world could be portrayed with realism and sophistication.

The Division of Labor in Society is by all odds the clearest illustration of Durkheim's own variety of materialist analysis. In it he makes use of generically materialist arguments to reject the causal priority of the economic factor per se in the generation of modern forms of social cohesion. Despite the title of the book, the division of labor is not seen as the ultimate determinant of organic solidarity but merely as a mediating variable which is itself the result of changes in the volume and density of the raw material of society. The degree and mode of concentration of the social mass— demographic fluctuations, urbanization, improved communications and transport, and so on—bring about heightened rates of social interaction. The rate of social interaction is the mediator between what Durkheim calls the social "substratum" and the patterns of behavior which result from it, the key variable on which the analysis of social facts seems to turn. According to the argument of this book, interaction engenders competition, and from the latter emerges the differentiation of function, the division of labor, on which organic solidarity is based.[50] It was Durkheim's preoccupation with the determining role which the structural element of social life plays in the development of social order and institutions which led him to focus on the concept of *concentration*, conceived in terms much broader than the purely economic. We shall see that his notion of concentration remains a recurrent theme in his later work.[51]

"Two Laws of Penal Evolution" makes liberal use of this sort of structural analysis. The notable improvement over *The Division of Labor*'s analysis of penal institutions discussed above is achieved because Durkheim's first law makes quantitative variations in the intensity of punishment depend not only on the level of social development but also on the degree of political centralization, defined as "the more or less complete concentration of all society's controlling functions in one and the same hand." This intensification of state power "releases a social force sui generis," a force sufficiently strong to counteract the putative long-term mitigating tendency of general social development.[52] Though Durkheim errs in assigning to political centralization a secondary role in the determination of penal evolution, very real gains in explanatory power result from the application of the logic of concentration.

This same line of reasoning contributes to the originality of his second law, that of qualitative variations. Durkheim replaced the earlier division of penal systems according to whether they rely primarily on repressive or restitutive sanctions with the far more useful and subtle distinction between "religious" and "human" criminality. The former progressively gives way to the latter as the result of changes in social densities. As population becomes more concentrated, clanic and tribal groups lose their autonomy to the larger scale aggregates which absorb the former's functions. In consequence of the clan's decline, a shift must occur from collective to individual responsibility in order to guarantee the availability for trial and punishment of individuals accused or convicted of crimes. No longer able to depend upon primary groups for aid in enforcing norms through preventive detention, the society must develop alternative means of insuring conformity with the law. Thus, concentration is shown to be the underlying cause of the need for prisons as an instrument of justice.[53]

At the same time, this very concentration provides the necessary means for the satisfaction of that need. The more intense and continuous collective life which it calls forth creates a differentiated public sphere. To the exalted position of persons upon whom centralized political authority devolves correspond new architectural forms which make the practice of incarceration possible.

On first examination, it doubtless seems quite obvious that, from the day when prisons became useful to societies, men had the idea of constructing them. However, in reality, the existence of prisons assumes that certain conditions, without which they are not possible, have been realized. Prisons imply the existence of public establishments, sufficiently spacious, militarily occupied, arranged in such a way as to prevent communications with the outside, and so on . . .

But as the social horizon is extended, as collective life, instead of being dispersed into a vast number of minor foci where it can manage only a meager existence, is concentrated about a more restricted number of points, it simultaneously becomes more intense and more continuous. Because it takes on greater importance, the dwellings of those who are in charge are transformed. They are extended and are organized in view of the more extensive and permanent functions which are incumbent upon them. The more the authority of those who live in them grows, the more those dwellings are singularized and distinguished from the rest. They take on a grandiose air, they are sheltered by higher walls and deeper moats in such a way as to denote visibly the line of demarcation which thenceforth separates the holders of power and the mass of their subordinates. At that point, the pre-conditions of the prison come into being.[54]

It is concentration, in short, which makes the institution of the prison both necessary and possible.

The logic of concentration remains a touchstone of Durkheim's analytical strategy in his later work as well. *L'Evolution pédagogique en France*, a historical study of the institutional basis of the French educational system, provides several valuable examples. In one particularly striking instance, Durkheim considers the crucial period of the founding of the university system in the late twelfth and early thirteenth centuries. With the consolidation of the Capetian monarchy and its permanent establishment in Paris, French society was given a focus, a center of gravity. The rapid growth of the new capital lent enormous prestige to its school, which had previously been just one among many. The scholars and students attracted to Paris soon achieved the critical mass necessary for the emergence of new institutional forms in education. As Durkheim describes the process of concentration in the late twelfth century, the explanatory power of his enduring preoccupation with the relationship between "substratum" and human institutions is given new scope.

> From then on the scholarly life of France and also of the other European societies had a fixed, definite, immovable center which owed its importance not to the authority and prestige of a famous master, of an evanescent personality who could leave to teach elsewhere, who would disappear sooner or later, and to whom the destiny of the school was linked. The preponderance of what in this period comes to be called the "Paris School" rests above all upon impersonal, enduring causes, on its geographical situation, on the place which it occupied at the very center of the state ... With a stable, regular, impersonal organization, an uninterrupted development became possible, and from it a new system of instruction, a new form of scholarship which had been hitherto unknown.
>
> The causes—at least the impersonal causes—of these transformations, the consequences of which we are going to observe, can therefore be reduced to two. There was, in the first place, a general stimulation of intellectual activity in all Europe. [This occurred] through a double concentration of this activity, first in a certain number of dispersed locations, later about a unique but stable location. And it is from the life awakened around this central and privileged point that arose the pedagogical innovations which we shall witness. From it emerged this university organization within which medieval civilization was actually elaborated and which, while undergoing transformations, was to perpetuate itself down to our own day.[55]

Here again, definite institutional innovations have been imputed to an increase in the density of certain specialized forms of social interaction.

It would be an easy task to multiply examples of this same line of reasoning in Durkheim's work. We will limit ourselves to one additional instance, drawn from *The Elementary Forms of the Religious Life*, to show that this analytical style survived even into work of the later period, that is, into what some scholars have considered Durkheim's idealist phase. It is true that Durkheim had become convinced more than ever that religion was a, and perhaps the, primordial social phenomenon. But it is for the light which the origins of religion shed on the problem of social solidarity, the problem which never ceased to occupy his mind, that he pursued the analysis of its simplest forms. His approach to the problem is, moreover, hardly idealist. On the contrary, the main thesis of this book is that religious forms are faithful reflections of such factors as the system of kinship relations or the distribution of political authority—in short, of the existing social structures. In fact, Durkheim makes the claim that through its religious character, our entire conceptual apparatus, including such notions as time, genus, force, and causality, is grounded in concrete social relations and ultimately in the nature of the social "substratum."[56] If the book consists in part in the celebration of the sacred, the symbolic and transcendent aspect of the social, and locates the primary source of social change in this distinct realm, it does so with due regard for the importance of broadly materialist factors. In particular, Durkheim contends that at critical junctures, societies undergo periods of "effervescence," when deep-seated conflicts suddenly surface. "There are periods in history when, under the influence of some great collective shock, social interactions have become much more frequent and active. Men look to each other and assemble together more than ever. The general effervescence results which is characteristic of revolutionary or creative epochs. Now this greater activity results in a general stimulation of individual forces. Men see more and differently now than in normal times. Changes are not merely of shades and degrees; men become different."[57] In such periods, group relations are set in turmoil and the restraining influence of the normative system is relaxed, allowing the creative resolution of social strains. At the most concrete level, this effervescence results from the concentration of the social mass, for it is precisely the intensification of human relations which liberates the impulse and energy for change. The consequences of effervescence, though more short-term and acute, are described in much the same terms Durkheim used in *The Division of Labor* to explain the transformation from one to another form of social solidarity.

In brief, the concentration image appears so frequently in Durkheim's writing as to constitute a leitmotiv, an implicit model of social development which bears strong evolutionary overtones. He seems to conceive of social systems as economies of human energy, in which the reciprocal reinforcement of interaction at nodal points results in an intensification of activity beyond normal levels and produces emergent phenomena with innovative potential. Despite the criticisms which Durkheim levels at the overly literal use of organismic analogies and at unlinear evolutionary perspectives, it seems that he has, consciously or not, transposed many of the elements of the Darwinian view of biological evolution into the sphere of social analysis. It is precisely because concentation induces competition and thus differentiation, but within a normative order which allows for the generation of consensus, that new social forms can emerge. If Durkheim stops short of the belief that selection among the resulting social forms operates "naturally" or results in the survival of only "superior" types, his general perspective never manages to divest itself entirely of a frankly evolutionary cast.

Social Morphology and Structural-Functionalist Analysis

There exists yet another reason to believe that Durkheim's interest in a generically materialist mode of analysis was genuine and enduring: he tells us so himself. Durkheim's initially informal use of the logic of concentration was given a more systematic expression in the late 1890s as the subdiscipline of "social morphology."

After 1895, Durkheim was actively engaged in revising his perspective to assign a more prominent role to the understanding of religious phenomena. The review of Labriola, in which the latter are presented as being more basic than the economic phenomena on which Marxist analysis relied so heavily, was composed early in that same period. But 1897 was also the moment, and *L'Année sociologique* the forum, which Durkheim chose to give more formal status to the study of the broadly material basis of social life. Introduced as a new rubric of the review section of *L'Année*, social morphology was to discuss works which focused upon the structural basis of social behavior. Drawing upon a wide variety of social science disciplines—Durkheim mentions geography, demography, and history in particular—social morphology was to derive its unifying theme from the attempt systematically to relate elements of what could be called the infrastructure and superstructure. As he himself described it:

Social life rests upon a substratum which is determinate both in its extent and in its form. It is composed of the mass of individuals who comprise society, the manner in which they are disposed upon the earth, and the nature and configuration of objects of all sorts which affect collective relations. Depending on whether the population is more or less sizable, more or less dense; depending on whether it is concentrated in cities or dispersed in the countryside; depending on the way in which the cities and the houses are constructed; depending on whether the space occupied by the society is more or less extensive; depending on the borders which define its limits, the avenues of communication which traverse it, and so forth, this social substratum will differ. From another point of view, the constitution of this substratum directly or indirectly affects all social phenomena just as all psychic phenomena are placed in mediate or immediate relationship with the brain. Thus, we have a whole collection of problems which are of obvious interest to sociology and which, because they all refer to a single and identical object, must come within the jurisdiction of a single science. It is this science which we propose to call *social morphology.*[58]

This emphasis on a mode of analysis which few associate with his name was neither unique nor transitory. In "Sociology and the Social Sciences," published in 1909 and therefore clearly located in Durkheim's so-called later period, he sketched the organization of the field of sociology toward which he had been working for two decades. There he proposed a tripartite division, the first section of which was to be social morphology, the study of society "in its external aspect."[59] The term "morphology" originated as part of an analogy from medicine, which Durkheim completed by labeling the second great subdivision "social physiology." As in the life sciences, the former was to study anatomy and structure, the latter function. The third and overarching category, "general sociology," was to synthesize the findings of the other two, combining their insights within a structural-functionalist perspective. Though separable for analytical purposes, the study of morphology and physiology merely constituted alternative and complementary strategies for achieving an understanding of social behavior; to develop an appreciation for the complexity and ultimate unity of social action, it remained essential that they finally be reintegrated.

Implicit in his rationale for thus dividing the field is Durkheim's assumption that the study of structure is a convenient point of departure because it presents us with a concrete and easily accessible aspect of reality which can be examined "objectively." [60] But however convenient the initial consideration of concrete factors for certain research questions, the wholistic social systems envisioned by Durkheim practically precluded the ultimate efficacy of either a narrow idealism or a narrow materialism. A properly structural-functionalist perspective must end by recognizing that both elements are real and have independent causal impact. While we may choose to gain explanatory leverage in the investigation of social phenomena by adopting one or the other point of view as circumstances demand, such a choice can only be justified as heuristic. Durkheim took full advantage of both strategies of analysis, and while this often neglected materialist aspect of his work should not be carried too far, the characterization of his thought as one-sidedly idealist constitutes a more serious, because more common, obfuscation and distortion.

Normality and the Concept of "Social Health"

From his structural-functionalist orientation Durkheim also derived a characteristic stance on a broad range of social and political issues. Though he has frequently been styled a conservative, his opposition to many of the orthodoxies of his day suggests otherwise. He was, for example, a staunch supporter of the Third Republic at a time when this alone placed one in the liberal camp, an active and committed Drefusard, and an energetic proponent of social reform, particularly in the field of education. Similarly, in the intellectual realm, his advocacy of the new discipline of sociology was from the first a heretical and daring enterprise which his personal capacity for innovative action, no less than his methodical nature, helped to crown with success.

In short, stock labels fail to capture the character of Durkheim's thought. It is quite true that on occasion he could evince an almost Burkean reverence for constituted norms and institutions, for the corollary of his belief in the organic nature of social order was the conviction that both present and future existed as extensions of the past. But Durkheim was a moderate rather than a reactionary, more historically conscious than backwards yearning, and he displayed these traits primarily as matters of style and personal orientation, and not in the form of some global political or social ideology.

In the final analysis, it is his almost obsessive desire to discover a measured and temperate course of action which has sometimes been mistaken for a frank conservatism. Despite his liberal politics, despite his positivist orientation, Durkheim's emphasis on consensus over conflict and on continuity over change resulted in the conservative tone most apparent in his discussion of moral issues. Although he could be highly sensitive to the need for social change, and explicitly acknowledged the special potential of periods which broke with established norms, his preference for the balanced viewpoint and for meliorative solutions gave his thought a reformist cast.[61] Viewed in this light, the Durkheimian notion of "social health" proves revealing of his attitude, for its very ambiguities express the difficulty he experienced in reconciling these anomolous tendencies.

The definition of normality which Durkheim developed in *The Rules of the Sociological Method* adopted the criterion of universality as an empirical indicator. In his view, a given social state was normal not because its consequences were wholly or necessarily beneficial, but, in a more strictly etymological sense, because it tended to converge with an observable statistical norm. For Durkheim, the generality of a social fact indicated that it was "bound to the fundamental conditions of social life."[62] One advantage of this positive approach was to dissociate his perspective from the dominant normative system and from the moralistic judgment which the constituted authorities might render with respect to widespread practices of which they disapproved. The standard of universality, moreover, alerted him to the possibility of latent functions, for especially when encountered in the face of normative sanctions, the very generality of a social phenomenon suggests the existence of some pressing, hidden need. A statistical rather than a judgmental criterion also helped underscore the dynamic quality of social norms and the fact that deviations often indicate a beneficial degree of flexibility in the social order, since every ultimately successful innovation begins by being characterized as criminal or deviant, only later to win acceptance by virtue of its compatibility with emerging social conditions.

But Durkheim also used the concept of normality to mask the imposition of his personal predilections. Though he claimed that social forms could be classed as healthy or pathological in strictly scientific terms, we today, with a fuller understanding of how the process of labeling can be bent to the purposes of a supposedly objective observer, have grounds for skepticism. When, for example, he offers an operational definition of crime as any act which elicits punishment, or when he simply assumes, upon repeatedly encountering a pattern of social behavior in diverse settings, that "so universal a fact is not without a reason for existing," he seems suddenly negligent of the problems of circularity or teleology in his reasoning. We cannot, in short, escape the conclusion that the notion of normality was a flexible standard which Durkheim manipulated almost at will.

These translations, in short, will help complete and correct the acquired wisdom regarding Durkheim's thought. They show him to have been a scholar with an intense sense of vocation, one whose combative spirit was quickly aroused by the least opportunity to plant the triumphant banner of sociology on new territory. His singlemindedness, far from detracting from the power of his intellectual system, was its greatest asset. No other figure in the sociological tradition possessed a disciplinary program of comparable clarity and scope. This very intensity of purpose, more than any other factor, accounts for the enduring nature of his work.

The claim that Durkheim's sociology largely consists of myriad approaches to a single central issue, social solidarity, is in no way intended to dismiss or diminish its import. Our point is, on the contrary, that Durkheim unerringly focused his intellectual energy on *the* crucial problem in the investigation of which sociology could address and resolve the principal difficulties it would encounter along the path to acceptance in the pantheon of the social sciences.

A studied eclecticism is also characteristic of his thought. If he has come to be known as a founder of the quantitative tradition in sociology, it is a judgment fully justified by the brilliance of his pioneering work in statistical inference; but his skill in this area should not obscure his methodological versatility. Indeed, to take him at his word, it is from comparative history that he expected the most gratifying results. Similarly, he made use of variables drawn from every realm of the differentiated social world as elements of both materialist and idealist arguments. Yet he achieved a general integration of these varied techniques and strategies of research within a structural-functionalist perspective.

All his efforts to elucidate the nature of social behavior were intended to serve a broader program: to restore the overarching normative order to a state of health and vitality; on that basis to recreate a nonantagonistic relationship between the individual and the social group; and thus to rescue modern man from the pervasive sense of isolation and meaninglessness into which he had been plunged by the transition to organically organized social forms. The moral regeneration and transcendence at which Durkheim aimed remain the unachieved ideal of many sociologists today. No better model of the synthesis of imaginative social science and enlightened pursuit of the amelioration of social conditions can yet be found. These translations will hopefully serve to broaden our collective grasp of Durkheim's intellectual posture. The reader already familiar with the acknowledged classics, and whose appetite this sampling of the more obscure Durkheim merely whets, will be pleased to learn that a further treasure of French sources still lies waiting.

THE ORIGINS
AND OBJECTIVES OF SOCIOLOGY

1

COURSE IN SOCIOLOGY: OPENING LECTURE

Charged with the task of teaching a science born only yesterday, one which can as yet claim but a small number of principles to be definitively established, it would be rash on my part not to be awed by the difficulties of my task. Moreover, I make this avowal without difficulty or timidity. Indeed, I believe that there is room in our universities, beside those chairs from which established science and acquired truths are taught, for other courses in which the professor in part creates the science even as he is teaching it; in which his listeners are almost as much collaborators as pupils; in which they join him in searching, in feeling the way, and sometimes even in wandering astray. I do not, therefore, come before you to reveal a doctrine which is the privilege and the secret possession of a tiny school of sociologists nor, above all, to propose ready-made remedies to cure our modern societies of the ills from which they suffer. Science does not move so quickly. It needs time, a great deal of time, to become of practical use. Moreover, the inventory of what I bring to you is far more modest and easier to set forth. I believe that I am able to pose with some precision a certain number of special questions which are related to each other in such a way as to form a science set among the other positive sciences. To resolve these problems, I shall propose to you a method with which we shall experiment together. From my studies of these matters, I have drawn a few orienting ideas, a few general perspectives, a little

Originally published as "Cours de science sociale: Leçon d'ouverture," *Revue internationale de l'enseignement* 15 (1888): 23-48.

experience, if you like, which I hope will serve to guide us in our prospective research.

Still, I hope that these reservations will not have the effect of awakening or reawakening in some of you the skepticism of which sociological studies have sometimes been the object. A young science should not be overly ambitious, and it enjoys greater credibility among scientific minds when it presents itself with greater modesty. However, I cannot forget that there are still some thinkers, though in fact few in number, who have doubts about our science and its future. Obviously we cannot ignore them. But I feel that to discuss in an abstract way the question of whether or not sociology is viable is not the best manner of convincing them. Such a discussion, however excellent, never converted a single disbeliever. The only way to demonstrate movement is to take a step. The only way to demonstrate that sociology is possible is to show that it exists and that it lives. That is why I am going to devote this first lecture to setting before you the succession of transformations through which sociology has passed since the beginning of this century. I shall show you the progress which has been made and that which remains to be accomplished, how sociology has developed and how it is now developing. From this exposition, you will decide for yourselves what service this discipline can render and to what public it must address itself.

I

Since Plato and his *Republic*, there has been no lack of thinkers who have philosophized about the nature of societies. But until the beginning of this century, most of this work was dominated by an idea which radically prevented the establishment of sociology. In effect, nearly all these political theorists saw society as a human creation, a product of art and reflection. According to them, men began to live together because they found that it was useful and good; society is an invention which they thought up in order to better their condition a little. According to this view, a nation is not a natural product, like organisms or plants, which are born, which grow and develop through some internal necessity. Rather, it resembles the machines which men make by assembling parts according to a preconceived plan. If the cells of an adult animal's body become what they are, it is because it was in their nature to become that. If they are aggregated in a specific way, it is because, given the existing milieu, it was impossible for them to be aggregated in any other. On the other hand, the fragments of metal from which a watch is made have no special affinity either for a given form or for a given mode of combination. If they are arranged in one way rather than another, it is because the artisan willed it. It is not their nature but his will which explains the changes which they underwent; it is he who has arranged them in the way which conformed most closely to his plans. Well, shouldn't it be the same way with society as with this watch?

According to this perspective, there is nothing in the nature of man which necessarily predestined him to collective life; he himself invented it and established it. Whether it is everyone's creation, as Rousseau argues, or that of a single man, as Hobbes thinks, it derived in its entirety from our brains and from our imaginations. In our hands it is but a convenient instrument, one which we could do without, if necessary, and which we can always modify at will. For we can freely undo what we have freely done. If we are the creators of society, we can destroy it or transform it. All we have to do is exert our wills.

Such is the conception which has reigned until recent times. The opposite view, to be sure, has come to light at rare intervals, but only briefly and without leaving behind lasting traces. The illustrious example of Aristotle, who was the first to see society as a natural fact, remained almost without imitators. In the eighteenth century, the same idea was indeed reborn with Montesquieu and Condorcet. But Montesquieu himself, who so firmly declared that society, like the rest of the world, is subject to necessary laws which are derived from the nature of things, let the consequences of his principle escape him even as he posed it. Under such circumstances, there can be no place for a positive science of societies, but only for the art of politics. Science, in effect, studies what is; art combines means in view of what should be. If, therefore, societies are what we make them, we needn't ask what they are, but only what we should make of them. Since it is not necessary to account for their nature, there is no reason we should know it; it is enough to determine the end which they must fulfill and find the best way to arrange things so that this goal is indeed fulfilled. For example, we might suppose that the aim of society is to assure each individual the free exercise of his rights, and from that we could deduce sociology in its entirety.

The economists were the first to proclaim that social laws are as necessary as physical laws and to make this axiom the basis of a science. According to them, it is just as impossible for competition not to level off prices little by little or for the value of merchandise not to augment when population increases as it is for objects not to fall in a vertical line or for rays of light not to be refracted when they pass through media of unequal density. As for the civil laws made by princes or voted by assemblies, they are merely the expression, in a sensible and clear form, of these natural laws. Civil laws can neither create nor change natural laws. One cannot give value to a product which has none—that is, which no one needs—by issuing a decree. And all the efforts of governments to modify societies at their will are useless when they are not outright harmful. It would be better that they abstain from such attempts. Their intervention can hardly be anything but harmful. Nature does not need them. She follows her own course all on her own. It would not be necessary, even if it were possible, to help or to hinder her.

Extend this principle to all social facts and sociology is established. In effect, any special order of natural phenomena subjected to regular laws can be the object of a methodical study, that is to say, of a positive science. All skeptical arguments founder on this very simple truth.

"But," the historians say, "we have studied societies and have not discovered the most insignificant of laws. History is but a series of accidents which are, no doubt, interrelated according to the laws of causality but are never repeated. Essentially local and individual, these accidents pass and never return and are, therefore, refractory to any generalization, that is to say, to any scientific study, since there is no science of the idiosyncratic. Political, economic, and legal institutions depend on the race, the climate, and all the circumstances in which they develop: these are all heterogenous factors which do not lend themselves to comparison. In each civilization they have their own physiognomy, which can be studied and described with great care; but we have said all we can when we have produced a well-executed monograph."

The best way to answer this objection and to prove that societies, like everything else, are subject to laws would assuredly be to discover those laws. But, without waiting until that has been accomplished, a very legitimate induction permits us to affirm that they exist. If today there exists any point settled beyond question, it is that all natural entities from the mineral world up through man come within the province of positive science, that is to say that all that concerns them occurs according to necessary laws. This proposition no longer partakes of conjecture; it is a truth which experience has demonstrated, for these laws have been found, or at least we are discovering them little by little. In succession, physics and chemistry, then biology, and finally psychology have been established. We can even say that of all laws, the one based on the best experimental evidence—for not a single exception is known, though it has been verified in an infinite number of cases—proclaims that all natural phenomena evolve according to laws. If, then, societies are part of nature, they must also obey this general law, which simultaneously results from and dominates science. Social facts are, without doubt, more complex than psychic facts, but are not the latter infinitely more complex than biological and physico-chemical facts? Yet there can be no question today of setting apart conscious life from the rest of the world and from science. When the phenomena are less simple, their study is less easy; but it is a question of ways and means, not of principle. Moreover, because they are more complex, they are more flexible and more easily take on the stamp of the least circumstances which surround them. That is why they appear more individual and are mutually distinct to a greater extent. But the differences must not blind us to the similarities. There is, no doubt, an enormous gap between the consciousness of a savage and that of a cultivated man; and yet both are human consciousnesses between which there are resemblances and between which comparisons can be made. The psychologist who draws from these comparisons so much useful information knows this well. The same is true of the flora and fauna amid which man evolves. As different as they may be from one another, the phenomena produced by the actions and reactions among like individuals placed in analogous circumstances must necessarily resemble one another in some respect and lend themselves to useful comparisons. Will someone allege, in an effort to escape this consequence, that human liberty excludes any idea of law and makes any scientific prediction impossible? That objection can hardly interest us, and we can ignore it, not out of disdain, but through the application of method. The question of knowing whether or not man is free is no doubt of interest, but it belongs to metaphysics, and the positive sciences can and must ignore it. There are philosophers who have discovered in organisms and even in inanimate objects a sort of free will and contingency. But neither the physicist nor the biologist has changed his method because of such findings; they have peacefully gone their way without concerning themselves with these subtle arguments. Similarly, psychology and sociology need not wait until the question of man's free will has finally been resolved before they can establish themselves. This question has been pending for centuries, and everybody recognizes that it is not about to be resolved. Metaphysics and science both have an interest in remaining independent of one another. We can, therefore, conclude that one must choose between two alternatives. Either one recognizes that social phenomena are accessible to scientific investigation, or else one admits, for no reason and contrary to all the inductions of science, that there are two worlds within the world: one in which reigns the law of causality, the other in which reign arbitrariness and contingency.

That is the great service which the economists have rendered to social studies. They were the first to sense all that is living and spontaneous in societies. They understood that collective life could not brusquely be established by some clever artifice; that it did not result from an external and mechanical impulsion but is slowly elaborated in the very heart of society. In this way they were able to ground a theory of liberty on a foundation more solid than a metaphysical hypothesis. In effect, it is obvious that if collective life is spontaneous, it must not be deprived of its spontaneity. Any fetter would be absurd.

Still, one must not exaggerate the merit of the economists. Even while saying that economic laws are natural, they understood the word in a sense that diminished its import. According to them, there is nothing real in society but the individual. Everything emanates from him, and it is toward him that everything converges. A nation is only a nominal entity; it is a word which serves to designate a mechanical aggregate of juxtaposed individuals. But it has no specific properties which distinguish it from other things. Its properties are those of the elements which compose it, merely enlarged and amplified. The individual is, therefore, the only tangible reality which the observer can get at, and the only question which science can set for itself is to investigate how the individual should conduct himself in the principal circumstances of economic life, given his nature. Economic and, more broadly, social laws are not, then, very general facts which the scholar induces from the observation of societies, but logical consequences deduced from the definition of the individual. The economist does not say, "Things happen in this way because experience has established that fact." Rather he says, "Things should happen in this way because it would be absurd if it were otherwise." The word *natural* should therefore be replaced by the word *rational*, which is not the same thing. If only this concept of the individual, which is supposed to contain in itself the entire science, were adequate in reality! But in an attempt to simplify things, the economists have artificially impoverished the concept. Not only have they ignored all circumstances of time, place, and country in order to conceive of man's abstract type in general, but in this ideal type itself they have neglected everything which does not bear upon strictly individual life to such an extent that, passing from abstraction to abstraction, nothing is left but the sad portrait of an isolated egoist.

In this way, political economy lost all the benefits of its founding principle. It remained an abstract and deductive science, concerned not with the observation of reality, but with the construction of a more or less desirable ideal. For this abstract man, this systematic egoist whom it describes, is solely a creature of reason. Real man—the man whom we all know and whom we all are—is complex in a different way: he is of a time, of a country; he has a family, a city, a fatherland, a religious and political faith; and all these factors and many others merge and combine in a thousand ways, converge in and interweave their influence without it being possible to say at first glance where one begins and the other ends. It is only after long and laborious analyses, barely begun today, that it will one day be possible to determine in an approximate way the role of each. The economists did not yet, therefore, have a sufficiently correct idea of societies to serve as a basis for sociology. For the latter, taking as its point of departure an abstract creation of the mind, could surely result in a logical demonstration of the metaphysical possibilities but could not establish laws. What was still lacking was a natural realm to observe.

II

If the economists stopped at the halfway point, it was because they were poorly prepared for this sort of study. They were, for the most part, jurists, businessmen, or statesmen and rather unfamiliar with biology and psychology. In order to be able to integrate social science into the general system of the natural sciences, one must at least have practiced one of them. It is not enough to possess general and practical intelligence. To discover the laws of the collective consciousness, one must know those of the individual consciousness. It is because Auguste Comte was current with all the positive sciences, with their method and their results, that he was in a position to found, this time on a definitive basis, sociology.

Auguste Comte revived the proposition of the economists: like them, he declared that social laws are natural. But he gave the word its full scientific meaning. He assigned to sociology a reality which it would seek to know: societies. For him, society was as real as a living organism. To be sure, it cannot exist except through the individuals who serve as its substratum; it is, however, something more than a collection of individuals. A whole is not identical to the sum of its parts, even though without them it would be nothing. In the same way, by coming together in a definite structure and through lasting bonds, men form a new entity which has its own nature and its own laws. This is the social entity. The phenomena which take place within assuredly have their roots in the consciousness of the individual. Collective life is not, however, simply a duplicate, on an enlarged scale, of individual life. It presents characteristics which are unique and which the inductions of psychology alone do not permit us to foresee. Thus, mores and the prescriptions of law and morality would be impossible if man were not capable of acquiring habits; they are, nonetheless, something other than individual habits. That is why Comte marks off for the social organism a determinate place in the scale of all organisms. He places it at the summit of the hierarchy because of its greater complexity and because the social order implies and includes within itself all the other realms of nature. Because this being cannot be reduced to any other, it cannot be deduced from them, and to know it one must observe it. This time, sociology found itself in possession of both an object of study which belonged to it alone and of a positive method for studying it.

At the same time, Auguste Comte called attention to a characteristic of societies which is their distinctive mark and which the economists had nonetheless ignored. I am speaking of "this universal consensus which characterizes all the phenomena of living bodies and which social life necessarily manifests to the highest degree."[1] For the economists, moral, legal, economic, and political phenomena unfold along parallel lines, without intersecting, so to speak. Similarly, the corresponding sciences can develop without mutual contact. We know, indeed, what jealous care political economy has always taken to defend its independence. For Comte, on the contrary, social facts are too tightly integrated for it to be possible to study them separately. The result of this relatedness is that each of the social sciences loses some of its autonomy but gains in vitality and vigor. The facts which each had studied when the analytical framework had detached them from their natural milieu seemed to have no connection and to exist in a vacuum. They were abstract and dead. Now that they have been brought together according to their natural affinities, they appear as what they are: the various facets of a single, living reality, namely, society. Instead of dealing with phenomena arranged, so to speak, in linear series, external to one another and meeting only by chance, now we are presented with an enormous system of actions and reactions in the sort of ever-changing equilibrium which characterizes life. At the same time, because he had a better sense for the complexity of social phenomena, Auguste Comte was proof against those absolute solutions so dear to the economists and, with them, the political ideologues of the eighteenth century. When one sees in society only the individual and reduces the concept of that individual to a simple idea which admittedly is clear, but also dry and empty, a concept from which everything living and complex has been extracted, it is natural that nothing very complex can be deduced from it and that one ends up with simplistic and radical theories. If, on the contrary, each phenomenon studied is related to an infinity of others, if every point of view is integrated with several others, then it is no longer possible to settle questions categorically. A certain kind of eclecticism, the method of which I need not describe, becomes indispensable. There are so many different things in life! One must know how to fit each into its proper place. That is how Auguste Comte, even in agreeing with the economists that the individual had the right to a large share of liberty, would not accept it without limits and declared that collective discipline was necessary. In the same way, even in recognizing that social facts could not be arbitrarily created or changed, he believed that, as the result of their greater complexity, they were more easily altered and, consequently, could be, to a certain extent, usefully directed by human intelligence.

These were great and serious triumphs, and it is with good reason that tradition dates the beginning of sociology from Auguste Comte. You must not think, however, that the preliminary work was thereupon complete and that sociology now needed only to pursue peacefully its career. It now had an object, but how indeterminate it remained! It must study, we were told, *Society*. But *Society* did not exist. There were societies classed into types and species like plants and animals. With what species was it, then, to be concerned? With all at once or just one in particular? For Comte the question did not even arise, for he believed that there existed only one social species. An adversary of Lamarck, he did not think it possible that the mere fact of evolution could differentiate organisms to the point of giving birth to new species. According to him, social facts are always and everywhere the same, with variations in intensity, while social development is always and everywhere the same, with variations in rate. The most savage nations and the most cultivated peoples are but different phases of a single and identical evolution, and it was the laws of this unique evolution which he sought. Humanity, viewed in its totality, develops in a straight line, and the various societies are only the successive stages of this rectilinear advance. Moreover, the words *society* and *humanity* were used interchangeably by Comte. This is because his sociology is far less a special study of social beings than a philosophical meditation on human sociology in general. This same reason explains for us another peculiarity of his method. If human progress everywhere follows the same law, the best way to recognize it is naturally to observe it in its sharpest and most complete form, that is to say, in civilized societies. That is why, in order to verify this famous law of three stages, which is supposed to summarize the entire life history of humanity, Auguste Comte was content summarily to pass in review the principal events of the history of the German-Latin peoples, never perceiving how strange it was to establish on so narrow a base a law of such amplitude.

Comte was encouraged in this perspective by the state of imperfection in which the ethnological sciences were to be found in his time and also by the lack of interest which these studies inspired in him. But today it is manifestly impossible to maintain that there is a human evolution which is everywhere identical and that societies are all just different versions of a single and identical type. Zoology has already renounced the linear classification whose extreme simplicity once seduced scholars. It is increasingly accepted that the genealogical tree of organized beings, instead of having the form of a geometric line, resembles more nearly a very bushy tree whose branches, issuing haphazardly all along the trunk, shoot out capriciously in all directions. It is the same way with societies. Despite Pascal's famous formulation, which Comte wrongly revives, humanity cannot be compared to a solitary man who has lived all these past centuries and still survives. Rather, it resembles an immense family, the various branches of which, as they diverge more and more from one another, gradually detach themselves from the common source to live their own lives. What assures us that this common source ever existed? Is there not, in fact, at least as much distance between a clan or a tribe and our great European nations as between the human species and the immediately inferior animal species? To speak of only a single social function, what relationship is there between the barbarous mores of a miserable tribe in the Tierra del Fuego and the refined ethics of modern society? It is doubtless possible that very general laws which apply to all may be obtained through the comparison of these social types; but it is not the observation, however attentive, of a single one that will reveal them.

This same error produced another consequence. I told you that for Comte society was a being sui generis. But because he rejected the philosophy of evolutionary descent, he assumed that a break in continuity existed between each species of being just like that between each species of science. He therefore found it difficult to define and provide a mental representation of this new being which he added to the rest of nature. Where did it come from and what did it resemble? He often called it an organism, but all that he saw in this expression was a metaphor of limited value. Since his philosophy forbade him to see in society the continuation and extension of inferior beings, he was unable to define it in terms of the latter. And at that point, where could he look for the elements of a definition? To remain consistent with his principles, he was obliged to admit that this new realm did not resemble the preceding ones; and, in fact, even while comparing sociology and biology, he claimed for the former a special method different from those pursued in the other positive sciences. Sociology had therefore been annexed to the rest of the sciences, rather than integrated with them.

III

It was only with Spencer that this integration was definitively achieved. Spencer was not content just to call attention to a few specious analogies between societies and living organisms: he clearly declared that society is a sort of organism. Like other organisms, it is born of a seed, evolves over a period of time, and ends in a final dissolution. Like other organisms, it results from a convergence of differentiated elements, each of which has a special function, and which, by complementing one another, all conspire toward a single goal. There is more: in virtue of the general principles of his philosophy, these essential resemblances were for Spencer an indication of a veritable relationship of consanguinity. If social life recalls the general traits of individual life, it is because the former arises from the latter. If society has traits in common with organisms, it is because it is itself an organism, transformed and perfected. Cells, when aggregated, form living beings, just as living beings, when aggregated, form societies. But the second evolution is a consequence of the first, and the whole difference is that, by refining its procedures more and more, it manages little by little to render the organic aggregates more flexible and freer without compromising its own unity.

This very simple truth has nonetheless been the occasion for a rather lively polemic. It is certain that it loses some of its value if it is taken too literally and if its importance is exaggerated. If, like Lilienfeld in his *Thoughts on the Social Science of the Future* (*Gedanken über die Socialwissenschaft der Zukunft*), we imagine that this one comparison will dissipate in an instant all the mysteries which still surround the origins and the nature of societies, and that to do so, it will be enough to import into sociology the better-known laws of biology by plagiarizing them, we are deluding ourselves. If sociology exists, it must have its own method and laws. Social facts can truly be explained only by other social facts, and they have not been accounted for just because their resemblance to biological facts, the science of which seems already complete, has been pointed out. The explanation which is appropriate to the latter cannot be exactly adapted to the former. Evolution is not a monotonous repetition. Each realm of nature manifests some novelty which science must discover and reproduce, rather than erase. In order that sociology have the right to exist, there must be in the social realm something which escapes biological investigation.

But, on the other hand, we cannot forget that analogy is a precious instrument for knowledge and even for scientific research. The mind cannot create a new idea out of nothing. Should we discover an entirely new being without analogue in the rest of the world, it would be impossible for the mind to grasp; it could only be represented in terms of something else that the mind already knows. What we call a new idea is in reality but an old idea which we have touched up in order to accommodate it as exactly as possible to the special object which it must express. There was, then, a real point in calling attention to the analogy between the individual organism and society, for not only did the imagination thenceforth know how to grasp it and have the means to conceive of the new being, but for the sociologist, biology became a veritable treasure trove of perspectives and hypotheses, which he doubtless had no right brutally to pillage, but which at least he might wisely exploit. There had previously existed no conception of the science which, to a certain extent, by that very fact was established. In effect, if social and biological facts are only different facets of a single evolution, there must, from that very fact, exist sciences which explain them. In other words, the framework and the procedures of sociology should recall those of biology, even though they do not duplicate them.

Spencer's theory is, therefore, very fertile in applications if one knows how to use it. In addition, Spencer determined the object of sociology with more precision than Comte had done. He no longer speaks of society in a general and abstract way, but distinguishes different social types, which he classifies into divergent groups and subgroups. To discover the laws which he seeks, he does not choose one of these types in preference to the others, but deems them all of equal interest to the scholar. If we wish to obtain the general laws of social evolution, we cannot neglect a single one. Moreover, in his *Principles of Sociology* we find an imposing abundance of documents taken from the histories of various peoples and attesting to this philosopher's rare erudition. He ceases to pose the sociological problem in the vague and general manner of Auguste Comte. Instead, he distinguishes special questions, which he examines one after another. Thus, he successively studies the family, ceremonial government, political government, and ecclesiastic functions, and he proposes, in the still unpublished part of his work, to pass on to economic phenomena, language, and morality.

Unfortunately, the execution of this vast and beautiful program does not live up to the expectations to which it gave rise. The reason for this is that Spencer, like Auguste Comte, worked less as a sociologist than as a philosopher. He was not interested in social facts for their own sake; he does not study them just to know them but to use them in verifying the grand hypothesis which he conceived and which was supposed to explain everything. All the documents which he accumulated, all the special truths which he encountered along the way were intended to demonstrate that, like the rest of the world, societies develop in conformity with the law of universal evolution. In a word, we must not expect to find a sociology in his book, but, rather, a philosophy of sociology. It is not for me to ask whether there can be a philosophy of the sciences and what its interest might be. In any case, this is possible only for established sciences, while sociology has only just been born. Before taking up these lofty questions, one would first have to resolve a multitude of others, both special and particular, which have only recently been posed. How is it possible to find the supreme principle of social life when we do not yet know what the different types of society are or what their principal functions and laws might be? Spencer believed, it is true, that he could deal with these two orders of problems at the same time. He felt he could push forward both analysis and synthesis—found the science and simultaneously create its philosophy. But wasn't it rather foolhardy to attempt such an enterprise? And what came of it? He observed the facts, though rather hurriedly, in view of his desire to attain the objective which led him on. He ran through a number of problems, stopping only momentarily for each, even though they were all loaded with difficulties. His *Sociology* is a sort of bird's-eye view of societies. Organisms no longer present the sort of relief or sharply defined pattern which they have in reality. Instead, they become indistinguishable as they blur into a single, uniform tint which permits only indecisive features to show through.

We can guess what solutions result from so precipitate an examination and what this unique formulation, embracing and summarizing all these specific solutions, can be like. Ungrounded and vague, it expresses only the external and most general form of things. Whether it is a matter of the family or of governments, of religion or of commerce, everywhere Spencer believes he is rediscovering the same law. Everywhere he thinks he sees societies pass more or less slowly from the military to the industrial type, from a state in which social discipline is very strong to another in which everyone constructs his own self-discipline. Is that really all there is to history? And did humanity undergo such hardships just to suppress a few customs regulations and to proclaim freedom of speculation? That would be a rather small result for so colossal an effort. Is the solidarity which unites us to other men so burdensome that the whole aim of progress is to render it a little lighter? In other words, is the ideal for societies the ferocious individualism which Rousseau made their point of departure? Is positive politics just the *Social Contract* all over again? Carried away by his eagerness to generalize and perhaps also by his English preconceptions, Spencer has taken the form for the content. No doubt the individual is freer today than he was formerly, and it is good that it should be so. But if liberty is so highly valued, it is not for its own sake, by the sort of inherent virtue which the metaphysicians willingly attribute to it, but which the positive philosopher cannot recognize. It is not an absolute good of which one cannot get enough. Its value arises from the fruit which it bears and, by that fact, is narrowly limited. Though necessary to permit the individual to arrange his personal life according to his needs, it extends no further. Beyond this first sphere, there is another far more vast, where the individual also acts, but here in view of goals which transcend him, of which he usually is not even aware. Here he obviously can no longer assume the initiative for his actions, but can only be the recipient or sufferer of them. Individual liberty is, therefore, always and everywhere limited by social constraint, whether this takes the form of customs, mores, laws, or regulations. And, since to the extent that societies become more voluminous, the sphere of the society's action grows at the same time as that of the individual, we have every right to reproach Spencer for having seen only one side of reality and perhaps the lesser; to have misunderstood the properly social elements to be found in society.

IV

The failure of this attempt at synthesis demonstrated the necessity for sociologists at last to come around to detailed and precise studies. That is what Alfred Espinas understood, and that is the method which he followed in his book *Animal Societies*. He was not the first to have studied social facts in order to ground a science rather than just to maintain the symmetry of some grand philosophical system. Instead of limiting himself to overviews of society, he forced himself to study a specific social type; then, within this type, he distinguished classes and species and described them with care. It is from this attentive observation of the facts that he induced a few laws, the generality of which he carefully restricted to the special order of phenomena which he had studied. His book constitutes the first chapter of sociology.

What Espinas did for animal societies, a German scholar undertook to do for human society, or rather for the most advanced peoples of contemporary Europe. Albert Schaeffle devoted the four large volumes of his *Bau und Leben des Socialen Körpers* to a scrupulous analysis of our great modern societies. Here we find few or no theories. Schaeffle begins, it is true, by positing as a basic principle the fact that society is not a simple collection of individuals but an entity which has its own life, consciousness, interests, and history. Moreover, this idea, without which sociology cannot exist, has always been very much alive in Germany and was eclipsed only during the brief period when Kantian individualism held undisputed sway. The Germans have too profound a sense for the complexity of things to be easily content with so simplistic a solution. The theory which compares society with living organisms was therefore well received in Germany because it permitted the Germans to become more fully aware of an idea which had long been dear to them. Schaeffle also accepts it without hesitation, but he does not make it the touchstone of his method. He does indeed borrow from biology a few technical expressions of occasionally questionable propriety. But his dominant concern is to place himself as close as possible to social facts, to observe them in themselves, to see them as they are, and to reproduce them as he sees them. He takes apart, piece by piece, the enormous mechanisms which are our modern societies, counting the gears and explaining their functions. He distinguishes and classifies the many and diverse bonds which, though invisible, link us one to another. He shows us how social units are coordinated with one another in such a way as to form ever more complex groups, and how, from the actions and reactions produced within these groups, a certain number of common ideas issue little by little. These ideas are like the consciousness of society. After reading this book, how scanty and insubstantial seems Spencer's construction, and how much the elegant simplicity of his doctrine suffers by comparison to this patient and laborious analysis! We could, no doubt, object to the somewhat vague eclecticism of Schaeffle's doctrine. We could, in particular, reproach him for believing too strongly in the influence of rational thought on human conduct, for having intellect play too great a role in the evolution of mankind, and, consequently, for according too prominent a place in his method to reason and logical explanation. Finally, we might find that the scope of studies which he undertakes is still quite vast, too vast perhaps to permit him everywhere to conduct his observations with the same rigor. It is nonetheless certain that his entire book employs a properly scientific method and constitutes a veritable treatise of positive sociology.

This same method has been applied by other scholars, also from Germany, to the study of two social functions in particular: law and political economy. Instead of starting with human nature and deducing science from it, as the orthodox economists did, the German school attempts to observe economic facts as they present themselves in reality. That is the principle of the doctrine which they indiscriminantly call "socialism of the chair" or "state socialism." If this school openly leans toward a certain form of socialism, it is because, when we seek to see things as they are, we observe that, in fact, in all known societies, economic phenomena transcend the individual's sphere of action, that they constitute a function which is not domestic and private but social. Society, represented by the state, cannot, therefore, without qualification and control, entirely ignore and abandon this function to the free enterprise of individuals. That is how the method of Wagner and Schmoller, to name only the heads of this school, necessarily led them to make political economy a branch of sociology and to adopt a mitigated socialism as their doctrine.

At about the same period, certain jurists discovered the subject matter for a new science in law. Until then, law had been the occasion for only two types of work. On the one hand, there were the professional jurists, who were solely concerned with annotating legal formulations in order to establish their meaning and import. On the other hand, there were the philosophers, who attributed little significance to these human laws, which they saw as the contingent manifestation of the universal moral law. They undertook to discover, by force of intuition and reason alone, the eternal principles of law and ethics. But the interpretation of texts constitutes an art and not a science, since it does not lead to the discovery of laws; and, as for these grand speculations, their value and interest could only be metaphysical. Legal phenomena were, therefore, the object of no science, properly speaking, and for no good reason. It was this lack which Ihering and Post attempted to remedy. Though they belonged to very different philosophical schools, they both tried to induce the general principles of law from the comparison of texts on laws and customs. This is not the place for me either to set forth nor, above all, to evaluate the results of their analyses. But, whatever they may be, it is certain that this double movement, economic and legal, achieved an important advance. From that point on, sociology ceased to be a sort of universal science, general and confused, including just about everything. It was divided into a certain number of special sciences which attacked ever more determinate problems. The study of political economy had long since been established, even though it had long been languishing. The science of law, though newer, was basically but a transformation of the old philosophy of law. Sociology, thanks to its relationship to these two sciences, lost that erstwhile air of sudden improvisation which had sometimes cast doubt upon its future. It no longer seemed to have miraculously appeared out of nowhere one sunny day. Thenceforth, it had its historical antecedents and its links with the past, and it became possible to show how, like the other sciences, it emerged by a slow and steady process of development.

V

That is what sociology has become in our time, and those are the principal stages of its development. We have seen its birth with the economists, its founding with Comte, its consolidation with Spencer, its orientation with Schaeffle, and its specialization with the German jurists and economists. And from this brief summary of its history, you can deduce for yourselves what progress remains to be achieved. It has a clearly defined object and a method for studying it. The object consists of social facts. The method is observation and indirect experimentation, or, in other words, the comparative method. What is necessary at present is to outline the general framework of the science and to mark off its essential divisions. This work is not simply useful in properly ordering such studies but has a higher purpose. A science has truly been established only when it has been divided and subdivided, when it includes a certain number of problems which are distinct and at the same time integrated with one another. It must pass from this state of confused homogeneity in which it originates to a distinct and ordered heterogeneity. As long as it amounts to one or a few questions, it attracts only very synthetic minds; these people lay hold of it and mark it with their strong imprint to such an extent that it becomes their own property and seems to become confused with them. Being a personal work, it involves no collaboration. One may accept or reject these grand theories, modify them in their details, and apply them to a few specific cases, but one cannot add anything to them because they include everything, embrace everything. Conversely, by becoming more specialized, science comes closer to things which are themselves specialized. It thus becomes more objective, more impersonal, and, consequently, accessible to the full range of individual talents and to all workers of good will.

It might be tempting to proceed logically with this operation and, as Plato would say, dismantle the science into its component parts. But this would obviously mean failing in our goal, for we wish to analyze something real, not just a concept. A science is itself a sort of organism. We can observe its form and study its anatomy, but we cannot impose upon it one or another plan of composition just because it is more logical. It creates its own subdivisions in the course of establishing itself, and we can only reproduce those created naturally and render them clearer by bringing them to full awareness. Above all, it is necessary to proceed with this sort of caution in dealing with a science which has only just matured and whose features are still somewhat tender and inconsistent.

If, then, we apply this method to sociology, we obtain the following results:

1. In every society, there exists a certain number of common ideas and sentiments. These are passed from one generation to another and simultaneously assure the unity and the continuity of collective life. Among these are popular legends, religious traditions, political beliefs, language, and so on. All these phenomena are psychological in nature, but they do not have their source in individual psychology, since they infinitely transcend the individual. They must, therefore, be the object of a special science charged with their description and the investigation of their preconditions. This science could be called *social psychology*. This is the Germans' *Völkerpsychologie*. If we said nothing a moment ago about the interesting work of Lazarus and Stanthal, it is because no results have yet been produced. *Völkerpsychologie*, as they understood it, was but a new word to designate general linguistics and comparative philology.

2. Moreover, some of the judgments which everyone accepts have a two-sided character, in that they are both oriented to practical matters and are obligatory. They exert a sort of ascendancy on men's wills, constraining them to conform. This trait permits us to recognize those propositions, the sum of which constitutes morality. Ordinarily, we see morality as merely an art whose aim is to outline for men an ideal pattern of conduct. But the science of morality must precede the art. This science attempts to study moral maxims and beliefs as natural phenomena and to investigate their causes and laws.

3. Some of these maxims are obligatory to such an extent that society employs specific measures to prevent them from being disobeyed. It does not rely on public opinion to insure respect for them, but charges specially authorized representatives with that task. When they assume this particularly imperious character, moral judgments become legal formulations. As we have said, there is a science of law just as there is a science of morality, and these two sciences are in continual relationship. If we wish to push the distinction even further, we might divide the science of law into two

specialized sciences corresponding to the two types of law, one of which is penal and the other of which is not. I intentionally use very general expressions which do not prejudge the important question which we shall confront another time. We may therefore distinguish the science of law, properly so called, on the one hand, and criminology on the other.

4. Finally, there are what by convention are called economic phenomena. The science which studies them no longer needs to be created; but, for it to become a positive and concrete science, it will have to renounce the autonomy of which it was so proud and become a social science. It is not a simple catalog reform to tear political economy from its isolation and make it a branch of sociology. Its method and its doctrine will be changed at the same time.

This inventory fails to be complete. But any classification which, in the present state of sociology, claims to be definitive could only be arbitrary. The framework of a science which is only in the process of developing can in no way be rigid; it is important that it remain open to future acquisitions. Thus, we have discussed neither the army nor diplomacy, both of which are, nonetheless, social phenomena susceptible to scientific study. But these scientific studies do not yet exist, even in an embryonic state. I believe that it is better to do without the facile pleasure of sketching in broad outline the plan of an entire science waiting to be created, a sterile operation unless performed by the hand of a genius. We shall undertake a more useful piece of work by concerning ourselves only with phenomena which have already served as the subject matter of established sciences. There, at least, we have only to continue work that has already been begun and in which, to a certain extent, the past guarantees the future.

But each of the groups of phenomena which we have just distinguished could be examined from two different points of view and thus give rise to two sciences. Each of them consists in a certain number of actions coordinated in view of a goal, and one could study them as such. Or one might prefer to study the entity charged with accomplishing these actions. In other words, sometimes one will investigate what its role is and how it accomplishes it, and sometimes how it is itself constituted. In this way, we rediscover the two great divisions which dominate all biology: functions on the one hand, and structures on the other; physiology on one side, morphology on the other. What happens if the economist, for example, adopts the physiological point of view? He would ask himself what are the laws of the production of commodities, of their exchange, their circulation, and their consumption. From the morphological point of view, on the other hand, he would investigate how the producers, the workers, the merchants, and the consumers are grouped. He would compare the guilds of former times to the unions of today and the workshop to the factory by determining the laws of these various modes of grouping. The same holds for law: either one studies how it functions or one describes the bodies charged with making it function. This division is, to be sure, quite natural; however, in the course of our research we will remain almost exclusively within the physiological perspective, and the reasons for that preference are the following. Among lower organisms there exists a narrow and rigid relationship between the organ and the function. A modification in the function is impossible unless it produces a corresponding change in the organ. The latter is set in its role because it is fixed in its structure. But it is not the same with the superior functions of superior beings. Here the structure is so flexible that it is no longer an obstacle to changes: it can happen that an organ or a part of an organ accomplishes different functions. We know that among living organisms different lobes of the brain can replace each other with great facility; but it is above all among societies that this phenomenon manifests itself most strikingly. Again and again, we find that social institutions, once created, serve ends which no one foresaw. They could, therefore, hardly have been organized with these ends in view. We know that a constitution cleverly arranged with despotism in mind can sometimes become a haven for liberty, or vice versa. Did not the Catholic church, in the great moments of its history, adapt to the most diverse circumstances of time and place, yet always and everywhere remain the same? How many mores and practices remain today what they were formerly, even though their goal and their raison d'être have changed. What these examples attest to is a certain suppleness of structure in the organs of society. Of course, because they are so flexible, the forms of social life are somewhat vague and indeterminate. They offer fewer opportunities for scientific observation and are less easily accessible. It would be better, then, not to begin with them. Moreover, they are less important and less interesting, for they are only a secondary and derived phenomenon. Structure presupposes function and derives from it, and such a statement is never more true than in speaking of societies. Institutions are not established by decree but result from social life and merely translate it externally through overt symbols. Structure is function consolidated; it is action which has become habit and which has crystallized. Therefore, unless we wish to see things only in their most superficial aspect, and if we desire to reach down to their very roots, we must apply ourselves above all to the study of functions.

VI

As you see, my principal concern is to limit and circumscribe as much as possible the extent of our research, for I am quite convinced that it is necessary for sociology finally to end the era of generalities. But, however restricted these studies may be—or rather, because in being more restricted they will be more precise—they can, I believe, be of use to rather different audiences.

First, we have the students in philosophy. If they run through their programs of study, they will find no mention of sociology. But, if, instead of sticking to the traditional rubrics, they go to the heart of the matter, they will observe that the phenomena which philosophy studies are of two sorts: the first relates to the consciousness of the individual, the other to the consciousness of the society. Here we are concerned with the latter. Philosophy is in the process of dissociating itself into two groups of positive sciences: psychology on the one hand, sociology on the other. To be more precise, it is sociology which is the source of the problems which heretofore belonged exclusively to philosophical ethics. We shall recapture them in our turn. Of all the areas of sociology, morality is the one which attracts us by preference and holds our attention before all else. We shall, however, try to deal with it scientifically. Instead of constructing it according to our personal ideal, we shall observe it as a system of natural phenomena whose causes we seek and which we shall subject to analysis. Experience will teach us that these causes are social in nature. We shall not, to be sure, forbid ourselves to speculate in any way about the future, but it should be clear that before investigating what the family, property, or society should be, we must know what they are, to what needs they correspond, and to what conditions they must conform in order to survive. We shall begin in this way and thereby resolve an antinomy which has sorely troubled men's minds. For a century past, men have argued whether morality must precede science or science morality. The only way to end this antagonism is to make morality a science like the others and related to them. It has been said that there is today a crisis in morality and, indeed, there is so great a break in continuity between the moral ideal, as some minds have conceived of it, and factual reality that, depending on circumstances and temperaments, morality oscillates between these two poles without knowing where to come to rest. The only way to end this state of instability and unrest is to view morality as a fact, the nature of which we must scrutinize attentively and, I would even say, respectfully, before we dare to change it.

But the philosophers are not the only students to whom this course of study is addressed. I mentioned in passing the services which the historian could render to the sociologist, but it is difficult for me to believe that the historians have nothing to learn from sociology in return. In a general way, I have always found that there was a sort of contradiction in making history a science, yet not asking future historians to undergo any scientific apprenticeship. The general education which is required of them has remained what it always was: philological and literary. Is mediation upon the chefs-d'oeuvres of literature a sufficient initiation into the spirit and practice of the scientific method? I am quite aware that the historian is not a generalizer; his very special role is not to discover laws but to render to each period and to each people its own individuality and its particular physiognomy. He remains and must remain in the realm of the particular. But as particular as the phenomena which he studies may be, he is not content to describe them, but links them one to another and investigates their causes and preconditions. To do that, he makes inductions and hypotheses. How could he help often going astray if he proceeds empirically, if he feels his way along by trial and error, if he is not guided by any notion about the nature of societies, their functions, and the relationship among those functions? In this enormous mass of facts which constitutes the thread of life of great societies, how will he make a choice? Some of those facts have no more scientific interest than the trifling incidents of our daily life. If he accepts them all indiscriminately, he falls into vain erudition. He may still hold the interest of a small circle of learned men, but he is no longer doing useful and vital work. To make a selection, he needs an orienting idea, a standard which he can expect to come only from sociology. It is sociology which will teach him which of society's functions are vital and which of its organs are essential. It is to the study of these functions and these organs that he will apply himself by preference. Sociology will pose for him the questions which will limit and guide his research. In return, he will furnish sociology with the elements of the answer, and the two sciences can only gain from this exchange of assistance.

There is a final category of students whom I would be happy to see represented in this room: law students. When this course was created, people wondered whether it didn't belong in the law school. The question of where the course is to be given is, I believe, unimportant. The boundaries which separate the various parts of the university are not so sharply drawn that certain courses may not equally well be placed in one or another curriculum. But what this scruple does prove is that today the best minds recognize that it is necessary that the law student not close himself off in the study of pure exegesis. If he spends all his time commenting on texts and if, consequently, his sole preoccupation with each law is to investigate and speculate about the legislator's intent, he will come to see the legislative will as the sole source of the law. But he would thus be taking the letter for the spirit and the appearance for the reality. It is in the very guts of society that the law is elaborated, and the legislator only consecrates a work which is accomplished without him. The student must, therefore, learn how the law is formed under the pressure of social needs, how it is molded little by little, through what degrees of crystallization it successively passes, and how it is transformed. He must be shown in actual practice how the great legal institutions like the family, property, and contract are born, what their causes are, how they have varied, and how they are likely to vary in the future. Then he will no longer see legal formulations as sentences or oracles whose sometimes mysterious meaning must be divined. He will know how to determine their import, not according to the obscure and often unconscious intent of a man or an assembly, but according to the very nature of reality.

These are the theoretical services which our science can render. But it can also have a salutary influence on practice. We live in a country which recognizes no master but public opinion. Unless this master is to become a mindless despot, it must be enlightened. And how are we to do this if not through science? Under the influence of causes which we have no time to analyze here, the collective spirit has been weakened in us. Each of us has so overwhelming a sense of self that he no longer perceives the limits which hem him in on all sides. Deluding himself about his own power, he aspires to suffice unto himself. That is why we make our personal worth depend on distinguishing ourselves as much as possible from one another and on each pursuing his own course. We must react with all our energy against this dispersive tendency. Our society must regain awareness of its organic unity. The individual must develop a sense for this social mass which envelops and penetrates him; he must sense it always near and active. And this sentiment must always rule his conduct, for it is not enough that he be inspired by it only once in a while in particularly critical circumstances. I believe that sociology, more than any other science, is in a position to restore these ideas. It is sociology which will make the individual understand what society is, how it completes him, and how little he really is when reduced to his own forces alone. It will teach him that he is not an empire embedded within another empire but the organ of an organism. It will show him all that is beautiful in conscientiously performing his role as an organ. It will make him feel that there is no diminution in being integrated with others and in depending on them, in not belonging quite entirely to himself. No doubt these ideas will become truly effective only if they spread among the lower strata of the population. But for that to happen, we must first elaborate them scientifically at the university. To contribute to the accomplishment of this result, to the extent of my ability, will be my principal concern, and I could know no greater joy than to achieve some measure of success in this attempt.

2

SOCIOLOGY AND THE
SOCIAL SCIENCES

When dealing with a new science such as sociology, which, born only yesterday, is merely in the process of being constituted, the best way to understand its nature, object, and method is to retrace its genesis in a summary fashion.

The word *sociology* was created by Auguste Comte to designate the science of societies.[1] If the word was new, it was because the thing itself was new; a neologism was necessary. To be sure, one could say in a very broad sense that speculation about political and social matters began before the nineteenth century: Plato's *Republic*, Aristotle's *Politics*, and the innumerable treatises for which these two works served as models—those of Campanella, of Hobbes, of Rousseau and of so many others—already dealt with these questions. But these various studies differed in one fundamental respect from those which are designated by the word *sociology*. They took as their object not the description or explanation of societies as they exist or as they have existed, but the investigation of what societies *should be, how they should be organized* in order to be as perfect as possible. The aim of the sociologist is entirely different; he studies societies simply *to know them* and *to understand them*, just as the physicist, the chemist, and the biologist do for physical, chemical, and biological phenomena. His sole task is properly to determine the facts which he undertakes to study, to discover the laws according to which they occur, leaving it to others

Originally published as "Sociologie et sciences sociales," in *De la méthode dans les sciences* (Paris: Alcan, 1909), pp. 259-85.

to find, if there is need, the possible applications of the propositions which he establishes.

That is to say that sociology could not appear until men had acquired the sense that societies, like the rest of the world, are subject to laws which of necessity derive from and express their nature. Now this conception was very slow to take form. For centuries, men believed that even minerals were not ruled by definite laws but could take on all possible forms and properties if only a sufficiently powerful will applied itself to them. They believed that certain expressions or certain gestures had the ability to transform an inert mass into a living being, a man into an animal or a plant, and vice versa. This illusion, for which we have a sort of instinctive inclination, naturally persisted much longer in the realm of social phenomena.

In effect, since they are far more complex, the order which inheres in social phenomena is far more difficult to perceive and, consequently, one is led to believe that they occur in a contingent and more or less disordered way. At first sight, what a contrast exists between the simple, rigorous sequence with which the phenomena of the physical universe unfold and the chaotic, capricious, disconcerting aspect of the events which history records! From another viewpoint, the very part which we play therein disposes us to think that, since they are done by us, they depend exclusively on us and can be what we want them to be. In such circumstances, there was no reason to observe them, since they were nothing by themselves but derived any reality they had from our will alone. From this point of view, the only question which could come up was to know not what they were and according to what laws they operated but what we could and must desire them to be.

It was only at the end of the eighteenth century that people first began to perceive that the social realm, like the other realms of nature, had its own laws. When Montesquieu declared that "The laws are the necessary relationships which derive from the nature of things," he well understood that this excellent definition of natural law applied to social as well as to other phenomena; his book, *The Spirit of Laws*, attempts to show precisely how legal institutions are grounded in man's nature and his milieu. Soon thereafter, Condorcet undertook to reconstruct the order according to which mankind achieved its progress.[2] This was the best way to demonstrate that there was nothing fortuitous or capricious about it but that it depended on determinate causes. At the same time, the economists taught that the phenomena of industrial and commercial life are governed by laws, which they thought they had discovered.

Although these different thinkers had prepared the way for the conception on which sociology rests, they had as yet only a rather ambiguous and irresolute notion of what the laws of social life might be. They did not wish to say, in effect, that social facts link up according to definite and invariable relations which the scholar seeks to observe by procedures analogous to those which are employed in the natural sciences. They simply meant that, given the nature of man, a course was layed out which was the only natural one, the one mankind should follow *if it wished to be in harmony with itself and to fulfill its destiny*; but it was still possible that it had strayed from that path.

And in fact, they judged that mankind had ceaselessly strayed as the result of deplorable aberrations which, moreover, they did not take much trouble to explain. For the economists, for example, the true economic organization, the only one which science should undertake to know, has, so to speak, never existed; it is more ideal than real. For men, under the influence of their rulers and as a result of a veritable blindness, have always let themselves be led astray. That is to say that the economists far more often constructed it deductively than observed it; and in this way they returned, though in an indirect way, to the ideas which were the basis of the political theories of Plato and Aristotle.

It is only at the beginning of the nineteenth century, with Saint-Simon at first, and especially with his disciple, Auguste Comte, that a new conception was definitively brought to light.[3]

Proceeding to the synthetic view of all the constituted sciences of his time in his *Cours de philosophie positive*, Comte stated that they all rested on the axiom that the phenomena with which they dealt are linked according to necessary relationships, that is to say, on the determinist principle. From this fact, he concluded that this principle, which had thus been verified in all the other realms of nature from the realm of mathematical splendors to that of life, must be equally true of the social realm. The resistances which today are opposed to this new extension of the determinist idea must not stop the philosopher. They have arisen with regularity each time that it has been a question of extending to a new realm this fundamental postulate and they always have been overcome. There was a time when people refused to accept that this principle applied even in the world of inanimate objects; it was established there. Next it was denied for living and thinking beings; now it is undisputed there as well.

One can therefore rest assured that these same prejudices which this principle encountered in the attempt to apply it to the social world will last only for a time. Moreover, since Comte postulated as a self-evident truth—a truth which is, moreover, now undisputed—that the individual's mental life is subject to necessary laws, how could the actions and reactions which are exchanged among individual consciousnesses in association not be subjected to the same necessity?

Viewed in this way, societies ceased to appear as a sort of indefinitely malleable and plastic matter that men could mold, so to speak, at will; thenceforth, it was necessary to see them as realities whose nature is imposed upon us and which, like all natural things, can only be modified in conformity with the laws which regulate them. Human institutions could be considered no longer as the product of the more or less enlightened will of princes, statesmen, and legislators, but as the necessary result of determinate causes that physically imply them. Given the composition of a nation at a given moment in its history, and the state of its civilization at this same period, a social organization results which is characterized in this or that manner, just as the properties of a physical body result from its molecular constitution. We are thus faced with a stable, immutable order of things, and pure science becomes at once possible and necessary for describing and explaining it, for saying what its characteristics are and on what causes they depend. This purely speculative science is sociology. In order better to suggest the relationship in which it stands to the other positive sciences, Comte often calls it social physics.

It has sometimes been said that this conception implies a sort of fatalism. If the network of social facts is so solid and so resistant a web, does it not follow that men are incapable of modifying it and that, consequently, they cannot act upon their own history? But the example of what has happened in the other realms of nature demonstrates to what extent this reproach is unjustified. As we were saying a moment ago, there was a time when the human mind did not know that the physical universe had its laws. Was it then that man held greatest sway over things? No doubt, the sorcerer or the magician believed that he could transmute at will various bodies one into another; but the powers which he thus attributed to himself were, we know today, purely imaginary. On the contrary, since the positive natural sciences were established (and they too were established by taking the determinist postulate as a foundation), what changes we have introduced into the universe! It will be the same way in the social realm. Until yesterday we believed that all this was arbitrary and contingent, that legislators or kings could, just like the alchemists of yore, at their pleasure change the aspect of societies, make them change from one type to another. In reality, these supposed miracles were illusory; and how many grave errors have resulted from this yet too widespread illusion! On the contrary, it is sociology which by discovering the laws of social reality will permit us to direct historical evolution with greater reflection than in the past; for we can change nature, whether moral or physical, only by conforming to its laws. Progress in political arts will follow those in social science, just as the discoveries of physiology and anatomy helped perfect medical arts, just as the power of industry has increased a hundredfold since mechanics and the physico-chemical sciences have sprung to life. At the same time that they proclaim the necessity of things, the sciences place in our hands the means to dominate that necessity.[4] Comte even remarks with insistence that of all the natural phenomena, social phenomena are the most malleable, the most accessible to variations and to changes, because they are the most complex. Therefore, sociology in no way imposes upon man a passively conservative attitude; on the contrary, it extends the field of our action by the simple fact that it extends the field of our science. It only turns us away from ill-conceived and sterile enterprises inspired by the belief that we are able to change the social order as we wish, without taking into account customs, traditions, and the mental constitution of man and of societies.

But, as essential as this principle may be, it was not a sufficient basis on which to found sociology. For there to be substance to a new science called by this name, it was yet necessary that the subject matter which it undertakes to study not be confused with those which the other sciences treat. Now on first consideration, sociology might appear indistinguishable from psychology; and this thesis has in fact been maintained, by Tarde, among others.[5] Society, they say, is nothing but the individuals of whom it is composed. They are its only reality. How, then, can the science of societies be distinguished from the science of individuals, that is to say, from psychology?

If one reasons in this way, one could equally well maintain that biology is but a chapter of physics and chemistry, for the living cell is composed exclusively of atoms of carbon, nitrogen, and so on, which the physico-chemical sciences undertake to study. But that is to forget that a whole very often has very different properties from those which its constituent parts possess. Though a cell contains nothing but mineral elements, these reveal, by being combined in a certain way, properties which they do not have when they are not thus combined and which are characteristic of life (properties of sustenance and of reproduction); they thus form, through their synthesis, a reality of an entirely new sort, which is living reality and which constitutes the subject matter of biology. In the same way, individual consciousnesses, by associating themselves in a stable way, reveal, through their interrelationships, a new life very different from that which would have developed had they remained uncombined; this is social life. Religious institutions and beliefs, political, legal, moral, and economic institutions—in a word, all of what constitutes civilization—would not exist if there were no society.

In effect, civilization presupposes cooperation not only among all the members of a single society, but also among all the societies which interact with one another. Moreover, it is possible only if the results obtained by one generation are transmitted to the following generation in such a way that they can be added to the results which the latter will obtain. But for that to happen, the successive generations must not be separated from one another as they arrive at adulthood but must remain in close contact, that is to say, they must be associated in a permanent fashion. Thus, this entire, vast assembly of things exists only because there are human associations; moreover, they vary according to what these associations are, and how they are organized. These things find their immediate explanation in the nature of societies, not of individuals, and constitute, therefore, the subject matter of a new science distinct from, though related to, individual psychology: this is sociology.[6]

Comte was not content to establish these two principles theoretically; he undertook to put them into practice, and, for the first time, he attempted to create a sociological discipline. It is for this purpose that he uses the three final volumes of the *Cours de philosophie positive*. Little remains today of the details of his work. Historical and especially ethnographic knowledge was still too rudimentary in his time to offer a sufficiently solid basis for sociological inductions. Moreover, as we shall see below, Comte did not recognize the multiplicity of the problems posed by the new science: he thought that he could create it all at once, as one would create a system of metaphysics; sociology, however, like any science, can be constituted only progressively, by approaching questions one after another. But the idea was infinitely fertile and outlived the founder of positivism.

It was taken up again first by Herbert Spencer.[7] Then, in the last thirty years, a whole legion of workers arose—to some extent in all countries, but particularly in France—and applied themselves to these studies. Sociology has now left behind the heroic age. The principles on which it rests and which were originally proclaimed in a very philosophical and dialectical way have now received factual confirmation. It assumes that social phenomena are in no way contingent or arbitrary. Sociologists have shown that certain moral and legal institutions and certain religious beliefs are identical everywhere that the conditions of social life are identical. They have even been able to establish similarities in the details of the customs of countries very distant from each other and between which there has never been any sort of communication. This remarkable uniformity is the best proof that the social realm does not escape the law of universal determinism.[8]

II. The Divisions of Sociology: The Individual Social Sciences

But if, in a sense, sociology is a unified science, still it includes a multiplicity of questions and, consequently, a multiplicity of individual sciences. Therefore, let us examine these sciences of which sociology is the corpus.

Comte already felt the need to divide it up; he distinguished two parts: social statics and social dynamics. Statics studies societies by considering them as fixed at a given point in their development; it seeks the laws of their equilibrium. At each moment in time, the individuals and the groups which shape them are joined to one another by bonds of a certain type, which assure social cohesion; and the various estates of a single civilization maintain definite relations with one another. To a given degree of elaboration of science, for example, corresponds a specific development of religion, morality, art, industry, and so forth. Statics tries to determine what these bonds of solidarity and these connections are. Dynamics, on the contrary, considers societies in their evolution and attempts to discover the law of their development. But the object of statics as Comte understood it is very indeterminate, since it arises from the definition which we have just given; moreover, he devotes only a few pages to it in the *Cours de philosophie*. Dynamics take up all the rest. Now the problem with which dynamics deals is unique: according to Comte, a single and invariable law dominates the course of evolution; this is the famous Law of Three Stages.[9] The sole object of social dynamics is to investigate this law. Thus understood, sociology is reduced to a single question; so much so that once this single question has been resolved—and Comte believed he had found the definitive solution—the science will be complete. Now it is in the very nature of the positive sciences that they are never complete. The realities with which they deal are far too complex ever to be exhausted. If sociology is a positive science, we can be assured that it does not consist in a single problem but includes, on the contrary, different parts, many distinct sciences which correspond to the various aspects of social life.

There are, in reality, as many branches of sociology, as many individual social sciences, as there are different types of social facts. A methodical classification of social facts would be premature and, in any case, will not be attempted here. But it is possible to indicate its principal categories.

First of all, there is reason to study society in its external aspect. From this angle, it appears to be formed by a mass of population of a certain density, disposed on the face of the earth in a certain fashion, dispersed in the countryside or concentrated in cities, and so on. It occupies a more or less extensive territory, situated in a certain way relative to the seas and to the territories of neighboring peoples, more or less furrowed with waterways and paths of communications of all sorts which place the inhabitants in more or less intimate relationship. This territory, its dimensions, its configuration, and the composition of the population which moves upon its surface are naturally important factors of social life; they are its substratum and, just as psychic life in the individual varies with the anatomical composition of the brain which supports it, collective phenomena vary with the constitution of the social substratum. There is, therefore, room for a social science which traces its anatomy; and since this science has as its object the external and material form of society, we propose to call it *social morphology*. Social morphology does not, moreover, have to limit itself to a descriptive analysis; it must also explain. It must look for the reasons why the population is massed at certain points rather than at others, why it is principally urban or principally rural, what are the causes which favor or impede the development of great cities, and so on. We can see that this special science itself has a multitude of problems with which to deal.[10]

But parallel to the substratum of collective life, there is this life itself. Here we run across a distinction analogous to that which we observe in the other natural sciences. Alongside chemistry, which studies the way in which minerals are constituted, there is physics, the subject matter of which is the phenomena of all sorts for which the bodies thus constituted are the theater. In biology, while anatomy (also called morphology) analyzes the structure of living beings and the mode of composition of their tissues and organs, physiology studies the functions of these tissues and organs. In the same way, beside social morphology there is room for a social physiology which studies the vital manifestations of societies.

But social physiology is itself very complex and includes a multiplicity of individual sciences; for the social phenomena of the physiological order are themselves extremely varied.

First there are religious beliefs, practices, and institutions. Religion is, in effect, a social phenomenon, since it has always been a property of a group, namely, a church, and because in the great majority of cases the church and the political society are indistinct. Until very recent times, one was faithful to certain divinities by the very fact that one was the citizen of a certain state. In any case, dogmas and myths have always consisted in systems of beliefs common to an entire collectivity and obligatory for the members of that collectivity. It is the same way with rituals. The study of religion is, therefore, the domain of sociology; it constitutes the subject matter of the *sociology of religion*.

Moral ideas and mores form another category, distinct from the preceding. We shall see in another chapter how the rules of morality are social phenomena; they are the subject matter of the *sociology of morality*.

There is no need to demonstrate the social character of legal institutions. They are to be studied by the *sociology of law*. This field is, moreover, closely related to the sociology of morality, for moral ideas are the spirit of the law. What constitutes the authority of a legal code is the moral idea which it incarnates and which it translates into definite formulations.

Finally, there are the economic institutions: institutions relating to the production of wealth (serfdom, tenant farming, corporate organization, production in factories, in mills, at home, and so on), institutions relating to exchange (commercial organization, markets, stock exchanges, and so on), institutions relating to distribution (rent, interest, salaries, and so on). They form the subject matter of *economic sociology*.

These are the principal branches of sociology. They are not, however, the only ones. Language, which in certain respects depends on organic conditions, is nevertheless a social phenomenon, for it is also the product of a group and it bears its stamp. Even language is, in general, one of the characteristic elements of the physiognomy of societies, and it is not without reason that the relatedness of languages is often used as a means of establishing the relatedness of peoples. There is, therefore, subject matter for a sociological study of language, which has, moreover, already begun.[11] We can say as much of aesthetics, for, despite the fact that each artist (poet, orator, sculptor, painter, and so on) puts his own mark on the works that he creates, all those that are elaborated in the same social milieu and in the same period express in different forms a single ideal which is itself closely related to the temperament of the social groups to which they address themselves.

It is true that certain of these facts are already studied by disciplines long since established; notably, economic facts serve as the subject matter for the assembly of diverse research, analyses, and theories which together are designated as political economy. But just as we said above, political economy has remained to the present a hybrid study, intermediate between art and science; it is much less concerned with observing industrial and commercial life such as it is and has been in order to know it and determine its laws than with reconstructing this life as it should be. The economists have as yet only a quite weak sense that economic reality is imposed upon the observer just like physical realities, that it is subject to the same necessity, and that, consequently, the science which studies it must be created in a quite speculative way before we undertake to reform it. What is more, they study facts, which are dealt with as if they formed an independent whole which is self-sufficient and self-explanatory. In reality, economic functions are social functions and are integrated with the other collective functions; they become inexplicable when they are violently removed from that context. Workers' wages depend not only on the relationships of supply and demand but upon certain moral conceptions. They rise or fall depending on the idea we create for ourselves of the individual. More examples could be cited. By becoming a branch of sociology, economic science will naturally be wrenched from its isolation at the same time that it will become more deeply impregnated with the idea of scientific determinism. As a consequence of thus taking its place in the system of the social sciences, it will not merely undergo a change of name; both the spirit which animates it and the methods which it practices will be transformed.

We see from this analysis how false is the view that sociology is but a very simple science which consists, as Comte thought, in a single problem. As of today, it is impossible for a sociologist to possess encyclopedic knowledge of his science; but each scholar must attach himself to a special order of problems unless he wishes to be content with very general and vague views. These general views may have been useful when sociology was merely trying to explore the limits of its domain and to become aware of itself, but the discipline can no longer dally in such a fashion. This is not to say, however, that there is no place for a synthetic science which will manage to assemble the general conclusions which all these other specific sciences will reveal. As different as the various classes of social facts may be, they are, nonetheless, only species of the same genus; there is, therefore, reason to seek out what makes for the unity of the genus, what characterizes the social fact *in abstracto*, and whether there are very general laws of which the very diverse laws established by the special sciences are only particular forms. This is the object of general sociology, just as general biology has as its object to reveal the most general properties and laws of life. This is the philosophical part of the science. But since the worth of the synthesis depends on the worth of the analyses from which it results, the most urgent task of sociology is to advance this work of analysis.

In summary, table 1 represents in a schematic way the principal divisions of sociology.

III. THE SOCIOLOGICAL METHOD

Having determined the domain of sociology and its principal subdivisions, we must now try to characterize the most essential principles of the method employed in this science.

The principal problems of sociology consist in researching the way

Table 1. Principal divisions of sociology

SOCIAL MORPHOLOGY

{
The study of the geographic base of various peoples in terms of its relationships with their social organization.

The study of population: its volume, its density, and its disposition on the earth.
}

SOCIAL PHYSIOLOGY

{
Sociology of Religion

Sociology of Morality

Sociology of Law

Economic Sociology

Linguistic Sociology

Aesthetic Sociology
}

GENERAL SOCIOLOGY

in which a political, legal, moral, economic, or religious institution, belief, and so on, was established, what causes gave rise to it, and to what useful ends it responds. Comparative history, understood in the sense which we are going to try to specify, is the only instrument of which the sociologist disposes to resolve these kinds of questions.

In effect, to understand an institution, one must know of what it is made. It is a complex whole, comprised of parts; one must know these parts and be able to explain each of them separately as well as the way in which they are combined. To discover all this, it is not enough to consider the institution in its completed and recent form, for, being accustomed to it, we find it rather simple. In any case, there is nothing in it which indicates where the various elements of which it is formed begin or end. There is no line of demarcation which separates them from one another in a visible way, any more than we perceive with our naked eyes the cells which form the tissues of the living being or the molecules which compose inert bodies. We need an instrument of analysis to make them appear. It is history which plays this role. In effect, the institution under consideration was established gradually, piece by piece; the parts of which it is formed were born one after another and were added more or less slowly. Therefore, all we need to do to see the various elements from which it results naturally dissociated is to follow its genesis in time, that is, in history. They then present themselves to the observer one after another in the very order in which they were formed and combined. For example, there is nothing simpler, it would seem, than the notion of kinship. Yet history shows us that it is extremely complicated: the idea of consanguinity plays a role, but many other things enter in, for we find types of families in which consanguinity plays only a very accessory role. Matrilineality and patrilineality are qualitatively distinct phenomena which depend on entirely different causes, consequently requiring that they be studied separately, for we find in history types of families in which only one of the two types of kinship existed. In a word, history plays a role in the order of social realities analogous to that of the microscope in the order of physical realities.

What is more, it alone allows us to create explanations. In effect, to explain an institution is to account for the various elements which served in its formation; it is to show their causes and their raisons d'être. But how are we to discover these causes if not by carrying ourselves back to the moment when they were operative, that is to say, when they gave rise to the facts which we seek to understand? For it is only at that moment that it is possible to grasp the way in which they acted and engendered their effect. But this moment is in the past. The only way to succeed in knowing how each of these elements came into being is to observe it at the very instant when it was born and to be present at its genesis. But this genesis took place in the past and, consequently, can only be known through history. For example, today kinship is bilateral: both the paternal and the maternal lines count. In order to discover the determining causes of this complex organization, one would first observe societies in which kinship is essentially or exclusively uterine and would try to find its cause; then, one would consider peoples among whom agnatic kinship was established.[12] Finally, since the latter, when it appears, often relegates the former to a secondary role, one would investigate civilizations in which both have begun to be placed on an equal footing and would attempt to discover the conditions which determined this equality. It is in this way that sociological questions are graded, so to speak, into different stages of the past, and it is only on condition of situating them in this way, of relating them to the various historical milieux in which they were born, that it is possible to resolve them.

Sociology is, therefore, in large part a form of history which has been extended in a certain way. The historian also deals with social facts; but he considers, above all, the way in which they are peculiar to a determinate people and time. In general, he proposes to study the life of a given nation or of a given collective individuality taken at a given moment in its evolution. His immediate task is to rediscover and to characterize the particular, individual physiognomy of each society and even of each of the periods which comprise the life of a single society. The sociologist sticks solely to discovering the general relationships and verifiable laws of different societies. He does not especially try to find out what religious life or property law was like in France or in England, in Rome or in India, in a particular century; but these specialized studies, which are, moreover, indispensable to him, are but the means of arriving at the discovery of a few of the factors of religious life in general. We have only one way to demonstrate that a logical relationship (for example, a causal relationship) exists between two facts; we would have to compare cases in which they are simultaneously present or absent and to see if the variations which they present in these different combinations of circumstances bear witness to the dependence of one on the other. Experiment is, fundamentally, just a form of comparison; it consists in making a fact vary, of producing it in various forms which are subsequently methodically compared. The sociologist cannot, therefore, limit himself to the consideration of a single people or even of a single era. He must compare societies of the same type and also of different types. Thus, the variations in the institution or the practice for which he wishes to account—once brought together with the parallel variations which are observed in the social milieu, in the state of ideas, and so on—allow him to perceive the relationships which unite these two groups of facts and to establish some causal relationship between them. The comparative method is thus the preeminent instrument of the sociological method. History, in the usual sense, is to sociology what Latin grammar or Greek grammar or French grammar, taken and treated separately from one another, are to the new science which has taken the name "comparative grammar."[13]

There are, however, cases in which the material for sociological comparisons must be requested of a discipline other than history. One sometimes investigates not how a legal or moral rule or religious belief was formed, but what determines whether it is more or less well observed by the collectivities which practice it. For example, instead of wondering where the rule prohibiting homicide originates, one would undertake to discover the various causes which make peoples and groups of all sorts more or less inclined to violate it. In the same way, one could propose to find some of the factors which make marriages more or less frequent, more or less early, more or less easily dissolved by divorce, and so on. To resolve these kinds of questions, one must essentially address oneself to statistics. One would investigate how the frequency of homicides, marriages, or divorces varies with societies, religious confessions, professions, and so on.[14] Problems related to the various conditions on which peoples' morals depend must notably be dealt with according to this method.[15] With the help of the same procedure one can, in economic sociology, study the causes, in function of which wages, rents, interest rates, the value of monetary exchanges, and so on, vary.

But, whatever the particular technique to which he has recourse, there is a rule of which the sociologist must never lose sight: before beginning the study of a determinate category of social phenomena, he must begin by making *tabula rasa* of the notions of them which he may have formed in the course of his life; he must accept as a matter of principle the fact that he knows nothing about them or about their characteristics or of the causes on which they depend. He must, in a word, place himself in a state of mind like that of physicists, chemists, physiologists, and today even psychologists when they enter a previously unexplored region of their scientific domain.

Unfortunately, as necessary as this attitude may be, it is not easy to maintain vis-à-vis social reality; inveterate habits lead us astray. Because every day we practice the rules of morality and of law, because we buy, sell, and exchange sums, and so forth, we necessarily have some idea of these various phenomena; without them we could not manage our daily tasks. A quite natural illusion derives from this: we believe that with these ideas we grasp all the essentials of the things to which they may refer. The moralist takes no great pains to explain what the family, kinship, paternal power, contract, or the right of property may be; the economist proceeds in the same way as far as value, exchange, or rent are concerned. It seems that the science of these things is innate; all we need is to be aware as clearly as possible of the notions which are commonly held of these complex realities. But these notions, which are formed without any method in order to answer practical exigencies, are devoid of any scientific value. They express social phenomena no more exactly than the notions which the layman has of physical bodies—of their properties, of light, sound, heat, and so on— represent exactly the nature of these bodies and their objective characteristics. The physicist and the chemist set aside these everyday representations, and reality, as they make us see it, is, in fact, singularly different from what the senses perceive directly. The sociologist must do the same; he must place himself face to face with social facts, forgetting all that he believed he knew about them, as if he faced an unknown. Sociology must not be a simple illustration of ready-made and deceptive truisms; it must fashion discoveries which, moreover, cannot fail often to upset accepted notions. We know nothing at all of these social phenomena amid which we move; the task of progressively revealing them to us belongs to the various social sciences.

3

NOTE ON SOCIAL MORPHOLOGY

Before analyzing the works which we have assembled under this rubric, we must first indicate the meaning of the term.

Social life rests upon a substratum which is determinate both in its extent and in its form. It is composed of the mass of individuals who comprise the society, the manner in which they are disposed upon the earth, and the nature and configuration of objects of all sorts which affect collective relations. Depending on whether the population is more or less sizable, more or less dense; depending on whether it is concentrated in cities or dispersed in the countryside; depending on the way in which the cities and the houses are constructed; depending on whether the space occupied by the society is more or less extensive; depending on the borders which define its limits, the avenues of communication which traverse it, and so forth, this social substratum will differ. From another point of view, the constitution of this substratum directly or indirectly affects all social phenomena, just as all psychic phenomena are placed in mediate or immediate relationship with the brain. Thus, we have a whole collection of problems which are of obvious interest to sociology and which, because they all refer to a single and identical object, must come within the jurisdiction of a single science. It is this science which we propose to call *social morphology*.

The works which deal with these questions now have their origin

Originally published in *L'Année sociologique* 2 (1897-98): 520-21. The reader should bear in mind that this note introduced a newly created rubric within the book review section of the journal.

in different disciplines. It is geography which studies the territorial forms of nations. It is history which retraces the evolution of rural or urban groups. It is demography which covers all that concerns the distribution of population. We believe there is an advantage to be gained by drawing these fragmentary sciences out of their isolation and placing them in contact by assembling them under a single rubric. They will thus achieve an awareness of their unity. The reader will learn below of how a school of geography is now attempting an analogous synthesis under the name of *political geography*.[1] But we fear that this expression may create certain confusions. In effect, this new field will study, not the forms of the earth, but the forms which affect societies as they establish themselves on the earth, which is quite a different matter. There is no doubt that watercourses, mountains, and the like enter as elements in the constitution of the social substratum; but they are neither the only nor the most essential elements. Now the word *geography* almost fatally leads to according them an importance which they do not have, and we shall have occasion to see that this is so. The number of individuals, the way in which they are grouped, and the form of their habitations in no way constitute geographic facts. Why then should we retain a term which has been so changed from its ordinary meaning? For these reasons, a new rubric seems necessary. The one we propose has the advantage of placing in sharp relief the unity of the object upon which all this research bears, namely the tangible, material forms of societies or, in other words, the nature of their substratum.

Moreover, social morphology does not consist in a simple science of observation which describes these forms without accounting for them. It can and must be explanatory. It must investigate the conditions which cause variations in the political territory of different peoples, the nature and aspect of their borders, and the unequal density of the population. It must ask how urban agglomerations are born, what the laws of their evolution are, how they are recruited, what their role might be, and so forth. It does not, therefore, merely consider the social substratum already established in order to present a descriptive analysis; it observes it in the process of creation in order to see how it is constituted. This is not a purely static science; rather, it quite naturally includes the movements from which result the conditions which it studies. In addition, it, like all the other branches of sociology, finds indispensable auxiliaries in history and comparative ethnography.

REVIEWS AND CRITICAL ANALYSES

4

REVIEW OF ALBERT SCHAEFFLE,
Bau und Leben des Sozialen Körpers:
Erster Band

Though Schaeffle's name is known in France, he does not seem to have been much read. In any case, he is very little discussed. Espinas has praised him on several occasions, but only in passing.[1] Fouillée has said a few words about this "capable German" lost in the petty details of social life.[2] And that's all. The exposition which we are about to undertake is, therefore, tardy but timely.

I

This book, the most important of *Bau und Leben des Sozialen Körpers*, is a sort of social statics.[3] Comte devoted only one lecture of his course (the fiftieth) to this part of the discipline. Spencer was primarily concerned with the evolution of societies. Schaeffle proposes to subject contemporary societies (*nations*) to analysis and to resolve them into their principal elements.

The author is clearly a realist. Society is not a simple collection of individuals, it is an entity which preceded those who comprise it at present and which will survive them, which acts more on them than they on it, which has its own life, own consciousness, own interests and destiny. But what is its nature?

To be sure, great analogies exist between individual organisms and societies. To all those which have already been pointed out, Schaeffle adds another. It has been objected that the parts of an

Originally published in *Revue philosophique* 19 (1885): 84-101. This piece is the first that Durkheim published. The pagination in Durkheim's footnotes refers to the second edition. See "A Note on the Translations," p. xi-xii.

animal are continuous, while society is a discrete entity. Schaeffle calls attention to the fact that in living bodies cells are separated from one another by an intercellular substance such as blood serum or neuroglia. In the same way, the roads, the paths of communication and transport, and, in a word, all the riches which circulate in the society link its citizens to one another. Moreover, we should no longer see the cell as the simple and indivisible element of the organism but as the center of a tiny elementary organism whose field of action extends over an entire territory, over an entire intracellular world. The social unit is similarly not the physical individual fully stripped but one tied to a certain amount of matter which he animates, which he organizes, and which participates through him in social life.

And yet society is not an organism. To be sure, no sociologist has truly claimed that these terms are identical: for Spencer and Espinas they are similar but distinct. But where others see only a difference of degree, Schaeffle finds an opposition in their basic nature. At the time of the first edition of his book, he was taken to be a faithful disciple of Spencer and Haeckel. He protests in a lively way against such an interpretation.[4] When he speaks of social histology, of social organography, it is pure metaphor. The reader is warned.

In fact, the members of human societies are not attached to one another by a material link but by ideal bonds. Espinas, it is true, also said that a society was an organism of ideas. But at the same time, he attributed a more or less diffuse sort of psychological life to the elements of the living body; thus, he covered himself both ways. Schaeffle does not accept this conception; it appears to him to have just barely the value of a metaphysical hypothesis.[5] There is a break in continuity between the organism and the society. One is formed mechanically, the other under the influence of ideas. In the former, efficient causes reign; in the latter, final causes.[6] There is a clearly drawn line of demarcation. It is only with man that this new form of existence appears. It is without historical antecedent. The study of animal societies is doubtless of interest, and Schaeffle renders full justice to Espinas' book, which he summarizes in his Introduction. Such studies are, however, not an effective preparation but merely a prelude (*Vorspiel*), a prefiguring of the human societies which were later to appear.[7] Moreover, at the same time that he has a sort of vague consciousness penetrate every cell of the body, Espinas, in order not to stray too far in that direction, tries to restrict the role of lucid consciousness and of rational thought in social life.[8] In fact, whether or not man is free, when he deliberates before acting he stamps his actions with a personal imprint which does not lend itself to generalization, and he becomes a source of unexpected changes which lead scientific forecasts astray. In order that first the individual, then the society fall within the province of scientific study, ideas and sentiments, shielded from criticism, must be fixed in men's minds in the form of instincts, habits, traditions, and prejudices. In a word, social evolution must become automatic and reflexive. Schaeffle rejects this doctrine,[9] which he terms an historical mysticism. For him, the collective consciousness is above all constructed from lucid ideas. Societies are no doubt born spontaneously; but this spontaneity is well thought out. He goes so far as to see social consensus as a product of art and the result of conscious adaptations.[10]

If this is true, then sociology is not a simple extension, not just the final chapter of biology. Between these two sciences, just as between their respective subject matters, there exists a break in continuity. We must return to Comte's conception. It is, moreover, remarkable "that no one has seriously undertaken to create the theory of social man as if it were a part of zoology." A knowledge of the vital functions could assuredly furnish the sociologist with an orienting concept and with fertile suggestions. It is no less certain that sociology (*la science sociale*), since it studies a new world, must have a new method.

This method is not simple and cannot be defined in a word. It includes a cluster of procedures which one must be able to use individually and to combine as situations demand. It is, nonetheless, possible to say that the method will be essentially inductive. Induction is, no doubt, difficult to practice in social matters. We cannot isolate by experimentation phenomena which are presumed to be causally related. Moreover, each fact results from an infinity of causes, and it is far from easy to determine what part each has taken in the production of the common effect. Nevertheless, there is reason to hope that statistics will soon attenuate this double inconvenience. It is true that it has thus far rendered little service. But we must not forget that it is of quite recent origin. When it will have been methodically applied for several centuries, it cannot possibly fail to furnish rich matter for sociological induction. Moreover, by a fortunate interaction, science will render methods more efficacious. When sociology will have discovered the principal elements of the social body and the intercorrelations, it will, by the same token, have traced the framework within which the information of statistics will thenceforth be arrayed. Statistics will no longer be a mass of poorly related bits of knowledge but a systematically arranged collection of facts which will represent, so to speak, the natural relationships among things.

It is with this aim and with this hope that Schaeffle undertakes his meticulous analysis, the principal conclusions of which are here presented.

II

Two elements comprise the substance of which society is made: one passive, the other active—on the one hand, things, on the other, persons.

This is one of the book's innovative ideas. Ordinarily, wealth seems to serve only as nourishment for the society. Schaeffle discovers a new role for it: he makes it one of the histological elements of the social body. It is the link which unites, one to another, the consciousnesses of which the society is composed. It transmits ideas from one mind to another. It even places generations in communication with one another. It is in this way that the mind of the ancients has survived to this day, fixed in their historical and literary monuments. Wealth is, therefore, a symbol. But all symbols have two sides. On the one hand, they express the consciousness from which they emanate; they are like its equivalent. On the other hand, thanks to this very equivalence, they provoke in others a movement analogous to that which produced them. Wealth also presents this double aspect: it is at once a means of expression and a means of communication (*Güter der Darstellung und Mittgeilung*).

But the source of life which wealth transmits is the individual. We are not dealing with man as Rousseau conceived of him—that abstract being, born to solitude, renouncing it only very late and by a sort of voluntary sacrifice, and then only as the issue of a well-deliberated covenant. Every man is, on the contrary, born for society and in a society. What proves this is not only his marvelous aptitude for defining himself within it and, consequently, for uniting himself with it; still more, it is his inability to live in isolation. What remains if, from the sum of our knowledge, our sentiments, and our customs we take away all that comes to us from our ancestors, our masters, and the milieu in which we live? We will have removed at the same time all that makes us truly men. But aside from all that thus reaches us from outside, there is within us, or so it appears, something intimate and personal which is our own creation; this is our ideal. This is, in the final analysis, a world in which the individual reigns supreme and into which society does not penetrate. Doesn't the cult of the ideal presuppose an entirely internal life, a spirit turned inward on itself and detached from other things? Is idealism not at once the most elevated and the most prideful form of egoism? Quite the contrary, there is no more powerful link for uniting men to one another. For the ideal is impersonal; it is the common possession of all mankind. It is toward this dimly glimpsed goal that all the forces of our nature converge. The more we are clearly aware of it, the more we feel that we are in solidarity with each other. This is precisely what distinguishes human society from all others; it alone can be moved by this need for a universal ideal.

An objection might be that under such conditions man no longer belongs to himself, and one might ask what becomes of his liberty and personality. If by these words we mean the ability to violate the principle of causality, to set oneself up as an absolute by abstracting oneself from any social context, then we lose nothing by sacrificing that ability. For that would be a sterile independence and the plague of all morality. The only thing to which one must cling is the right to choose, among all the alternatives, the one which we judge best suited to our nature. The ability to specialize without restraint is the only freedom of value; and this is possible only in a society.

Living beings are made up of material molecules; but the

molecules are not living. Similarly, society is made up of individuals and of wealth; but neither the wealth nor the individuals manifest social life. That appears only with the family, which is like the cell of the society.

It is naturally composed of those two elements which we have just defined and which we will rediscover everywhere; on the one hand, persons (spouses, children, servants) and on the other, things, the analysis of which presents a difficulty and raises a question. In the organic cell, we distinguish one intracellular and one intercellular substance. The former is directly subject to the action of the cell and participates in its life; it is its property, its thing. The latter, without belonging to any particular cell, serves to interrelate them all and thus is the indivisible property of the community. We should encounter the same distinction in the family. And, in effect, there are goods whose role is uniquely to maintain domestic life: the social cell appropriates them for itself, and it has that right. For, otherwise, it would die. But there are others—Schaeffle calls them, in a word, capital—which are destined above all to permit families to communicate with one another. They are necessary to transport life in every direction. They must, therefore, circulate freely; they belong to no one, yet they belong to everyone. Unfortunately, it is difficult to distinguish the former from the latter. Where does capital begin and where does it end? Without doubt, it is necessary as sustenance for all social enterprises; but it is also, at least in part, the source of the revenue which nourishes the family. These two sorts of riches, however different, interpenetrate each other so intimately that they are commonly confused; they have been subjected to the same regimen, and capital has remained what it was at the beginning of history, the property of the family. But the following are the sad effects of this confusion: some cells absorb all society's wealth, others are forever disinherited. Hypertrophy on the one hand, anemia on the other. Whence the proletariat, the class struggle, unbridled competition, the all-powerfulness of money with its deplorable consequences. That is the evil. What is the remedy? There can be no question of suppressing property, but it can be generalized. Monopoly must be prevented and life must reach the least elements of the organism. But there is only one way to do that:

to render the instruments of production to the nation, to make economic life a social function, and to submit it to a collective and conscious orientation.

Since the family is the seed from which society is born, we should find in it a miniature version of society itself. And, in effect, it has its tissues and its organs. It occupies a portion of the earth which it appropriates for its needs. It has its protective and defensive institutions (clothing, heating, shelter, and so on). It has an economic organization, an industry, an intellectual life. If the family is thus a sort of complete organism, it is because it was formerly self-sufficient and was itself the entire society. From this primitive state, it has even preserved an expansive and invasive tendency. As soon as there appears an empty place in society, it takes it over; if a function is abandoned by the community, it seizes it. In this way, it became mistress of capital. But to the extent that the society becomes organized, the functions of the family become specialized. In an adult society, its only role would be to insure the survival of physical and intellectual life. It alone can fulfill this task. And that is why, despite the communist utopias, there will never be a state without families.

III

Ordinarily, we distinguish in society only individuals and families on the one hand, great institutions on the other. Such institutions as the Church, the university, and the state can truly be called the organs of the society. But we thus omit an intermediate level. Here, as among the animals, the anatomical elements begin by juxtaposing themselves to form tissues. These tissues are what form the organs. A complete sociology must, therefore, include a histology.

There are two types of social tissues. Some are meant just to link social cells among themselves, to unite them in compact and coherent masses—in a word, to protect the social unit against any dissolution. They are amorphous and indifferent of themselves. Neither their functions nor their forms are special. Ordinarily, they leave the individuals whom they unite in a state of repose; but the least stimulus is enough to irritate them and to incite sudden activity, which is covert and becomes organized as if by magic. In times of peace, patriotism lies dormant in the depths of men's consciousnesses. Should war break out, however, it will take precedence over everything.

These sorts of tissues or social bonds (*Binde-Gewebe*) are eight in number. They derive from the unity of (1) origins, (2) territory, (3) interests, (4) opinions, (5) religious beliefs, (6) social instincts, (7 and 8) the community of historical traditions and language.

These various bonds do not run through society in a parallel fashion, but interlace in a thousand ways. They interweave in the heart of each individual. Moreover, if one of them is destroyed, the others suffice to maintain the mass which tends to detach itself from the organism. That is why a people which presents these eight characteristics, pure and free of contamination—which has a national language, a cult of its history, an exclusive patriotism, a perfect religious, political, economic, geographical, and ethno-graphic unity—would form a solid, unshakable whole that no enemy force, internal or external, could manage to penetrate. But it would pay dearly for this solidarity, for it could be acquired and main-tained only at the price of an enormous centralization and by a government which would be internally oppressive and externally bellicose. Yet, especially in these times, a society can and must have an ideal other than this artificial concentration, other than this jealous and perpetually aggressive egoism. And in effect, if we allow these natural sentiments to occur and develop freely, they show themselves to be less narrow and less exclusive. Among the bonds which we were just passing in review, there are more than one which, if not forcibly restrained, will cross borders and bring together men of different nationalities. Can we not have friends in foreign countries? Is science, are the modern religions, the property of any single society? Don't various peoples have, in general, the same economic interests? Thus, new ideas are born. Cosmopolitanism comes to combat the effects of blind patriotism. From the fact that these two sentiments are opposed, it does not follow that one day one will strangle the other. They are both necessary. It is certain that in the future international relations are destined to become more and more important and extensive; but they will not, for all that, suppress national life any more than the latter will, by developing, suppress domestic life. It would be best that these two tendencies remain in eternal equilibrium. A society in which they were harmoniously combined would be whole even while remaining free; it would be strong without being overwhelming.

The unique raison d'être of all these tissues is to assemble and to keep the members of the society united. But, within the heart of this homogenous mass, a differentiation is established. The individuals who have been brought together group themselves in such a way as to fulfill the functions necessary for communal life. Thus, new tissues are formed. These are not yet organs because they are just composed of similar elements, and, indeed, it is from their combinations that all the organs result. But these tissues differ from the preceding in that each of them has a determinate form and a determinate role. They are, what's more, independent unities which can live their own, personal life without being absorbed by the milieu of which they are a part.

They are five in number:

1. Each organ occupies a space which it adapts to its functions. Cities, villages, farms, and roads thus form an immense tissue which runs through society in all directions and calls to mind our own skeletal system. A capital without its inhabitants resembles a skull; the secondary cities link up behind it in order, like the vertebrae.

2. Among animals, most of the organs are protected by the epidermis, the epithelium, the mucous membranes, and so on. In society, too, there are protective tissues. That is the role of clothing for the individual, of ramparts for the city, of police for the state.

3. In the third place, there are tissues charged with feeding all the anatomical elements of the social body. They do the job of the capillary vessels.

4. Others have the function of putting each organ in condition to act externally. They correspond to our muscular system (the army, the navy, and so on).

5. Finally, there is nervous tissue with its two essential elements: the fibers and the ganglionary corpuscles. The latter are constituted by the nervous systems of various individuals who sometimes act in isolation, sometimes in unison, grouped to form more voluminous

and more powerful ganglions. As for the fibers, their place is taken by the various means of communication and transport; but, instead of transmitting nervous movements, they convey symbols which serve as vehicles for ideas. The variety of these symbolic signs is infinite; they can, however, be divided into two classes. One group expresses thought by certain movements of the body; the other represents thought by means of external things. Language, song, and gestures are examples of the first; writing, art, and monuments illustrate the second.

Thanks to this organization, ideas can be exchanged among individuals and groups. It is in this way that society's psychological life develops. But that side of society deserves to be studied separately. Psychology comes after histology.

IV

There exists a social consciousness of which individual consciousnesses are, at least in part, only an emanation. How many ideas or sentiments are there which we obtain completely on our own? Very few. Each of us speaks a language which he has not himself created: we find it ready-made. Language is, no doubt, like the clothing in which thought is dressed up. It is not, however, everyday clothing, not flattering to everyone's figure, and not the sort that anyone can wear to advantage. It can adapt itself only to certain minds. Every articulated language presupposes and represents a certain articulation of thought. By the very fact that a given people speaks in its own way, it thinks in its own way. We take in and learn at the same time. Similarly, where do we get both the rules of reasoning and the methods of applied logic? We have borrowed all these riches from the common capital. Finally, are not our resolutions, the judgments which we make about men and about things, ceaselessly determined by public mores and tastes? That is how it happens that each people has its own physiognomy, temperament, and character. That is how it happens that at certain moments a sort of moral epidemic spreads through the society, one which, in an instant, warps and perverts everyone's will. All these phenomena would be inexplicable if individual consciousnesses were such independent monads.

But how are we to conceive of this social consciousness? Is it a simple and transcendent being, soaring above society? The metaphysician is free to imagine such an indivisible essence deep within all things! It is certain that experience shows us nothing of the sort. The collective mind (*l'esprit collectif*) is only a composite of individual minds. But the latter are not mechanically juxtaposed and closed off from one another. They are in perpetual interaction through the exchange of symbols; they interpenetrate one another. They group themselves according to their natural affinities; they coordinate and systematize themselves. In this way is formed an entirely new psychological being, one without equal in the world. The consciousness with which it is endowed is infinitely more intense and more vast than those which resonate within it. For it is "a consciousness of consciousnesses" (*une conscience de consciences*). Within it, we find condensed at once all the vitality of the present and of the past. But is it not just the manifestation of an invisible substratum? That is what human understanding cannot know, no more than individual psychology can teach us whether the soul exists and what its nature may be. But that is no reason to refuse social psychology the right to exist. All these hypotheses are matters of faith, not of science. However, we must not conclude from this comparison that the individual and the society are psychologically equivalent. To be sure, the imagination likes to represent the individual consciousness as a social consciousness; the nerve cells would play the role of citizens; the brain would take the place of the state. But these supposed explanations are only metaphors, fictions which are convenient for the mind but without scientific merit. We do not know what the "stuff" of thought actually is. Neither do we know how the nerve ganglions communicate with one another. We have no more right to create dogmas about the cellular consciousness than about the spiritual soul. Metaphysics on the one hand, metaphysics on the other. Once we spoke of the soul; now we speak only of organisms. One hypothesis has been replaced by another, one word by another. But science gains nothing by such substitutions. [11]

But as far as society is concerned, we are not bound by the same constraints. Here there is nothing unconscious or mysterious. To know how the social units act upon one another we have only to open our eyes. We can, therefore, affirm that a collective consciousness is nothing but an integrated system, a harmonic consensus. And the law of this organization is the following: each social mass gravitates about a central point and is subject to the action of a directing force which regulates and combines the elementary movements. Schaeffle calls this force authority. The various authorities are subordinated one to another in their turn, and that is how a new life, at once unified and complex, arises out of all the individual activities.

Authority can be represented by a man or by a class or by a slogan. But whatever form it takes, it is indispensable. What would become of individual life without innervation? We would have chaos. Always and everywhere it is faith that provides the force of authority. If we obey when authority commands, it is because we believe in it. Faith can be freely given or imposed; with progress, it will no doubt become more intelligent and more enlightened, but it will never disappear. If, by the use of violence or trickery, it is suffocated for a time, either the society breaks apart or new beliefs are reborn without delay—beliefs less correct and worse than those which preceded them because they are less ripe and not so well tested, because, pressed by the necessity of living, we seize upon the first beliefs to happen along, without examining them. What's more, faith is nothing to be embarrassed about. We cannot know everything or do everything for ourselves; this is an axiom which every day becmes more true. It is, therefore, quite necessary that we address ourselves to someone else, someone more competent. Why stake our honor on being self-sufficient? Why not take advantage of the division of labor?

Authority is, nonetheless, a terrible thing if it is tyrannical. Everyone must be able to criticize it and need submit to it only voluntarily. If the masses are reduced to passive obedience, they will ultimately resign themselves to this humiliating role; they will become, little by little, a sort of inert matter which will no longer resist events, which can be molded at will, but from which it will no longer be possible to wrest the slightest spark of life. Yet the basis of a people's force is the initiative of the citizens; it is the activity of the masses. Authority directs social life but neither creates it nor replaces it. It coordinates its movements, but presupposes their existence. Imagine an individual in whom life retreats from the surface of the body: the nervous system may well try to survive in the midst of this ruin, but it will never succeed in shaking loose the least part of this dead substance amid which it is enslaved. Similarly, there where despotism has long reigned, nothing any longer manages to galvanize the society even in times of crisis. In democracies, on the contrary, the people hold in reserve a latent energy which is revealed suddenly, miraculously. This is because in democracies the least elements of the society are living and each day economize an energy and vitality which are recouped later, in a moment of danger.

Schaeffle verifies these general principles by a meticulous study of the facts. He analyzes the spirit of various peoples as if dismantling all their complicated gears and springs. We can only rapidly summarize the results of his observations.

In society as in the individual, the states of consciousness can be reduced to three principal types: intelligence, sensitivity, and will.

Social intelligence and social sensitivity have no special centers or determinate organs. They are not the property of certain citizens but are diffused throughout the entire organism. Everyone thinks and feels freely, and the ideas or the impressions spontaneously emitted from all points in the society also circulate without constraint. It is from this free intercourse that the heart and soul of the society is revealed. However, in order that it not remain sterile, this activity is regulated and ordered. Once they have survived the test of experience and time, these sentiments and opinions are little by little condensed into stock formulations; they are objectified in the form of principles to which everyone subscribes, which, in a word, have authority. Such are the great truths of science, the dogmas of religion, the aphorisms of everyday experience, the prescriptions of fashion, and so on. Often this authority is not that of an abstract judgment but that of a man. In matters of theoretical speculation as in matters of practice, in the factory and in the stock market, in parliaments and in high society, there are men who make the law, who set the tone, and whose advice and example everyone follows without question.

Unlike intelligence and sensitivity, social will does not result from the spontaneous fusion of individual wills; for, left to themselves, the latter attach themselves to a thousand different objects. And although two contradictory judgments can coexist without difficulty in the same consciousness, two contrary acts cannot occupy the same space. In the first case, variety is a richness; in the second, it is a cause for disorder and impotence. A broad-minded individual can, almost at the same time, think one thing and its opposite; but he cannot at once act and abstain from acting. One must choose between two courses of action. It is, therefore, necessary that someone in the society be charged with choosing and deciding. Some authority is no doubt also necessary to coordinate individual intellects and sensitivities. But this authority has no precise organization; it is established here or there according to needs and circumstances. It is, moreover, only consultative. On the other hand, that authority which is charged with guarding the interests of the country is made to command and must be obeyed. That is why it is concentrated at certain determinate points of the territory and belongs only to certain clearly designated persons. In the same way, the principles which regulate collective activity are not indecisive generalizations or vague approximations but positive laws, the formulation of which is sharply delineated once and for all.

However, the role of the public is not purely passive submission: it participates in this activity even though it does not direct it. The laws do not owe their existence to the solitary will of the legislator. They are immanent in society just as the laws of gravity are immanent in physical bodies. The state does not create the former any more than the scientist creates the latter. Law and morality are simply the conditions of collective life; it is, therefore, the people who make them, so to speak, and the people who determine them just by living. The legislator states and formulates them. Moreover, he is not indispensable. If he does not intervene, the law nonetheless exists in the form of custom—half unconscious, it is true, but no less efficacious for that. It loses its precision, not its authority. Moreover, most collective resolutions are directly prepared and almost imposed by public opinion. Once a question becomes the order of the day, opposing sides are organized, engage in battle, and fight for the majority. To be sure, in well-constituted societies, this entire movement, once it arrives on the threshold of social consciousness, stops there. At that point, the organ of the will begins to function. But who cannot see that the matter has already been decided, just as the human will has already been predetermined, by the time that deliberation is cut off? It is the stronger side which triumphs.

But if we concede so large a role to individual wills, will they not impart to the social body all sorts of disordered movements? This fear would be legitimate if egoism was man's only natural sentiment. If everyone pursued only his personal ends, the society would be done for; torn in all directions, it would soon break apart. But at the same time that we love ourselves, we love others. We have a certain sense of solidarity (*Gemeinsinn*) which prevents us from ignoring others and which predisposes us without difficulty to devotion and sacrifice. Of course, if we believe that society is an invention of men, an artificial combination, then there is reason to fear that it will perpetually be torn apart. For so fragile a bond can be broken at any moment.

Man is free, Rousseau said, and yet everywhere he is in chains. If this is true, there is reason to fear that at any moment he will break his chains. But this savage individualism is not part of nature. The real man—the man who is truly a man—is an integral part of a society which he loves just as he loves himself, because he cannot withdraw from it without becoming decadent.

V

Social psychology can ultimately be reduced to the special study of the nervous system: it is a chapter of histology. Schaeffle passes from the tissues to the organs.

Every organ is formed by the combination of five functional tissues, the nature of which we have specified above. These five elements are combined in different ways and in different proportions, but they are all necessary and are found everywhere. The Church, whose ends are not of this world, still has its economic organization; the shop and the factory have their intellectual lives.

Organs are divided into two types, according to whether they arise due to individual initiative or collective action. The latter are, in turn, divided into associations (*Gesellschaften, Genossenschaften, Vereine*) and corporations (*Koerperschaften*). In the former, the whole exists for the parts; in the latter, the parts exist for the whole. Moreover, the corporation is the preeminent agent of social activity. Associations, like individuals, are ephemeral. Born yesterday, they may dissolve tomorrow; they barely survive the members who compose them. Great social interests are, on the contrary, eternal; they change only slowly and through a continuous process of advancement. They must, therefore, be removed from the fluctuations, the failures, the sudden revolutions which too often occur in individual consciousnesses. Therefore, they must be incarnated in an institution which can live its own life, grow, and develop through the ages, leading generations along with it, rather than depending at every moment upon the good will of individuals. Moreover, when corporations are suppressed, the immediate result is a struggle among unrestrained egoisms the further consequences of which are all too easy to foresee—the strongest triumph of which is crushing the weak and reducing them to misery. That is what individualism produces. Or else the state intervenes, taking in its hands the general interests which have not been able to organize and defend themselves, substituting itself for those corporations which it would have done better to create or to maintain, meddling, consequently, in all the details of collective life. Thus, from the (rule of the) proletariat we fall into a despotic socialism. These are, in effect, the two chasms between which civilized societies today seem to waver. There is only one way to escape the danger which threatens in the immediate future and with which statesmen are beginning to concern themselves: that is to restore the corporations. Of course, there can be no question of reviving them such as they existed in the Middle Ages. But it is not impossible to find for them a new organization, less narrow and rigid, better adapted to today's fast-paced life and to the extreme division of labor.

We have arrived at the end of the analysis. Society is composed of cells which group themselves into tissues, which, in turn, form organs. But however real these similarities between living beings and societies may be, the latter nonetheless form a new world without analogy or precedent. In sum, what sets them apart is this threefold nature nowhere else to be found: consciousness, freedom, universality. As we have seen, consciousness, according to Schaeffle, clarifies all, penetrates all, moves all. And we do not speak of that weakened and nearly extinguished consciousness which is generously accorded to the cell but which is hard to distinguish from simple mechanical movement. We are speaking of the human faculty of thought, reflection, and deliberation. Social life does not take place in the penumbra of the unconscious; everything happens in broad daylight. The individual is not led by instinct; rather, he has a clear conception of the group to which he belongs and the ends which it is appropriate to pursue. He compares, discusses, and yields only to reason. Faith itself is but the free submission of an intellect which comprehends the advantages and the necessity of the division of labor. That is why there is something free and willed about the social organization. Societies are not, to be sure, the product of a contract, and they cannot be transformed from one day to the next. But, on the other hand, they are not the product of a blind necessity, and their history is not a fatal evolution. Consciousnesses are perpetually open to ideas and, consequently, to change. They can, therefore, escape their first impulse and modify the given direction, or, at any rate, if they persist in the original course, it is because they wished to. Finally, what sets human societies entirely apart is their remarkable tendency toward universality. Animal societies never extend beyond a tiny space, and colonies of a single species always remain distinct, often even enemies. Human societies (*les nations*), on the contrary, become more and more confused with one another; national characteristics, races, and civilizations mix and interpenetrate. Already science, art, and religions have no country. Thus, little by little a new society emerges from all the isolated and distinct groups, a society in which all others will fuse, and which will end by one day including the entire human race.

VI

We have not wished to break up the continuity of this exposition with discussions or remarks, desiring, above all, to reproduce the general argument of this beautiful analysis. Hopefully this summary, though a bit dry, will be faithful enough to give some idea of the character of this work, in which the richness of the details and of the observations does not exclude the unity of the whole, and in which the resources of a great erudition are set to work by a broadly independent mind. There are to be found in these nine hundred pages, aside from the social doctrines of which we have already spoken, a psychology, an ethics, a philosophy of law, a theory of religion, and the economic principles of collectivism. And yet, if our attention sometimes strays, it is certainly not because of the abundance of materials and the variety of questions, but rather because the book's development sometimes spreads out with considerable abandon. In sum, there are few readings more highly instructive for a Frenchman. It is by the practice of such patient and laborious studies that we shall fortify our spirit, now too slender, too thin, too fond of simplicity. It is by learning to face the infinite complexity of facts that we free ourselves of those too narrow frameworks in which we tend to compartmentalize things. It is perhaps no exaggeration to say that the future worth of French sociology depends on this.

But this work is not just good training for the mind. It also achieves an advance for sociology by claiming for it a complete independence. What a strange thing! The French philosophers who have spoken of Schaeffle have generally praised him in an entirely opposite way. Even recently, in an article in the *Revue des deux mondes*,[12] Fouillée said that Schaeffle's goal was to prove that the laws of biology applied to societies. It is possible to find in this author's book proofs in support of this thesis; but what is certain is that nothing is more contrary to his intentions. And we fail to understand what is gained by thus placing sociology in tutelage. We willingly recognize that society is a sort of organism, but we do not see how this aphorism founds the science. If we are to understand by it that a society is composed of coordinated and subordinated elements, we are only repeating a veritable truism. If we mean that the study of individual life is an excellent preparation for the study of social life, we are giving good advice to the sociologists of the future. But if we go further and see in sociology only a new application of biological principles—and, if these words mean anything, that is indeed what the expression "sociologist-biologist" signifies—then we impose upon this science conditions which can only slow its progress. The great service which Claude Bernard rendered to physiology was precisely to free it from any sort of yoke, from those of physics and chemistry as well as from that of metaphysics, reserving for a distant future the time for generalizations. It is fitting that we proceed with the same prudence in the study of societies. Before searching out what this new object of speculation resembles and from what it differs, we must know in what it consists. We must observe it in itself, for itself, and in conformity with an appropriate method. That is what Schaeffle wanted to do. From the fact that nature does not advance by leaps and bounds, it does not follow that all things are alike and can be studied with the same procedures. Evolution is not a monotonous repetition; continuity is not identity. To be sure, all the debates over the origin of societies have been far from useless. In this way the final blow was dealt to the doctrines of Hobbes and Rousseau; sociology has been shown to have a subject matter no less real than that of the life sciences; at the same time a word and an idea were brought into being which permitted men's minds to conceive of the new entity being discussed. But sociology has now left the heroic age. Its right to exist is no longer contested. Let it be founded and organized and let it outline its program and specify its method. If there is a real affinity between it and biology, these two sciences, by pursuing their natural development, will surely meet one day. But a premature fusion would be artificial and, consequently, sterile.

If any reproach of Schaeffle is valid, it is that he has not strongly enough maintained the independent position which he had so excellently chosen. An eclectic and complex mind, he frolics amid very diverse and often quite contradictory ideas. A practical man, once actively involved in politics, he seems to have retained a certain repugnance for systems too neatly designed and a fairly lively taste for conciliation. Thus, he constantly repeats that he does not accept the doctrine of the biologists, and yet he borrows important elements from biology. This extreme mobility renders the plan of the book somewhat indecisive. We cannot help but find strange the place relegated to social psychology, between histology on the one hand and organography on the other. If the life of societies is immanently conscious, psychology must apply everywhere. And what is the composition of, for example, those eight tissues whose role it is to keep the citizens of a single society united; do they consist of ideas and sentiments, the study of which belongs in psychology? Renan also managed to speak of these things at a public conference without thinking for a single moment that he was doing histology.[13] To reiterate, these metaphors and these analogies had their advantages at the beginnings of the science; as Spencer expressed it, they are a useful scaffolding, but one which masks reality from us. Is it not time to tear them down in order to face things as they really are?

Our author's eclecticism makes itself felt particularly with regard to one of the gravest questions which sociology has to resolve. Sociologists are divided into two schools according to whether they subordinate society to the individual or the individual to society. For the former, unfettered reason is the unique motive force of social life. They do not ask the individual to go beyond the narrow circle of his personal interests. For that, reason suffices: it is even the only basis of competence and nothing can replace it. Any constraint, clever or violent, would be useless and evil. But if society is a being which has a goal, then it may find the reasoning minds of individuals too independent and too mobile for the common destiny to be entrusted to them without fear. That is what led certain philosophers to make morality descend from the heights of full awareness to the lowly regions of instinct. They make of it a sort of mystery which they conceal from the gaze of the intellect. They count on education and heredity to imprint it upon the organism: these are, to be sure, two tendencies which are clearly opposed and which seem to exclude one another. Schaeffle tries, nonetheless, to reconcile them. On the one hand, he protests against individualism as a sort of social atomism which disaggregates society and makes the state of war not only the state of nature but the ideal of humanity as well. And yet we have seen that he expects the harmony of wills to follow from awareness alone. But by this point, objections press in from all sides. Let us assume that it is possible to have an adequate knowledge of the conditions of social life; still, we must recognize that it is accessible only to vigorous minds. The first person to come along is able easily to conceive of the group to which he immediately belongs: just moving about properly within this tiny sphere is enough to ask of a reasonable intellect. But to conceive of the thirty or forty million individuals who compose our contemporary peoples and of the conditions of equilibrium of these enormous masses, and to keep in mind at every instant the vast system of social harmonies, requires a power of concentration which not everyone possesses. What, then, will the masses do? How will you get them to devote themselves to the common interests? It is, no doubt, repugnant to us to admit an antimony between the heart and the mind. But, on the other hand, this sentiment appears to us to be too complex a thing for everyone to reflect upon without danger. Go and find an ordinary man and, through a scholarly education, unburden him of his instincts and his habits, give him full awareness of himself, make of him a pure reason. Thus transformed, he will no longer understand the grandeur of patriotism nor the beauty of sacrifice and disinterestedness. And if you succeed in giving him some idea of what these concepts are, the notion will be for him so indeterminate and vague that it will have no effect on his will. Individualism reasserts its hold over us once again. Each individual sees of society only the corner in which he lives, and, among all these sparse little worlds there is no longer anything in common.

As for the remedies which Schaeffle proposes, they are ineffective palliatives. What, for example, are these authorities about which he makes individual intelligence and sensibility gravitate? Is it not reason which creates and maintains them? It therefore remains their sovereign mistress and, with its supremacy, preserves all its disadvantages. A faith which is willed, reasoned, and which can be withdrawn at any time does not unify the mind; it can barely procure for it a few moments' rest. Schaeffle believed he had saved everything by protecting the organ of will from the action of the masses. But it is an error to believe that two contradictory judgments can safely coexist in the same consciousness. Every idea, once inflamed by emotion, tends toward action. If anarchy reigns in the realm of intellect and of sensitivity, it will soon penetrate into the realm of the will. History teaches us that peoples in which opinion is divided become incapable of any collective effort. As a last resource against individualism, we are left, it is true, with what Schaeffle calls the sense of solidarity, *Gemeinsinn*. Every man, no doubt, instinctively understands that he does not suffice unto himself. The child senses that he depends on his parents, the merchant on his clients, the worker on his boss, the boss on his workers. These relationships are simple, self-evident, tangible, and escape the awareness of no one. But the question is whether this sentiment can go so far as to include society in its entirety. But we have seen that most intellects are able to embrace only a restricted horizon. The heart can be no larger than the mind. If I do not perceive the invisible bonds which link me to the rest of the society, I will think that I am independent of it and I will act accordingly.

Not only does Schaeffle fail to answer these objections, but he passes them by as if he didn't even see them. This is because he has a robust faith in reason and the future of humanity. Moreover, nothing troubles the calm and serenity of his analyses. In them we do not even sense those fears, those vague anxieties, which are so familiar to our age. Such optimism is rare today, even here in France. We begin to feel that everything is not so straightforward and that reason does not cure all ills. We have reasoned so much! Moreover, was it not from Germany that we got the idea that unhappiness always increases with consciousness?

5

REVIEW OF FERDINAND TÖNNIES,
Gemeinschaft und Gesellschaft

Though this work is above all a sociological study (*une étude de science sociale*), it deeply blends views of very diverse nature. In it one finds an entire philosophy and an entire psychology as well as an entire sociology. The author was inspired, serially or simultaneously, by Schopenhauer, Karl Marx, Kant, Sumner Maine, and the evolutionists. So eclectic a synthesis naturally makes this book very laborious to read, and this is a pity; for we find in it quite interesting ideas, which we are going to try to sort out. We shall leave aside all concerns of general philosophy in order to extricate what is of particular interest to the sociologist.

As the title indicates, the author proposed to analyze two concepts, that of *Gemeinschaft* and that of *Gesellschaft*. These are the two modes of grouping, the two forces of social life, that are observed among men. The object of this study is to characterize each of them and to determine their interrelationships.

Gemeinschaft is community. It constitutes an absolute unity which excludes the distinction of parts. A group which merits this name is not a collection, even an organized collection, of different individuals in relation with one another; it is an undifferentiated and compact mass which is capable only of collective movements, whether these be directed by the mass itself or by one of its elements charged with the task of representing it. It is an aggregate of consciousnesses (*consciences*) so strongly integrated that none can act independently of the others. It is, in a word, community or, if you like, communism carried to its highest point of perfection. Only

Originally published in *Revue philosophique* 27 (1889): 416-22. The pagination that Durkheim uses refers to the edition published in Leipzig in 1887.

the whole exists; it alone has a sphere of action that is all its own. The individual parts have none.

What keeps the individuals united and indistinguishable is what the author calls *Verständniss* (consensus). It is the silent and spontaneous accord of many consciousnesses which feel and think alike; which are open to each other; which experience in common all their impressions, their joys and sorrows; which, in a word, resonate in unison. This harmony does not occur as a result of a prior understanding, of a previously worked out contract bearing upon specific matters. But it is a necessary product of the nature of things, of the state of men's minds (*l'état des esprits*). When conditions are favorable, and given the seed from which it is born, it grows and develops by a sort of spontaneous vegetation.[1]

For consciousnesses to be fused to this extent, for them thus to participate in each other's lives, they must be of the same nature, or there must at least exist among them great resemblances, and that is why the community of kin is the preeminent source of any sort of community. In other words, the most perfect example of the type of group which we are in the process of analyzing is the family, and the family is, at the same time, their source. From it is born every type of community, and, since it has its own source in the physiological constitution of man, the same is true of *Gemeinschaft*. The latter is, therefore, of an absolutely natural origin; it is an organic grouping and, as we shall see, this trait fundamentally distinguishes it from *Gesellschaft*.

Though the family is the most perfect form of *Gemeinschaft*, it is not the only one. Moreover, the family already harbors within itself certain properties, various elements and modes of combination which subsequently give birth to a certain diversity of groupings. Organic resemblance is not the only bond which ties the members of the family to one another. In fact, it is, as a rule, completely absent between spouses; it does not always exist among brothers and sisters. What assures the cohesion of domestic society, aside from consanguinity, is the fact of living together, near one another, in the same space. It is also the community of memories, a necessary consequence of a common existence. These two social bonds can develop even when the other, consanguinity, has been weakened, and they may even replace it. In this case, each of them gives birth to a particular kind of *Gemeinschaft*. For example, it happens that through the simple fact of neighboring and through the relationships which derive from neighboring, formerly independent families form firm collective aggregates. What then occurs is what Sumner Maine called the village community. Though this sort of community is more fully realized in the village than elsewhere, it is still to be found in the town as long as the town does not exceed certain dimensions, does not become the great city of our times. It is the community of memories and of occupations which gives birth to fraternal groups, to political, economic, or religious groups, to political, economic, or religious associations (*corporations*) in which all those who perform the same functions, have the same beliefs, feel the same needs, and so on, are united.

But in all these various forms, *Gemeinschaft* always presents the same general properties. We have indicated the most essential; others follow from them.

In such societies, where individuals are not distinguished from one another, property is naturally held in common. The whole group works in common and shares in common.[2] There is no property in the modern sense of the word but only possession (*Besitz*) and collective possession. Consequently, there is no exchange. Exchange between two or several independent families is conceived of without difficulty, it is true, but not among the members of a single family. The things possessed in common do not circulate but remain inalienable, attached to the group. Moreover, at this stage, the preeminent form of property is the land. The services of individuals are not paid for in wages, that is to say, sold for an arranged price. Each works not with a recompense in mind but because it is his natural function, and he receives a portion of the proceeds determined not by the law of supply and demand but by tradition, the feelings of the group generally being represented by the will of the chief.

Since there is no exchange, there can be no contract. A contract presumes the existence of two individuals, each with his own desires, interests, and sphere of action on the one hand, and on the other, an object which passes from the hands of one to those of the other. Now, we have just seen that these conditions are not realized in the pure *Gemeinschaft*. Within the group there are no shifts or changes in the distribution of the parts, since there are no parts, so to speak.

The life of the group is not the work of individual wills but is quite entirely directed by habits, customs, and traditions. The author contrasts the word *status* to the word *contract* and, in a general way, to any relationship which results from an agreement, and uses the former expression to characterize *Gemeinschaft*.

But we know of another mode of grouping: it is the one we can observe in the large cities of the great contemporary societies. It is there that one may observe, almost in its pure state, what Tönnies calls *Gesellschaft*.

Gesellschaft implies

> a circle of men who, as in *Gemeinschaft*, live and dwell in peace alongside each other, but instead of being essentially united are, on the contrary, essentially separated. While in *Gemeinschaft* they remain united despite all distinctions, here they remain separated in spite of all common ties. Consequently, in *Gesellschaft* we find no activities which can be deduced from a unity which exists *a priori* and of necessity, which expresses the will and spirit of this unity ... Here everyone is out for himself and hostile toward others. The various fields of activity and power are rigidly determined in relation to one another in such a way that each prohibits any contact or intermingling with the others.... No one will do anything for anyone else unless it be in exchange for a similar service or a recompense which he judges to be the equivalent of what he gives.... The prospect of a profit is the only thing which can lead him to give up a good which he possesses.[3]

One can see that this is the very opposite of *Gemeinschaft*. Here consciousnesses, formerly indistinguishable, are differentiated and even opposed to each other. While the first form of society is that which Hegel, for example, likes to describe, we recognize in the second the theory of Bentham. According to the author, these two types of social life, which are ceaselessly placed in opposition and presented as mutually exclusive, have both existed and developed successively in the course of history. The second was born of the first: *Gesellschaft* of *Gemeinschaft*. How did this filiation come about? It is because the interpenetration of consciousnesses which community presumes is only possible in groups of limited size. For it is only on this condition that people can know each other intimately.

As social aggregates have become more voluminous, society has weighed less heavily upon the individual. He has, therefore, quite naturally been emancipated, and it is this spectacle which we are witnessing today. The emancipation is, moreover, progressive; its beginnings go back quite far, and we have no reason to believe that we have the final and definitive result before our eyes.

Thus, while the whole previously took precedence over the parts, now the parts take precedence over the whole. The whole is formed only through the juxtaposition of the parts. That is why, while the composition of *Gemeinschaft* was organic, that of *Gesellschaft* is mechanical. That is the essential difference from which all others derive.

It is, moreover, unnecessary to deduce the principal characteristics of *Gesellschaft* in order to convey the concept to the reader. It is very nearly Spencer's industrial society. It is the reign of individualism in the sense in which this word is usually understood. The regime of *status* is now replaced by that of contracts. Since individual wills are no longer absorbed within the collective will, but are, so to speak, encamped face to face with one another in the fullness of their independence, nothing can end this state of war but a treaty of peace signed with full knowledge of the situation— that is to say, a convention or contract. The immanent and unconscious law of the *Gemeinschaft* is thus replaced by a deliberate, contractual law. The beliefs which reigned by the force of tradition are succeeded by opinions freely reflected upon, that is, by science. Property is also individualized and mobilized, and money appears. This is the era of commerce, of industry, especially of large-scale industry, of great cities, of free trade, and of cosmopolitanism. In short, the society which Tönnies portrays is the capitalist society of the socialists; and in fact, the author often borrows from Karl Marx and from Lassalle the somber colors in which he represents it to us.

Like them, he believes such a society impossible without a very powerful state. The state is necessary to insure the execution of individual agreements, to sanction contractual law, to hinder anything which might harm the general interests of society. The state must be strong in order to contain all these individual wills, all these unrelated individual interests, all these unrestrained desires. We can now understand the meaning of the book's subtitle: *Abhandlung des Communismus und Socialismus als empirischer Culturformen* (study of communism and socialism considered as empirical [historical?] forms of civilization). Communism is the regime of *Gemeinschaft*, just as socialism is the regime of *Gesellschaft*. Neither is, therefore, an ideological conception destined to be realized in the future; rather, they are real facts produced in history according to a determinate order. Just as *Gesellschaft* is born of *Gemeinschaft*, socialism arises from communism and replaces it.

But, while the socialists hail the regime of their choice as the ideal end-point of progress. Tönnies sees it as merely an inevitable stage of social evolution and even as the precursor of the final dissolution. He speaks of it, therefore, without enthusiasm but with impartiality, as of a natural and necessary phenomenon. It is indispensable that the state be formed and develop in order that *Gesellschaft* be able to endure; but, on the other hand, it can exert upon the members of the society only a mechanical action which cannot last indefinitely. By a quite artificial coercion, it can repress for a time all the internal contradictions, all the strains which rend society, but sooner or later they will manage to burst forth. It has true power only to the extent that it represents common ideas and common interests; but as *Gemeinschaft* regresses, the number of such ideas and the importance of such interests progressively diminishes. The state of war which society conceals within itself cannot help but fulfill itself, one day or another, and produce its natural consequences, namely, the rupture of all social relationships and the decomposition of the social body. Thus, the life of societies comprises two great phases, communism and socialism, but the latter is the beginning of a more or less proximate end. It is in this way that Greco-Roman society died, and right now we are again seeing the same process unfold before our eyes.

Such is the conclusion of the book. The material which it covers in one small volume is too vast for it to be possible to discuss the author's theories in depth. I only wish to bring out the points to which there are reasons to direct the discussion.

Like the author, I believe that there are two great types of societies, and the terms he uses to designate them indicate their nature rather well; it is regrettable that they cannot be translated. Like him, I believe that *Gemeinschaft* is the primary fact and *Gesellschaft* the derived end. Finally, I accept his analysis and description of *Gemeinschaft* in its general outline.

But the point at which I will differ with him is in his theory of *Gesellschaft*. If I have properly understood his thought, *Gesellschaft* is characterized by a progressive development of individualism, the dispersive effects of which can be prevented only for a time and through artificial means by the action of the state. It is essentially a mechanical aggregate; in it, all that remains of truly collective life results not from an internal spontaneity but from the entirely external impulsion of the state. It is, in a word, and as I have said above, society as Bentham imagined it. Now, I believe that the life of great social agglomerations is every bit as natural as that of small aggregates. It is neither less organic nor less self-contained. Aside from purely individual activities, there is in our contemporary societies a truly collective activity which is just as natural as that of the less extensive societies of former times. It is assuredly different; it constitutes another type. But there is no difference in nature between these two species of a single genus, as diverse as they may be. We would need an entire book to prove this; I can only formulate the proposition. Is it, moreover, likely that the evolution of a single being—society—would begin by being organic and would subsequently end as a pure mechanism? There is between these two modes of existence such a break in continuity that we cannot conceive how they could belong to the same line of development. Thus, to reconcile the theories of Aristotle and Bentham is quite simply to juxtapose opposites. We must choose: if society is originally a fact of nature, it remains so to the end of its career.

But in what does the collective life of *Gesellschaft* consist? The method pursued by the author did not allow for a response to this question, for it is altogether ideological. Especially in the second part of his work, Tönnies analyzes these concepts, systematically developing their content rather than observing the facts. He proceeds dialectically; in his work we find those distinctions, those symmetrical classifications of concepts which are so dear to German logicians. The only way to succeed would have been to proceed inductively, that is, to study *Gesellschaft* through the laws and mores which are associated with it and which reveal its structure. But, whatever our reservations, we cannot but recognize in this book a genuine vigor of thought and an uncommon power of intellectual construction.

6

REVIEW OF ANTONIO LABRIOLA,

Essais sur la conception matérialiste de l'histoire

This book has as its object to analyze the principle of historical philosophy which is the foundation of Marxism, to submit it to a new elaboration, not with the aim of modifying it, but in order to clarify it and to make it more precise. This principle states that historical evolution depends in the final analysis on economic causes. This has been called the dogma of economic materialism. Since the author believes that its best formulation is found in the *Communist Manifesto*, it is this document which serves as the theme of his study. The latter comprises two parts: the first explains the origin of the doctrine, the second comments upon it. An appendix contains the translation of the manifesto.

Ordinarily the historian sees only the most superficial layer of social life. Individuals, who are the agents of history, create for themselves a certain representation of the events in which they participate. In order to be able to understand their behavior, they imagine themselves to be pursuing one or another goal which seems desirable, and they make up rationalizations in order to prove to themselves and, as necessary, to others that this goal is worthy of being desired. It is these motives and these rationalizations which the historian considers to have been the determining causes of historical development. If, for example, he manages to discover what goal the men of the Reformation intended to achieve, he believes that he has

Originally published in *Revue philosophique* 44 (1897): 645–51. For an English translation of the book being reviewed, see Antonio Labriola, *Essays on the Materialist Conception of History* (New York: Monthly Review Press, 1966).

explained how the Reformation came about. But these subjective explanations are worthless, for men do not see the true motives which make them act. Even when our conduct is determined by personal interests which, being so close to us, are easier to perceive, we distinguish only a very small—and not the most important—part of the forces which motivate us. For the ideas and rationalizations which develop in our consciousnesses, and which, when they conflict, constitute our deliberations, most often arise from organic states, from hereditary tendencies, from inveterate habits of which we are no longer aware. This is even more true when we act under the influence of social causes, which escape our awareness to a greater degree because they are more distant and more complex. Luther did not know that he was "a moment in the development of the third estate." He believed that he was working for the glory of Christ and did not suspect that his ideas and his actions were determined by a certain state of society or that the respective class situations necessitated a transformation of the old religious beliefs. "All that has happened in history is the work of man, but it was only very rarely the result of critical choice or of rational will."[1]

If, therefore, one wishes to understand the true relationships among facts, one must renounce this ideological method. One must set aside the superficial level of ideas in order to reach the profound things which these ideas more or less unfaithfully express, to the underlying forces from which they derive. As the author puts it, "one must strip historical facts of those external guises which the facts themselves take on as they evolve." The only rational and objective explanation of events consists in discovering the way in which they are really produced, not the conception of their genesis created by the men who have been their instruments. It is this revolution in the historical method which the materialist conception of history claims to have realized.

If one proceeds in this manner, one observes, according to Marx and his disciples, that the living source of social evolution is the state of technology at each moment in history—that is to say, of "the conditions of work and of the instruments which are appropriate to it."[2] That is what constitutes the deeper structure or, as our author says, the economic infrastructure of society. Depending on whether production is agricultural or industrial, whether the machines used force it to be concentrated in a small number of large enterprises or, on the contrary, facilitate its dispersion, and so on, the relationships among the productive classes are quite differently determined. It is upon these relationships—that is, upon the various frictions and antitheses which result from this organization—that everything else depends. In the first instance, the state is the necessary consequence of the division of society into classes subordinated one to another, for the equilibrium can be maintained among these economically unequal entities only if it is imposed by violence and repression. That is the role of the state; it is a system of force used "to guarantee or to perpetuate a mode of association, the foundation of which is a form of economic production." [3] Its interests are, therefore, the same as those of the ruling classes. In the same way, law is never "anything but the customary, arbitrary, or legal defense of a definite interest"; [4] "it is simply the expression of the interests which have won out" [5] and, consequently, "it is almost immediately reduced to economics." Ethics is the sum of all the inclinations and habits that social life develops in individual consciousnesses, depending on the way in which it is organized. Finally, even products of art, of science, and of religion are always related to determinate economic conditions.

The scientific interest of this point of view, we are told, is that it has the effect of naturalizing history. It naturalizes it by the simple fact that, in explaining social facts, definite, real, resistant forces, namely, the distribution of men into classes—itself related to the state of economic technology—are substituted for those inconsistent ideals, for those phantoms of the imagination which until now were made out to be the motive forces of progress. But one must be careful not to confuse this naturalistic sociology with what is called Political and Social Darwinism. The latter consists simply in explaining the development of institutions by the principles and concepts which suffice for the explanation of zoological development. Since animal life unfolds in a purely physical milieu which has not yet been modified by any labor, this simplistic philosophy therefore finds itself accounting for social evolution with causes which are in no way social, namely, with the needs and appetites which are already found among animals. According to Labriola, the theory which he defends is entirely different. It seeks the motivating causes of historical development not in the cosmic circumstances which may have affected the organism, but in the artificial milieu which the work of associated men has created of whole cloth and then superimposed on nature. It makes social phenomena depend not on hunger, thirst, procreative desire, and so on, but on the state at which human art has arrived, on the ways of life which result from it—in a word, from collective works. In the beginning, no doubt, men, like other animals, had only their natural milieu for a field of action. But history need not go back to this hypothetical era of which we cannot now create any empirical representation. History begins only with a supernatural milieu, however elementary, for it is only then that social phenomena begin to appear; it need not concern itself with the way in which humanity has been led to raise itself above pure nature and to constitute a new world, for that is, moreover, indeterminable. Consequently, it can be said that the method of economic materialism applies to the whole of history.

Revolutionary socialism follows logically from these abstract principles. Over the last century, great changes have occurred in industrial technology; equally important changes in social organization should, therefore, result. And since everything which concerns the nature and form of production is fundamental and substantive, the perturbation which has thus been produced is not a local, restricted malady which partial correction of our collective economy can bring to a halt. It is a malady *totius substantiae* which can be cured only by a radical transformation of society. All the old frameworks must be broken; all the raw material of society must be set free so that it may be cast in new molds.

Such is the summary of this work which, in the preface, Sorel justifiably presents as an important contribution to socialist literature. One might, no doubt, regret the extreme diffusion of its development, the obvious insufficiency of its composition, and certain violences of language which are out of place in a scientific discussion. However, it is, to our knowledge, one of the most rigorous efforts which have been made to reduce Marxist doctrine to its elementary concepts and to give them greater depth. The analysis does not attempt, as too often happens, to conceal itself in indecisive nuances. It moves straight ahead with a sort of vigor. The author has no other preoccupation than clearly to see the mainspring of those beliefs whose logical consequences he accepts in advance and with resolve. Moreover, this exposé of the system is remarkably suited to making both its fecund views and its weaknesses stand out in relief.

We think it a fertile idea that social life must be explained, not by the conception of it created by those who participate in it, but by profound causes which escape awareness; and we also think that these causes must principally be sought in the way in which associated individuals are grouped. It even seems to us that it is on this condition, and on this condition only, that history can become a science and that sociology can, consequently, exist. For, in order that collective representations be intelligible, they must arise from something and, since they cannot form a circle closed upon itself, the source from which they arise must be found outside themselves. Either the collective consciousness floats in a vacuum, a sort of unrepresentable absolute, or it is related to the rest of the world through the intermediary of a substratum on which it consequently depends. From another point of view, of what can this substratum be composed if not of the members of society as they are socially combined? We believe this proposition is self-evident. However, we see no reason to associate it, as the author does, with the socialist movement, of which it is totally independent. As for ourselves, we arrived at this proposition before we became acquainted with Marx, to whose influence we have in no way been subjected. This is because this conception is the logical extension of the entire historical and psychological movement of the last fifty years. For a long time past, historians have perceived that social evolution has causes with which the authors of historical events are unacquainted. It is under the influence of these ideas that they tend to deny or to restrict the role of great men and look to literary, legal, and other movements for the expression of a collective thought which no specific personality completely incarnates. At the same time and above all, individual psychology taught us that the individual's consciousness very often merely reflects the underlying state of the organism and that the current of our representations is determined by causes of which the subject is unaware. It was then natural to extend this conception to collective psychology. But we are not able to perceive what part the sad class conflict which we are presently witnessing could have played in the elaboration or the development of this idea. No doubt, the idea came at a fitting time, when the conditions necessary for its appearance were present. It would not have been possible in just any era. But the question is to know what these conditions are, and when Labriola affirms that it has been roused "by the ample, conscious, and continuous development of modern technology, by the inevitable suggestion of a new world which is being born," he takes as self-evident a thesis without proof. Socialism has been able to employ the idea to its advantage, but it has not produced it, and, above all, it does not imply it.

It is true that if, as our author postulates, this objective conception of history were just the same as the doctrine of economic materialism, then, since the latter certainly has socialist origins, one might believe that the former was constituted under the same influence and inspired by the same spirit.[6] *But this confusion is devoid of all foundation, and it is important to bring it to an end.* There is no interdependence between these two theories, the scientific value of which is singularly unequal. Just as it seems true to us that the causes of social phenomena must be sought outside individual representations, it seems to that same degree false that they can be reduced, in the final analysis, to the state of industrial technology, and that the economic factor is the mainspring of progress.

Even without opposing any definite fact to economic materialism, how could one help but notice the insufficiency of the proofs on which it rests? Here is a law which pretends to be the key to history! To demonstrate it, a few sparse, disjointed facts are cited, facts which do not constitute any methodical series and the interpretation of which is far from being settled: primitive communism, the struggles of the patricians and the plebians, of the common people and the nobility, are advanced as having economic explanations. Even when a few examples borrowed from the industrial history of England are added to these rare documents, rapidly passed in

review, they will not have succeeded in demonstrating a generalization of such magnitude. On this issue Marxism is at variance with its
own principle. It begins by declaring that social life depends upon
causes which escape awareness and conscious reason. But then, in
order to get at these causes, one would have to employ procedures at
least as indirect and at least as complex as those used in the natural
sciences; all sorts of observations, experiments, and laborious
comparisons would be necessary to discover a few of these factors in
isolation, let alone to attempt to obtain at present a single representation of them. And here we are, in a twinkling, with all these
mysteries clarified and with a simple solution to these problems
which human intelligence appeared so hard pressed to penetrate!
Could we not say that the objective conception which we have just
summarily set forth has not been proved in an adequate way?
Nothing is surer. But what is more, it does not propose to assign a
definite origin to social phenomena; it limits itself to affirming that
they have causes. For, to say that they have objective causes has no
other meaning, since collective representations cannot have their
causes in themselves. It is, therefore, simply a postulate intended to
direct research and, consequently, forever suspect, for it is experience which must decide in the final analysis. It is a rule of method,
not a law from which one is authorized to deduce important
consequences, either theoretical or practical.

Not only is the Marxist hypothesis unproved, but it is contrary to
facts which seem well established. Sociologists and historians tend
more and more to meet in the confirmation that religion is the most
primitive of all social phenomena. From it, by successive transformations, have come all the other manifestations of collective activity:
law, ethics, art, science, political forms, and so on. Everything is religious in principle. We know of no way to reduce religion to economics,
nor of any attempt to accomplish this reduction. No one has yet shown
under what economic influences naturism arose out of totemism, as
a result of what modifications in technology it became the abstract
monotheism of Jahweh in one place and the Greco-Latin polytheism
in another; we strongly doubt that anyone will ever succeed in such
an enterprise. More generally, it is indisputable that in the beginning the economic factor is rudimentary while religious life is, on

the contrary, rich and overwhelming. How then could the latter result from the former, and is it not probable, on the contrary, that the economy depends on religion much more than the second on the first?

The preceding ideas, moreover, must not be pushed to an extreme where they lose all validity. Psycho-physiology, after pointing to the organic substratum as the basis of all psychic life, has often committed the error of refusing all reality to the latter; the resulting theory reduces consciousness to nothing but an epiphenomenon. We have lost from view the fact that, although representations originally depend on organic states, once they are constituted, they are, by that very fact, realities sui generis, autonomous and capable of being causes in turn, capable of producing new phenomena. Sociology must carefully refrain from making the same error. While the different forms of collective activity also have their own substratum, and while they derive from it in the last instance, once they exist, they become, in turn, creative sources of action, they have an effectiveness all their own, and they react on the very causes on which they depend. We are, therefore, far from maintaining that the economic factor is only an epiphenomenon: once it exists, it has an influence which is special to it; it can partially modify the very substratum from which it results. But we have no reason to confuse it, in some way, with this substratum and to make of it something particularly fundamental. Everything leads us to believe, on the contrary, that it is secondary and derived. From which it follows that the economic transformations which have occurred in the course of this century—the substitution of large-scale for small-scale in-dustry—in no way necessitate an overthrow and an integral renewal of the social order, and even that the malaise from which European societies may suffer need not have these transformations as their cause.

7

REVIEW OF GASTON RICHARD,

Le socialisme et la science sociale

The object of this book is to establish the concept of socialism and to confront it with the results of comparative sociology.

Richard looks for the elements of his definition not in the programs of political parties or in the deliberations of workingmen's congresses but in the great works of the masters. According to him, socialism is diminished when reduced to a mere list, short or long, of workers' demands and the practical reforms intended to bring them to realization. When one considers the doctrine only from this point of view, it is easy to have it one's own way, because it is always simple to demonstrate that the procedures recommended by the different systems as sovereign remedies for the ills from which we suffer are either inapplicable to existing conditions or would not have the expected consequences. A general and abstract formulation is, by definition, too distant from reality to be apprehended all at once and without resistance. The immediate inapplicability of a law of chemistry in no way demonstrates its falseness. In the same way, the fact that the applications deduced from socialist theories are unrealizable or would operate contrary to their expressed intent gives us no right to conclude that these theories are false. Socialism is, above all, a certain way of conceiving and explaining social facts, their evolution, and their future development. This conception must, therefore, be examined in its own terms; all considerations relating to the practical consequences which might result from it must be set aside.

Understood in this light, socialism, despite the unquestionable

Originally published in *Revue philosophique* 44 (1897): 200–205.

variations which it has presented historically, is far from lacking in unity. As diverse as may be the forms which it has successively assumed, there is at least one proposition on which all sects agree: this is the affirmation that a new society in which capital is no longer the motive force of economic life and in which values are no longer set by competition must necessarily emerge from present societies. Richard defines it as follows: "Socialism is the notion of the arrival of a society without competition, thanks to an organization of production without capitalist enterprises and to a system of distribution in which the length of work will be the sole measure of value." We see that socialism has been reduced to collectivism and nearly to Marxism. In fact, the only interpreters of socialist thought whom the author considers individually are Marx, Engels, and Proudhon. He denies this distinction to Saint-Simon, Fourier, agrarian socialism, and Christian socialism alike.

While certain of these exclusions are perfectly well grounded, others may seem insufficiently justified. While Christian asceticism has nothing in common with socialism, the same is not true of Saint-Simonism. Personally, I believe that the entire essence of socialist doctrine is to be found in the philosophy of Saint-Simon. However, an author is free to set up the object of his research as he wishes and to limit it at will. Still, the fact remains that socialism, thus defined, calls forth discussion on two fundamental questions, one of which concerns the past and the other of which looks to the future. It implies, in effect, a certain theory of how capital is established and another of the direction in which social evolution tends to move. What is the value of these theories?

According to Marx, the capitalist system is simply a transformation of feudalism; wage labor is just a new and aggravated form of serfdom. In former times, the serf worked openly for his master a part of the week; today the worker labors for his boss a part of his day. The exploitation is merely less visible. On a superficial level, his wages seem to represent his labor; in reality, they represent only a fraction of it. The rest is the employer's profit.

Now, says Richard, this conception of history is doubly in error. First, it is not true that wage labor is born of serfdom. The serf of former times became, not the industrial worker, not the wage-earning proletarian, but the small farmer and the small property owner of today. The worker's forerunner was the journeyman of the Middle Ages. The capitalist enterprise emerged out of the corporation, just as the corporation itself arose out of the home workshop.[1] All these comparisons between surplus labor time and corvées are thus devoid of any objective foundation. Second, this evolution, far from having worsened the condition of the worker, "corresponds to a real rise in personal freedom." The corporation is a system of hereditary monopoly under the control of authority. The masters keep the journeymen dependent on them, just as they themselves remain dependent on those with political power. Capitalist organization develops at the same time as the individual personality. It is the instrument whereby the individual is emancipated from the collective yoke and from the yoke of heredity. It is true that Marx calls upon these historical considerations only to confirm his theory of value, which is the basis of his entire system. But this theory implies a contradiction. Value can only be expressed as a function of the duration of labor and of it alone, as Marx would have it, if one does not take account of its degree of skill. But if one is to evaluate skill itself over time, one must adopt as a mediating factor the difficulty of the task. But the difficulty of the task can only raise the rate of pay of the worker if it makes competition more difficult. But if we return to competition, what remains of the doctrine? Richard even goes so far as to accuse the theory of surplus labor of leading to the negation of the notion of saving. To save is, after all, to capitalize; that is, to use the products of labor not as objects of consumption but in new production or, in what amounts to the same thing, as means of production.

The author then passes on to the second question. Whatever may be the origins of capitalist society, are there reasons to believe that it is destined to "give birth" to a new society in which capital would no longer be the basis of economic enterprises?

According to Marx, it is a law of history that capital comes to be concentrated in an ever more restricted number of hands. From this he concludes that in the end it must pass into the hands of the community. But, in reality, this supposed law of evolution has been obtained from the observation of a single case. His history of the progressive accumulation of capital is, above all and by his own admission, the economic history of England. A more narrowly based comparison cannot be imagined, especially when contrasted with the extreme generality of the law induced. The future of Europe cannot be read in the past of England alone. This entire philosophy of history is, moreover, vitiated by the famous dogma of economic materialism, which is devoid of any scientific value. It is not the economic organization which has determined the other social institutions. The proof is that the Incas of Peru were communists just like the confederation of the Iroquois, and yet the basic constitution of each of these two societies was quite different. Moreover, it is not true that the nutritive and generative functions have the preponderant role attributed to them. It is the relational function—that is, the conceptual function (*les fontions représentatives*)—which is the essential factor in human development.

But let us consider the law of accumulation in its own terms. If in truth capital comes more and more to be concentrated in fewer hands, we should observe the surplus value of capital diminish in a parallel fashion. Since the theory states that the workers cannot buy back all the product of their labor, the surplus which escapes them can only be consumed by the capitalists themselves. If those who possess the public wealth are in reality constantly decreasing in numbers, then the outlets would necessarily diminish. Moreover, this accumulation is possible only by virtue of a coercive action which imposes upon the worker an ever greater surplus labor. But where can we perceive the slightest trace of this constraint? Has not history shown us an ever more complete liberation of the individual? And statistics confirm the inductions of history. The number of property owners constantly increases.

But, with respect to these prophecies, socialism interjects not just the economic but also the political history of the human race. The present social condition results, it tells us, from the division of society into hostile classes—a division which is itself due to the present organization of commercial production. The one can disappear only along with the other. But this organization, replies Richard, is tied up with the social division of labor. Socialism, if it is to remain self-consistent, must therefore arrive at the conclusion that the division of labor is also destined to disappear, a conclusion which runs counter to the lesson of history. Despite the law that class consciousness develops with capitalism, it seems in fact to weaken to the extent that economic life is organized on the basis of private enterprise. The progress of the bourgeoisie is contemporaneous with that of science and free inquiry. Everything converges to prove that societies are developing in a direction quite different from that which socialists ascribe to them. To be sure, competition must slack off; it is imperative that legal regulation of contracts prevent undeniable abuses; the weak, notably women and children, must be protected. But for these results to be achieved, it is not necessary to overturn the present economic organization. On the contrary, the destruction of capitalism, should it actually come about, could only render them impossible.

These are the principal arguments which Richard cites in opposition to socialism. Whatever we may think of his discussion, there is one merit which we cannot deny him without injustice and which, in such matters, is already a mark of originality: this is his ardent desire to introduce into controversies which stir so much passion a degree of scientific calm and impartiality. We might also find at once surprising and regrettable the attacks to which he has been subject on the part of the authorized representatives of socialist doctrine. This despite the fact, as it seems to me, that socialism has every interest in receiving in a different fashion those who, in discussing it, treat it with the deference and respect due to any system of ideas which has played an important role in the history of the human spirit. Indeed, it is in everyone's interest that on both sides these discussions should in the future be conducted with greater composure and without the sort of mutual animosity which is the rule today and which deprives them of any scientific character. This would be, at the least, an initial step in the direction of conciliation, and this is the service which science can, in such matters, most immediately make practicable.

There is, moreover, something new in the point of view which Richard has adopted and which deserves to be retained. In leaving aside the traditional objections concerning the possible applicability of socialist theories, he has given proof, I believe, of his scientific spirit. There is nothing more vain than all this dialectic in which passion is given free play. The future gives no standard precisely because it does not exist and can to some extent be conceived of as we wish. Depending on whether a given provision is or is not attractive, it is easily found to be either practical or utopian. There is no reform of which it has not been said, on the very eve of its realization, that it was impossible. And though philosophers and statesmen alike have been warned by experience of the inanity of this method, they still use it willingly because it is the easiest and most readily within the reach of anyone. But if we wish to accomplish something useful, we must turn toward the past rather than the future. There, at least, because a given reality exists, there is room for objective research and, consequently, some chance for agreement.

In addition, we find in Richard's book a number of ingenious and interesting views. The author has here again displayed the qualities of the logician which distinguished his earlier *Essai sur l'origine de l'idée du droit*. It is true that his arguments sometimes have a rather formal character. This is perhaps because he has not taken, in regard to socialism, the only attitude appropriate for a sociologist. Of socialism, viewed as a theory of social facts, sociology has only one statement to make: it must, as a point of methodology and in order to remain true to itself, refuse to view it as a scientific enterprise. It must refuse to accord it this quality because the propositions which it sets forth are too broad. It is a complete system of society considered in terms of its past, its present, and, in reaction, its future. But it is impossible for a system of such breadth to be scientifically constructed. At present, science can only establish laws which are partial, restricted, but related one to another. As a result, the greatest circumspection is imposed in all that concerns practical matters. To be able to make judgments on the sum of our social institutions as categorical as those of the socialists, we would need to know a little better what these institutions are, the causes which have given rise to them, the needs to which they respond, and the relationships which they maintain with one another. But that would require all sorts of research which has, of necessity, barely begun. To speak with precision, socialism cannot, therefore, be scientific. It can only make use of certain incomplete and fragmentary scientific data in the service of a cause which it supports for reasons which are foreign to science because they go beyond its scope. Think, for example, of how much observation, how many statistical, historical, and ethnographic comparisons are assumed in the least of the theories of *Capital!* Yet not only had Marx not accomplished them in his time, but, for the most part, they still remain to be done. This is not to say that we won't find in his book some very suggestive philosophical perspectives. But we must not confuse worthy and fertile intuitions with definite and methodically demonstrated laws. The work of the scholar is not that of the philosopher. Moreover, of all the criticisms which Richard addresses to Marx, the strongest seems to me to be that which limits itself to placing in relief the gap which separates the fundamental proposition of the system and the observations on which it rests.

But, for all that, it does not follow from the foregoing that I believe that sociology must deal with socialism as a negligible quantity and ignore it. Though it is not a scientific theory of social facts, it is a social fact of the greatest importance and one which sociologists must seek to understand. After all, it exists and it is not without its causes; it expresses a state of society. We can, no doubt, rest assured in advance that it does not express it faithfully. It is not enough for one who is ill to inquire about the maladies from which he suffers in order to discover their causes, nature, and remedy. Socialism is, above all, the way in which certain strata of society which have been tested by collective suffering represent the latter to themselves. But it attests, at the very least, to the existence of social malaise and, though it may be an inadequate expression, it can help us to understand that malaise because it derives from it. For this reason, it is of the greatest interest. But from this perspective, the ways in which it justifies its formulation matter little. They are merely symbols. We must set aside this entire logical apparatus in order to penetrate to the underlying reality. Unless we proceed in this manner, it is difficult to see how the arguments devised, however ingenious, will fail to have a slightly artificial and academic flavor. For they do not bear upon something real but only on the external form of reality. Moreover, isn't this sort of objective study the only one of practical utility? For, once we have refuted the reasons which socialism alleges in support of its assertions, we are no better informed concerning the causes which brought it into being nearly a century ago or concerning the needs, whether or not they are normal, to which it responds. But isn't this what matters? It is true that the various parties have answers to this question at hand. But these hasty solutions have no more value when they deny socialism than when they affirm it. To arrive at the knowledge of what socialism is, how it is organized, and on what it depends, it is no more satisfactory to ask the socialists than to ask their adversaries. What we need is research, information, and methodical comparisons in which the confused and passionate intuitions of the common consciousness have no place.

8

REVIEW OF MARIANNE WEBER,
Ehefrau und Mutter in der Rechtsentwickelung

The object of this book is at once theoretical and practical. The author first proposes to recall for us the tableau of what has been the condition of women in the principal epochs of history. The major portion of the work is employed for this purpose.[1] But in the final chapters, she asks of this historical research the answer to the problems posed today concerning what at present should be the legal status of women in the family as well as in society.

An historical exposition which runs from the crudest societies of which we know to the recent reforms of German civil law naturally touches upon too many very complex questions to be very thoroughly elaborated. Weber is most often obliged to rely upon secondary works. However, it is only fair to recognize that, with respect to each of the numerous peoples which she discusses, she has informed herself as seriously as the magnitude of the subject which she strives to cover would permit. Most often she has been able to discover the most important works, and, in general, she uses them with a sense of judgment and a critical spirit to which it is fitting to render homage.

What this book lacks is, rather, an organizing concept which would set forth the facts according to a methodical plan and take account of the way in which they converge upon the conclusion to which one is led. The order in which questions are approached is rather arbitrary. A first chapter is concerned with all primitive forms

Originally published in *L'Année sociologique* 11 (1906–9): 363–69. The last word of the title of Weber's book appeared in the original under the preferred spelling *Rechtentwicklung*. I thank Fritz Traugott for pointing out the discrepancy, which is perhaps indirectly suggestive of Durkheim's command of an excellent, if somewhat academic, German.

139

of sexual commerce and of marriage. In the following chapter, we find thrown together the Egyptians, the Babylonians, the Hebrews, the Arabs before and after Islam, the Greeks, and the Romans. The third chapter deals exclusively with Germanic law, although it is not clear why it comes here, unless it is because it precedes (but no more than Roman law) medieval and modern law, which are dealt with next. Moreover, in each of these specific studies, the author has not been able to make her effort bear upon a restricted number of clearly determined ideas, selected for their importance for the general problem being treated. Rather, in a confusing way, she brings in everything to do with the ethics of the sexes, marriage, the family, the civil rights of women, and so on. This dispersion manages to render somewhat unclear the impression which the book leaves.

It is not that the whole work lacks a directing principle, for this principle, as we shall see, is fairly simple.

First of all, the author refuses to admit that there exists a definite relationship between the economic regimes which have succeeded one another in history and the social condition of women. She is doubtless aware that women are more or less well treated, depending on the greater or lesser importance of their economic role. But, according to her, the action of these factors is only secondary. In particular, she denies what certain socialists maintain, namely, that monogamy and the enslavement of women have as their fundamental cause the institution of private property. Here we sense that Weber is perpetually preoccupied with combatting the well-known theory of Engels. We find this preoccupation excessive and the place thus attributed to this theory entirely disproportionate to its scientific value.

It is principally domestic evolution which she presumes to have determined the way in which women's rights have developed. It is the woman's place in the family which is presumed to have determined her place in society. The principle is indisputable, but the author's conception of the history of the family is so simplistic that it hides from her the complexity of the problem being examined. Weber, following Grosse, recognizes just two types of family, clearly distinct from one another. One is the clan (*die Sippe*), a vast aggregate of individuals who are not necessarily consanguineous with one another. The second is the patriarchal family, which can be very extensive, as in the case of the Slavs, or less so, as in the case of the Romans, or yet more restricted when it includes only the descendants of a single couple, but which, in its various forms, reposes on the same principle and presents the same distinctive characteristics. It is formed by a group of relatives subjected to the authority of a male chief who is designated either by his age or by election or by his position on the family's genealogical tree. Not only are a large number of different types thus confused under the same rubric, but, what is more, it will be noted that there is no consideration of the matrilineal, or maternal, family. This is because the author sees therein not a determinate familial regime but a very contingent arrangement due to certain combinations of circumstances which can occur under all conceivable regimes. When the woman's family enjoys an economic or other superiority relative to the husband's family, the former naturally tends to lead the new household and the children who are born of it into her family's sphere of action. Moreover, it is rare that matrilineality not occur along with the contrary form of filiation in the same society. The former system would reign in a nearly exclusive manner and would be considered as the normal basis of domestic and conjugal relations in only a very small number of cases. Besides, according to our author, the form of filiation is presumed not to affect the internal structure of the family and would not suffice to give rise to a determinate familial type.

We think it useless to discuss a thesis which contradicts too many known facts. We cannot, moreover, help thinking that Weber would not so easily have accepted it if Engels' theory, which she has perpetually in view, had not attributed a primordial importance to the matriarchal family. Whatever the case on this particular point, here is how the author relates the history of women to the history of the family:

It is communism which characterizes the clan. The clan is an extensive grouping in which everything is common to everyone, in which the individual has no sphere of action which is proper to him alone; he cannot create a personality for himself. He is absorbed into the collectivity. The constitution of the patriarchal family corresponds to a first movement in the direction of individuation. The vast aggregate which constituted the clan is segmented into a certain number of individual, autonomous families. Each one administers its own interests as it sees fit. Thus, for the originally unified and homogenous life is substituted a plurality of heterogenous and independent centers of activity. Moreover, at the head of each of these groups is placed an individual who, thanks to the extent of the powers with which he is armed, achieves awareness of himself as a person. To the extent that familial groupings proceed to be segmented and to reduce themselves more and more, this movement of individuation itself develops and is accentuated until the family is normally composed of just the conjugal couple and its minor children. Then each man, once an adult, is found to exercise the full rights which accrue to a moral personality.

But this movement has profited only the masculine segment of humanity. The chiefs of individual families have always been men. The author does not deny that this hegemony has been necessitated by the very conditions of life. Notably, the importance of military functions explains the social primacy attributed to the stronger sex. However, the result has been a subjugation of women which persists today. The sovereignty of men, once established, has been maintained by the force of prejudices, and thus it is that today, though the old patriarchal power has lost its raison d'être, women are still treated as inferior beings and, by virtue of this, they are prevented from freely developing their personalities, as much within the household as in public life. Weber sees in this situation only a relic of the past, which we must strive to eliminate.

Since it is marriage which, by chaining the woman to the man, places the former in a state of dependence, some have proposed to suppress marriage as a social institution and to make of it a free contract quite entirely abandoned to the whim of the parties. A wisely conservative mind, the author rejects this remedy, which appears to her at once inefficacious and dangerous. The nuptial formalities seem to her indispensable as a means of declaring publicly and with certitude the will of a man and a woman to live together in a state of matrimony and to accept the legal consequences of that state. But, as marriage seems to her hardly useful except for this reason, Weber would be quite content with a regime in which the conjugal bond were singularly loosened, in which marriage were diminished in its stature. In the name of the moral individualism to which she appeals, she asks that it be possible to dissolve marriages simply by the will of the parties, when confirmed and duly declared. When one holds this conception of marriage, one easily sides with everything which can compromise the organic unity of conjugal society and of the family. This is why the author believes she can demand a total legal equalization of wife and husband: whether it be a matter of the children's education or of decisions which concern domestic affairs, neither spouse should have rights superior to those of the other.[2]

We are far from arguing that the legal status of women as it is determined by the civil law of European peoples does not call for important reforms. But from another perspective, we believe that Weber's simplistic argument and the conclusions which she draws from it fail to recognize the complexity of the problem.

Her entire theory rests on the principle that the patriarchal family has brought about a complete enslavement of women. In its absolute form, the proposition is most disputable. Assuredly, this domestic regime has given rise to the legal minority of women in civil life. But from another perspective, since in this same type of family, family life is much more intense and more important than in previous types, women's role, which is precisely to preside over this interior life, has itself taken on a greater importance, and the moral position of the wife and of the mother has been enlarged. At the same time and for the same reason, the husband and the wife have been brought more directly and more constantly in contact, because the center of masculine life has ceased to be, as much as in the past, outside the home. The greater the place occupied by the family in the man's preoccupations, the more he feels himself to be his wife's associate, the more he loses the habit of seeing in her an inferior. This result is the more marked as the patriarchal family is more strongly and more solidly organized. Thus, in Rome, where patriarchal power reached its furthest development, the woman was surrounded with respect and shared the condition of her husband. In this same regard, Rome was singularly more advanced than Athens.[3]

But who does not sense that everything which can contribute to the weakening of the organic unity of the family and of marriage must necessarily have the effect of eliminating this source of feminine grandeur? The respect shown her, a respect that has increased over historical time, has its origin mainly in the religious respect which the hearth inspires. If the family were henceforth considered only as a precarious union of two beings who could at any moment separate if they wished to, and who, as long as the association lasted, each had his or her own circle of interests and preoccupations, it would be difficult for this religion to subsist. And women would thereby be diminished. No doubt, some think that what they would lose on the one hand they would recover on the other in consequence of the more considerable role which they would play in civil life. It is still true that the gain which they would owe to the conquest of the rights which are claimed on their behalf would be compensated by important losses. This suffices to show that the problem is less simple than one would think, and that is all that we wished to establish.

9

REVIEW OF LUCIEN LEVY-BRUHL,

Les Fonctions mentales dans les sociétés inférieures

AND EMILE DURKHEIM,

Les Formes élémentaires de la vie religieuse

We shall not now undertake a complete analysis and critique of the works published in the "Travaux de *L'Année sociologique*" collection. However, we must at least put forth in summary fashion their principal conclusions in order that our depiction of sociological activity over the last three years not be incomplete.

The aim of Levy-Bruhl's book is to establish that human mentality does not exhibit the invariability which certain philosophers as well as the representatives of the anthropological school have attributed to it. Starting from the postulate that types of mentality must vary with types of society, he undertakes to establish the mental type which is peculiar to that poorly defined group of societies which are ordinarily termed "primitive" (*inférieures*). He is quite aware that because very different societies are subsumed under this rubric, the corresponding logical type will necessarily share the same relative indeterminacy. Proceeding in this way, we will only be able to obtain a very extensive genus which will contain a great number of distinct species. But, in the present state of research, only a preliminary attempt at a rough sketch is possible; only the future will render these results more precise.

According to Levy-Bruhl, what characterizes the primitive mentality is that it is essentially religious or, as the author puts it, mystical. Beings and things are represented in men's minds as having properties very different from those which sensory observation reveals. The primitive everywhere sees occult powers and

Originally published in *L'Annee sociologique* 12 (1909-12): 33-37.

mysterious forces, the existence of which is not and cannot be established by any experiment; they are matters of faith, and experiments can no more serve to impugn this faith than they can serve to demonstrate its validity. Moreover, it is characteristic of this mentality to be refractory to any experimental proof.

In that respect, the primitive mind is clearly differentiated from our own. The way in which it interrelates its ideas is no less specific, but its logic is not our own. The former is dominated by what Levy-Bruhl calls the law of participation. He formulates it as follows: "In the collective representations of the primitive mentality, objects, beings, and phenomena may be, in a way which is incomprehensible to us, at the same time themselves and something other than themselves. In a no less incomprehensible way, they give off and take on mystical forces, virtues, qualities and actions and make them felt outside themselves without ceasing to be where they are."[1] In a word, primitive thought does not obey the principle of contradiction, and that is why Levy-Bruhl terms it prelogical.

Having thus defined this mentality, Levy-Bruhl shows how it permits us to explain certain peculiarities of language, of enumeration, and of institutions specific to these kinds of societies.[2]

The work I have published on *The Elementary Forms of the Religious Life* naturally led me to pose questions which border upon or are related to those above; for primitive religions cannot be understood unless one studies the mentality of the peoples who practice them. While not dealing with the problem directly, I could not help but encounter it along the way and have not let pass these opportunities to grapple with it.

There is no need to say that my fundamental principles are the same as Levy-Bruhl's. Like him, I believe that different types of mentality have succeeded one another in the course of history. I also admit—and I have sought to establish it through factual analysis—that the primitive mentality is essentially religious, that is to say, that the notions which dominate the course of representations at that stage arise in the very heart of religion. On the other hand, since the principal object of this book is to show that the origins of religion are social, the result is that these notions and the corresponding logic have that same origin. This is what I have attempted to demonstrate in detail by passing in review the most important of these representations. However, my point of view is somewhat different from that of Levy-Bruhl. He is above all preoccupied with differentiating this mentality from our own and has gone so far as sometimes to present these differences in the form of a veritable antithesis. Religious and primitive thought on the one hand, scientific and modern thought on the other, would thus be set off as opposites. In the latter, the principle of identity and the sovereignty of experiment would be uncontested; in the former, a nearly complete indifference to experimental demonstration and to contradiction would reign. I, on the contrary, judge that these two forms of human mentality, as different as they may be, are far from arising from different sources; they are born one of the other and are two stages of a single evolution. I have shown, in effect, that the most essential notions of the human mind—the notions of time, of space, of genus and species, of force and causality, of personality—those, in a word, which philosophers call categories and which dominate the entire realm of logic, were elaborated in the very heart of religion. Science has borrowed them from religion. Between these two stages of the intellectual life of humanity, there is no break in continuity.[3]

At the same time that I established the religious origin of these categories, I showed that they were full of social elements, that they were even created in the image of social phenomena. The world was originally constructed on the model of the social space, that is to say, on the model of the territory occupied by the society and as the society represented it. Time expresses the rhythm of collective life. The idea of genus was at first just another aspect of the idea of human groups. The collective force and its influence on consciousnesses served as prototypes for the notions of force and causality, and so forth. True, it might seem that by virtue of these very origins, these fundamental representations necessarily lack any objective value and can only consist in artificial constructions without any basis in reality; for we generally see in society an alogical or illogical entity which was in no way constituted for the satisfaction of speculative needs. We do not, therefore, perceive at first glance how ideas which are the work of society and which express it can be called upon to play so preponderant a role in the history of thought and science. But I have applied myself to the task of demonstrating that, contrary to all appearances, the life of logic has its prime source in society. The essential characteristic of a concept, as opposed to a sensation or an image, is its impersonality: it is a representation which, to the extent that it is true to its nature, is common and communicable; it can pass from one mind to another. It is with concepts that intellects communicate. Now, a representation cannot be common to all the men of a single group unless it has been elaborated by them in common, unless it is the creation of the community. And if conceptual thought has a very special value for us, it is precisely because, being collective, it is rich in all the experience and all the science which the collectivity has accumulated in the course of centuries. The intellectual life of the society operates on an infinitely higher plane than that of the individual by the very fact that it is due to the concurrence, to the collaboration of a multitude of intellects and even of generations.[4] As for those concepts *sui generis* which are called categories, if they are social not only in their origins but also in their content, it is because they are eminent concepts: they dominate and envelop all other concepts. "Now, in order that they be able to embrace such an object, they must be based on a reality of equal magnitude."[5] A time which includes all particular durations, a space which embraces all specific distances, a total genus which takes in all known beings can only be the time, the space, the sum of things created by an object which consists of the totality of individual subjects and which surpasses them. It is society which taught man that there was a point of view other than that of the individual and which made him see things in their wholeness.

If, therefore, human mentality has varied with the centuries and with societies, if it has evolved, the various forms which it has successively assumed have been the source for one another. The higher and more recent forms are not juxtaposed to the lower and more primitive forms but are born of them. Even certain of the contrasts which have been pointed out should be attenuated. I have shown with examples that if the primitive mind is inclined to confusions, it is no less led to headlong oppositions and often applies the principle of contradiction in an exaggerated fashion. Inversely, the law of participation is not special to it: our ideas, today as previously, participate in one another. This is, indeed, the precondition of all logical life. The difference lies, above all, in the way in which this participation is established.[6]

LAW, CRIME, AND SOCIAL HEALTH

10

TWO LAWS OF PENAL EVOLUTION

In the present state of the social sciences, only the most general aspects of collective life can usually be translated into intelligible formulations. Because of this, we doubtless only manage to achieve what are sometimes gross approximations, but they are not without usefulness; for they constitute the mind's initial grasp of things and, as schematic as they may be, they are the necessary precondition of subsequent specification.

It is with this reservation that we shall seek to establish and explain two laws which seem to us to dominate the evolution of the repressive system.[1] It is quite clear that in this way we shall elucidate only the most general variations; but if we succeed in introducing a little order, however imperfect, into this confused mass of facts, our undertaking will not have been in vain.

The variations through which punishment (*la peine*) has passed in the course of history are of two kinds: quantitative and qualitative. The laws regarding each kind are, naturally, different.

THE LAW OF QUANTITATIVE VARIATION

It can be formulated as follows: *"The intensity of punishment is greater as societies belong to a less advanced type* (un type moins élevé)—*and as centralized power has a more absolute character."*

Let us first explain the meaning of these statements.

There is no great need to define the first. It is relatively easy to

Originally published as "Deux lois de l'évolution pénale," *L'Année sociologique* 4 (1899-1900): 65-95.

recognize whether a social species is more or less advanced than another: one has only to see which is more complex or, if equally complex, which is more organized. Moreover, this hierarchy of social species does not imply that the succession of societies forms a unique and linear series; on the contrary, it is certain that it is better represented as a tree with many more or less divergent branches. But on this tree societies are placed higher or lower and are found at a greater or lesser distance from the common trunk.[2] It is only on the condition of considering them in this way that it is possible to speak of a general evolution of societies.

The second factor which we distinguished above should detain us longer. We say of governmental power that it is absolute when it encounters in the other social functions nothing which by its nature balances and efficaciously limits it. In point of fact, a complete absence of all limitation is nowhere to be found; we can even say that it is inconceivable. Tradition and religious belief serve as restraints to even the strongest governments. What is more, there are always a few secondary social organs which, on occasion, are capable of asserting themselves and offering resistance. The subordinate functions to which the supreme function applies its regulatory force are never without some force of their own. But it happens that this de facto limitation involves no legal obligation for the government subjected to it; though the government maintains a certain moderation in the exercise of its prerogatives, it is not held to it by written law or convention. In such a case, it disposes of a power which we may call absolute. To be sure, if it allows itself to indulge in excesses, the social forces which it wrongs may coalesce to react and contain it. Foreseeing this reaction and in order to forestall it, the government may even restrain itself on its own. But this restraint, whether of its own doing or, for all intents and purposes, imposed upon it, is essentially contingent; it does not result from the normal functioning of institutions. When it is due to the government's own initiative, it appears as a gracious concession, as a voluntary surrender of legitimate rights; when it is the product of collective resistances, it has a frankly revolutionary character.

We can characterize absolute governments in yet another way. Legal affairs gravitate entirely about two poles: the relations which fix their pattern are either unilateral or, on the contrary, bilateral and reciprocal. Such are, at least, the two ideal types about which they oscillate. The first is constituted exclusively by the rights attributed to one of the parties of the relationship over the other, while the latter enjoys no rights corresponding to his obligations. In the second, on the contrary, the legal bond results from a perfect reciprocity between the rights conferred upon each of the two parties. "Real" rights, and, more particularly, the right of property, represent the most advanced form of relations of the first type: the owner has rights over the thing, but the latter has none over him. The contract, and especially the just contract—that is, one in which there is perfect equivalence in the social value of the objects or payments exchanged—is the ideal type of reciprocal relations. Now, the more the supreme power's relations with the rest of the society have a unilateral character—in other words, the more they resemble those which relate the person and the thing possessed—the more the government is absolute. Inversely, it is less absolute the more its relations with the other social functions are completely bilateral. Thus, the most perfect model of absolute sovereignty is the *patria potestas* of the Romans, as it was defined by the old civil law, since the son was the same as an object.

Thus, what makes the central power more or less absolute is the more or less radical absence of any countervailing force, regularly organized with a view toward moderating it. We can, therefore, foresee that what gives birth to a power of this sort is the more or less complete concentration of all society's controlling functions in one and the same hand. Because of their vital importance, they cannot be concentrated in one and the same person without giving him an exceptional preponderance over all the rest of society, and it is this proponderance which constitutes absolutism. He who wields such authority finds himself invested with a force which frees him from all collective restraints and makes him, at least to a certain extent, dependent only on himself and his pleasure and able to impose his will. This hypercentralization releases a social force *sui generis* so intense that it dominates all others and subjugates them to itself. And this preponderance exerts itself not only in fact but by right, for he who has this privilege is invested with such prestige that he seems to be of a superhuman nature; it is, therefore, not even conceivable that he can be subject to ordinary obligations like most men.

As brief and as imperfect as this analysis may be, it will at least suffice to forewarn us against certain still widespread errors. We see, in effect, that, contrary to the mistake committed by Spencer, governmental absolutism does not vary according to the number and importance of governmental functions. As numerous as its functions may be, the government is not absolute so long as it is not concentrated in a single person. This is what is happening today in our great European societies and particularly in France. Here the state's field of action has been extended differently than under Louis XIV; but the rights which it exercises over the society are not without reciprocal obligations and in no way resemble property rights. Not only are the supreme regulatory functions apportioned among distinct and relatively autonomous, though integrated organs, but they are not exercised without a certain amount of participation by the other social functions. Thus, it does not follow that the state has become more absolute just because it makes its action felt on a greater number of fronts. It is true that this may occur, but for that to happen, quite different circumstances are necessary than an increase in the complexity of the powers which have devolved upon it. Conversely, having functions of limited scope does not constitute an obstacle to its assuming an absolute character. In effect, if its functions are not very numerous nor often called into action, it is because social life itself, taken as a whole, is poor and languishing; for the more or less considerable development of the central regulatory organ only reflects the development of collective life in general, just as the dimensions of the nervous system in the individual vary according to the importance of organic exchanges. The controlling functions of the society are rudimentary only when the other social functions are of the same nature; and in this way the relationship among all of them remains the same. Consequently, the former retain all their supremacy, and it is enough that they be absorbed by one and the same individual to place him on a different plane and to elevate him infinitely above the rest of society. Nothing is more simple than government by a few uncivilized, petty kings; nothing is more absolute.

This observation leads us to another which more directly concerns our subject: the fact *that the more or less absolute character of the government is not an inherent characteristic of any given social type.* If, in effect, it can as easily be found where collective life is extremely simple as where it is extremely complex, it does not belong more exclusively to lower societies than to others. One might believe, it is true, that this concentration of governmental powers always accompanies the concentration of the social mass, either because the former results from the latter, or because the former contributes to the latter's determination. But this is in no way the case. The Roman city, especially after the fall of the monarchy, was until the last century of the Republic free from any absolutism; yet it was precisely under the Republic that the various segments, or partial societies (*gentes*), of which it was formed attained a very high degree of concentration and fusion. Moreover, we observe in the most diverse social types forms of government which deserve to be called absolute—in France in the seventeenth century, as at the end of the Roman state, or as in a multitude of uncivilized monarchies. Conversely, a single people, according to circumstances, can pass from an absolute government to another quite different type; however, a single society can no more change its type in the course of its evolution than an animal can change its species in the course of its individual existence. Seventeenth-century France and nineteenth-century France belong to the same type, yet the supreme regulatory organ has been transformed. It is as inadmissable to say that, from Napoleon I to Louis-Philippe, French society has passed from one social species to another, than it is to submit to an inverse change from Louis-Philippe to Napoleon III. Such transformations contradict the very notion of species.[3]

This special form of political organization—governmental absolutism—does not, therefore, arise from the congenital constitution of the society, but from individual, transitory, and contingent conditions. This is why these two factors of penal evolution—the nature of the social type and that of the governmental organ—must be carefully distinguished. This is because, being independent, they act independently of one another, sometimes even in opposite directions. For example, it happens that in passing from a lower species to other, more advanced types, we do not see punishment decrease, as could be expected, because at the same time the governmental organization neutralizes the effects of social organization. The process is, therefore, very complex.

Having explained the formulation of the law, we must show that it conforms to the facts. Since there can be no question of passing in review every society, we shall choose our comparisons from among those in which penal institutions have attained a certain level of development and are known with a certain degree of precision. Moreover, as we have tried to show elsewhere, the essence of a sociological demonstration is not to accumulate facts but to compose series of regular variations "the terms of which are related to one another by as continuous a set of gradations as possible and which, moreover, are of sufficient scope."[4]

In a very large number of ancient societies, death, pure and simple, did not constitute the supreme punishment; it was augmented, for those crimes held to be the most heinous, by supplementary penalties, which had the effect of making it more hideous. Thus, the Egyptians, aside from hanging and beheading, employed burning at the stake, torture by ashes, and crucifixion. In punishment by fire, the executioner began by making several incisions in the hands of the guilty party with sharp-ended cane stakes, and only then was the latter made to lie on a fire of thorns and burned alive. Torture by ashes consisted of suffocating the condemned man under a heap of embers. "It is even probable," Thonissen tells us, "that the judges usually inflicted upon the guilty party any accessory torments which they thought were required by the nature of the crime or the exigencies of public opinion."[5] The people of Asia appear to have pushed cruelty further. "Among the Assyrians, guilty parties were thrown to ferocious beasts or into a flaming furnace; they were roasted in a brass basin over a low fire; their eyes were put out. Strangulation and decapitation were rejected as insufficient measures! Among the various peoples of Syria, criminals were stoned, pierced with arrows, hanged, crucified, their ribs and entrails burned with torches, they were quartered, thrown from cliffs . . . . ., crushed under the feet of animals, etc."[6] Even the code of Manu distinguishes between simple death, which consisted of beheading, and aggravated or qualified death, of which there are seven kinds: impalement on stakes, fire, crushing under the feet of an elephant, drowning, boiling oil poured in the ears and mouth, being torn apart by dogs in a public square, and being cut into pieces with razors.

Among these same peoples, simple death is common. An enumeration of all cases which carry it as a penalty is impossible. One fact shows how numerous they were: according to an account by Diodorus, a certain king of Egypt managed to establish a new city in the desert by remanding those condemned to death; another, by using them for public works, succeeded in constructing numerous dams and in digging canals.[7]

Short of the death sentence, there were the expressive mutilations. Thus, in Egypt, counterfeiters—those who altered public documents—had their hands cut off; the rape of a free woman was punished by the ablation of the genitals; the spy's tongue was torn out, and so on.[8] Similarly, according to the laws of Manu, a man of the lowest cast who seriously insulted the Dwidjas had his tongue out, while the Sudra who had the audacity to seat himself next to a Brahmin was branded beneath the hip, and so on.[9] Besides these characteristic mutilations, all sorts of corporal punishments were employed by both peoples. Punishments of this sort were most often imposed at the discretion of the judge.

The Hebrew people certainly did not belong to a more advanced type than the preceding ones; the concentration of the social mass was achieved only at a relatively late date, under the monarchy. Until then there was no Israeli state, but only a juxtaposition of more or less autonomous tribes or clans, which coalesced only infrequently to face some common danger.[10] However, the Mosaic law is far less severe than that of Manu or than the sacred books of Egypt. Capital punishment is no longer surrounded with the same refinements of cruelty. It even appears that, for a long time, only lapidation was in use; it is only in the rabbinical texts that fire, decapitation, and strangulation are mentioned.[11] Mutilation—so liberally practiced by the other peoples of the Orient—is mentioned only once in the Pentateuch.[12] It is true that when the crime was a wound, retaliations could involve mutilations; but the guilty party could always escape this by means of a monetary settlement, forbidden only for murder.[13] As for the other corporal punishments, which amount to flagellation, they were certainly applied to a large number of offenses;[14] but the maximum was fixed at forty blows and in practice amounted to only thirty-nine.[15] Whence arises this relative lenience? It arises from the fact that, among the Hebrew people, absolute government never was able to establish itself in a lasting manner. We have even seen that for a long time they lacked political organization of any sort. Later, it is true, a monarchy was constituted; but the power of kings remained very limited: "There has always been among Israelites a lively feeling that the king was there for his people and not the people for its king; he was to help Israel, not use it for his own self-interest."[16] Though it sometimes happened that certain individuals acquired exceptional authority by virtue of their personal prestige, the spirit of the people remained profoundly democratic.

However, we have seen that their penal law was still very harsh. If we pass from the preceding societies to the pattern of the city-state, which is indisputably more advanced, we observe a more marked regression of penal law. In Athens, while capital punishment was augmented in certain cases, these were quite exceptional.[17] In principle, this consisted of death by hemlock, by the sword, or by strangulation. Expressive mutilations had disappeared. The same seems to hold for corporal punishments, except when used as punishments for slaves and, perhaps, for those low-born.[18] But Athens, even considered at its apogee, represents a relatively archaic form of the city-state. Never was the form of organization based on clans (genē or phratries) as completely obliterated as in Rome where, very early on, *curiae* and *gentes* became simple historical artifacts, the significance of which even the Romans no longer recognized very well. Moreover, the system of penalties was far more severe in Athens than in Rome. First, as we were saying, Athenian law was not wholly unfamiliar with aggravated death. Demosthenes alludes to guilty parties nailed to the gallows.[19] Lysias cites the names of assassins, thieves, and spies beaten to death;[20] Antiphon speaks of a poisoner dying on the rack.[21] Death was sometimes preceded by torture.[22] Moreover, the number of cases in which the death penalty was pronounced was considerable: "Treason, injury to the Athenian people, attacks upon their political institutions, the debasing of national law, lying before the tribunal of the people's assembly, the abuse of diplomatic functions . . ., extortion, impiety, sacrilege, etc., etc., incessantly required the intervention of the terrible minister of the Eleven."[23] In Rome, on the contrary, capital crimes were far less numerous, and the Porcian laws restricted the use of the ultimate punishment throughout the duration of the Republic.[24] In addition, except for quite exceptional circumstances, death was not associated with supplemental torture or any aggravation. The cross was reserved for slaves alone. Moreover, the Romans prided themselves on the relative mildness of their repressive system. Livy says, "*Nulli gentium mutiores placuisse pocuas,*"[25] and Cicero tells us, "*Vestram libertatem, non acerbitate supplicorum infestam, sed lenitate legum munitam esse voluerant.*"[26]

But when, with the Empire, governmental power tended to become absolute, penal law became more severe. First, more crimes carried capital punishment as a penalty. Adultery, incest, all sorts of attacks upon morality, but especially the ever growing number of cases of high treason were punishable by death. At the same time, more severe penalties were instituted. Burning at the stake, which had been reserved for exceptional political crimes, was now used against arsonists, the impious, sorcerers, parricides, and certain of those convicted of high treason. Condemnation *ad opus publicum* was established and mutilations practiced upon certain criminals (for example, castration for certain attacks upon morals or cutting off the hand of counterfeiters). Finally, torture made its appearance; it is from the period of the Empire that the Middle Ages later borrowed it.

If we pass from the city-state to Christian societies, we see penal law evolve according to the same law.

It would be an error to judge the penal law of feudal society by the reputation for atrocity which had been given to the Middle Ages. When we examine the facts, we note that it was far milder than previous social types, at least if we consider them at equivalent stages in their evolution, that is, in their periods of formation and, so to speak, of first youth; and it is only on this condition that the comparison can have a demonstrative value. Capital crimes were not very numerous. According to Beaumanoir, the only truly unpardonable deeds were manslaughter, treason, homicide, and rape.[27] The *Etablissements de Saint Louis* add to these abduction and arson.[28] These were the principal cases of *haute justice*. Nevertheless, while not formally qualified in that way, robbery was also a capital crime. The same was true of two offenses which were considered particularly prejudicial to seigneurial rights; these were crimes of commerce and highway robbery (violently robbing toll houses).[29] As for religious crimes, the only ones which were repressed with the ultimate penalty were heresy and irreligion. Sacriligious persons were simply made to pay a fine, as were the blasphemous; Pope Clement IV even censured Saint Louis for having decided, in the religious ardor of his youth, that these latter should have their foreheads branded and their tongues pierced. It was only later that the Church displayed an implacable severity toward its enemies. As for the penalties themselves, they were in no way excessive. The only aggravations of the death penalty consisted in being dragged on a hurdle and in being burned alive. Mutilations were rare. Moreover, we know how humane the Church's repressive system was. The punishments which it preferred to use were penances and mortifications. It rejected public humiliation, the iron collar, and the pillory, although similar punishments did not appear to exceed its jurisdiction. It is true that when it deemed a bloody repression necessary, it turned the guilty party over to secular justice. It is, nonetheless, a fact of the greatest significance that the highest moral power of the period thus evinced its horror for these kinds of punishments.[30]

This was the approximate situation until about the fourteenth century. From then on, the royal power was more and more firmly established. And as it was consolidated, penal law gathered strength. First to appear were crimes of treason; unknown under feudalism, the list of them now grew long. Religious crimes were classed in this way. As a result, sacrilege became a capital crime. Simple dealings with infidels and any attempt "to have people believe or to argue for anything which is or might be contrary to the holy faith of Our Lord" were also considered capital offenses. At the same time, punishments were applied more rigorously. Those found guilty of capital crimes could be broken on the wheel (it was then that torture by the wheel appeared), buried alive, quartered, flayed alive, or boiled to death. In certain cases, the children of the condemned shared his punishment.[31]

The apogee of absolute monarchy also marks the apogee of repression. In the seventeenth century, the capital punishments in use were still those we have just enumerated. Besides these, a new punishment, galley slavery, was instituted, one so terrible that the unfortunate condemned sometimes cut off an arm or a hand to escape it. This was so frequent that a declaration of 1677 made such mutilation punishable by death. As for corporal punishments, they were innumerable: there was the tearing out or piercing of the tongue, the cutting off of the lips, the cutting or tearing off of the ears, branding with a hot iron, beating with cudgels, the whip, the pillory, and so on. Finally, we must not forget that torture was often used, not only as a procedural device, but as a punishment. At the same time, capital crimes multiplied because crimes of treason became more numerous.[32]

Such was penal law until the middle of the eighteenth century. At that time the protest to which Beccaria gave his name took place all over Europe. To be sure, the Italian criminologist was hardly the cause of the reaction which has since been pursued without interruption. The movement had begun before him. Numerous works which demanded a reform of the penal system, forgotten today, had already appeared. It is, nonetheless, indisputable that his *Treatise on Crimes and Punishments* dealt the death blow to the old and hateful routines of criminal law.

An ordinance of 1788 had already introduced some important reforms, but it was with the Penal Code of 1810 in particular that the new aspirations finally received substantial satisfaction. Moreover, when it appeared, it was welcomed with unreserved admiration not only in France but in all the principal countries of Europe. It achieved important progress in the direction of mitigation. In reality, however, it still partook too much of the past. Demands for improvements were soon forthcoming. The complaint was raised that the death penalty, though it could no longer be as aggravated as it was under the *ancien régime*, was still too prevalent. It was considered inhumane to have preserved branding, the pillory, and the mutilation of the hand for parricides. The revision of 1832 took place in response to these criticisms. It introduced a much greater mildness into our penal organization by suppressing all mutilations, decreasing the number of crimes considered capital, and, finally, giving judges the means of lessening all punishments through the system of attenuating circumstances. It is not necessary to show that since that time this movement has proceeded in the same direction, because today we hear complaints about the too comfortable system created for criminals.

II. The Law of Qualitative Variations

The law which we have just established relates exclusively to the magnitude or quantity of punishments. That which we are now about to consider is related to their qualitative modalities. It can be formulated as follows: *Punishments consisting in privation of freedom—and freedom alone—for lengths of time varying according to the gravity of the crime, tend more and more to become the normal type of repression.* Lower societies are almost completely unacquainted with this kind of punishment. Even in the laws of Manu, there is at most one verse which mentions prisons. There it says, "The king shall place all prisons on the public highway so that criminals, chastened and hideous, may be exposed in view of all."[33] Moreover, such a prison had an entirely different character from those of our day; in theory, it was more like the pillory. The condemned was kept prisoner in order to be exposed to view and also because detention was the necessary condition for the punishments imposed upon him; but detention did not constitute the penalty itself, for this consisted primarily in the difficult existence created for those confined. Mosaic law is even more completely silent. In the Pentateuch, prison is not once mentioned. Later, in Chronicles and in the Book of Jeremiah, we find many passages which tell of prison, shackles, damp dungeons;[34] but in all these cases, it is a matter of preventive arrest, of places of detention in which accused persons and those suspected of having committed crimes were imprisoned while awaiting judgment, and in which they were subjected to a regimen more or less severe depending on the circumstances. These administrative measures, as arbitrary as they might have been, did not constitute definite punishments attached to definite crimes. It is only in the Book of Ezra that imprisonment is first presented as a punishment properly so called.[35] In ancient Slavic and Germanic law, punishments consisting purely of privation of freedom also appear to have been unknown. The same was true of the old Swiss cantons until the nineteenth century.[36]

Such punishments began to appear in the city-state. Contrary to what Schoemann says, it seems certain that in Athens imprisonment was inflicted as a special punishment in some cases. Demosthenes says explicitly that tribunals have the power to punish with imprisonment or any other penalty.[37] Socrates speaks of detention in perpetuity as a punishment which could be applied to his case.[38] Plato, outlining the plan of the ideal city in *The Laws*, proposed to repress a fairly large number of infractions with imprisonment, and we know that his utopia was closer to historical reality than has sometimes been assumed.[39] However, everyone recognizes that this type of punishment remained little developed in Athens. In the speeches of orators, prison was usually presented as a means of preventing the flight of accused persons or as a convenient procedure for constraining certain debtors to pay their debts or even as a supplementary penalty (*prostimēma*). When the judges limited themselves to inflicting a fine, they had the right to add a five-day detention in the public prison with feet shackled.[40] In Rome the situation was not very different. "Prison," says Rein, "was originally just a place for preventive detention. Later it became a punishment. However, it was seldom employed except for slaves, soldiers, and actors."[41]

It is only in Christian societies that it achieved its full development. In effect, the Church early adopted the custom of prescribing against certain criminals temporary or lifelong detention in a monastery. At first it was only considered as a means of surveillance, but there followed incarceration, or imprisonment, properly so called, which was treated as a genuine punishment. The maximum was perpetual and solitary detention in a cell which was walled in as a symbol of the irrevocability of the sentence.[42]

From this source, the practice passed into secular law. However, since imprisonment was simultaneously employed as an administrative measure, its penal significance long remained rather dubious. It was only in the eighteenth century that criminologists finally agreed to recognize the penal nature of prison in certain definite cases—when it was for life, when it had been substituted by commutation for the death penalty, and so on—in a word, whenever it had been preceded by a judicial investigation.[43] With the Penal Law of 1791, it became the basis of the repressive system which, aside from the death penalty and the pillory, included nothing but the various forms of detention. Nonetheless, simple imprisonment was not considered a sufficient punishment; privations of another order were added to it (for example, the belt or chain worn by the condemned, dietary restrictions). The Penal Code of 1810 did away with these aggravations, except for forced labor. The two other punishments consisting in privations of freedom differed only in the length of time the convicted person was shut up. Since then, forced labor has lost a large part of its characteristic traits and has tended to become a simple variety of detention. At the same time, the death penalty is more and more rarely applied; it has even completely disappeared from certain codes, with the result that temporary or lifelong privation of freedom occupies practically the entire domain of penal law.

III. EXPLICATION OF THE SECOND LAW

Having determined the way in which punishments have varied through time, we are going to investigate the causes of the stated variations, that is, to try to explain the two previously established laws. We shall begin with the second.

According to what we have just seen, detention first appeared in history as a purely preventive measure, only later to assume a repressive nature, and finally to become the prototype of punishment. To account for this evolution, we must first investigate what gave birth to prison in its original form and then what led to its later transformations.

The fact that preventive imprisonment is absent in less developed societies is easy to understand: it does not respond to any need there. In effect, responsibility is collective; when a crime is committed, it is not only the guilty party who is liable to punishment or for reparation, but the clan to which he belongs, either with him or in his place if he defaults. Later, when the clan has lost its familial character, it exists as a still extended circle of relatives. In such conditions, there is no reason to arrest and hold under surveillance the presumed author of the deed; for if he defaults for one reason or another, he leaves behind others who are answerable. Moreover, the moral and legal independence which is thus granted to each familial group limits the power to ask that it turn over one of its members on a simple suspicion. But as society becomes more concentrated, these elementary groups lose their autonomy and fuse with the total mass, and responsibility becomes individual. From that moment on, measures are necessary to prevent a person from avoiding punishment by fleeing. At the same time such measures shock established morality less, the prison makes its appearance. Thus, we find it in Athens, in Rome, and among the Hebrews after the exile. But it is so sharply contrary to the whole of the old social organization that it initially runs into opposition, at least everywhere that the power of the state is subject to some limitation, which narrowly restricts its use. Thus, in Athens, preventive detention was authorized only in particularly grave cases.[44] Even the murderer could retain his freedom until the day of sentencing. In Rome, the accused "was not at first kept prisoner except in cases of flagrant and manifest crime or when there was a confession; ordinarily, bail was sufficient."[45]

One must refrain from explaining these apparent restrictions on the right of preventive arrest as deriving from a sense of personal dignity and a sort of precocious individualism which the moral code of the city-state barely knew. What limited the right of the state was not the right of the individual, but that of the clan or family or, at least, what remained of it. It was not an anticipation of our modern morality but a vestige of the past.

However, this explanation is incomplete. In order to account for an institution, it is not enough to establish that at the moment it appeared, it responded to some useful end; for it does not follow from the fact that it was desirable that it was also possible. We must investigate beyond this, into how the conditions necessary to the realization of this end were created. A need—even an intense need—cannot create *ex nihilo* the means for its own satisfaction; we must therefore discover whence they came. On first examination, it doubtless seems quite obvious that, from the day when prisons became useful to societies, men had the idea of constructing them. However, in reality, the existence of prisons assumes that certain conditions, without which they are not possible, have been realized. Prisons imply the existence of public establishments, sufficiently spacious, militarily occupied, arranged in such a way as to prevent communications with the outside, and so on. Such arrangements are not improvised on the spur of the moment; no traces of them exist in less advanced societies. Public life is very meager, very intermittent, and has need of no special arrangements in order to develop except for some site where people can have meetings. Houses are built with exclusively private ends in mind; those of the chieftains—when there are permanent chieftains—are barely distinguishable from the others. Even temples are a rather late development. Finally, ramparts did not exist in less advanced societies; they appear only with the city. In such circumstances, the idea of a prison could hardly be conceived.

But as the social horizon is extended, as collective life, instead of being dispersed into a vast number of minor foci where it can manage only a meager existence, is concentrated about a more restricted number of points, it simultaneously becomes more intense and more continuous. Because it takes on greater importance, the dwellings of those who are in charge are transformed. They are extended and are organized in view of the more extensive and more permanent functions which are incumbent upon them. The more the authority of those who live in them grows, the more those dwellings are singularized and distinguished from the rest. They take on a grandiose air; they are sheltered by higher walls and deeper moats in such a way as to denote visibly the line of demarcation which thenceforth separates the holders of power and the mass of their subordinates. At that point, the preconditions of the prison come into being. What leads us to suppose that prisons originated in this way is that they often first appeared in the shadow of the king's palace or among the outbuildings of temples and similar institutions. Thus, in Jerusalem, we know of three prisons in the time of the invasion of the Chaldeans: one was "at the principal portal of Benjamin,"[46] and we know that the portals were fortified areas; another in the court of the king's palace;[47] the third in the house of a royal functionary.[48] In Rome, the most ancient prisons were found in the royal fortress.[49] In the Middle Ages, they were in the seigneurial castle, in the towers of the ramparts which surrounded the towns.[50]

Thus, at the very moment when the establishment of a place of detention became useful in consequence of the progressive disappearance of collective responsibility, edifices which could be used for this purpose were being constructed. Prisons, it is true, were as yet only preventive. But once constituted for this purpose, they quickly took on a repressive nature, at least in part. In effect, all those who were held prisoner in this way were suspects; they were, moreover, usually suspected of grave crimes. In addition, they were subjected to a severe regimen which was already almost a punishment. All the accounts of these primitive prisons, which did not yet constitute truly penetentiary institutions, portray them in the most unfortunate light.[51] In Dahomey, the prison was a hole in the form of a well in which the condemned squatted amid filth and vermin.[52] In Judea, we have seen that they constituted deep pits. In ancient Mexico, they consisted of wooden cages to which prisoners were bound; they were barely fed.[53] In Athens, persons detained were subjected to the infamous punishment of shackles.[54] In Switzerland, to make escape more difficult, prisoners were placed in an iron collar.[55] In Japan, prison was called "hell."[56] A stay in such places was naturally quite early considered a punishment. It was in this way that minor crimes were punished, especially those which had been committed by minor personnages, those whom the Romans called *personae humiles*. It was a correctional punishment which judges could use more or less arbitrarily.

To account for the legal fortunes which befell this new penalty from the very moment it was constituted, it is enough to combine the preceding considerations with the law regarding the progressive weakening of penal law. In effect, this weakening takes place from the top of the penal scale down. In general, it is the gravest punishments which are the first to be affected by this movement of retreat; that is, they are the first to be moderated, then to disappear. It is the aggravations of capital punishment which are the first to be attenuated, until the day when they are completely suppressed; it is cases of the application of capital punishment which are progressively restricted; mutilations are subject to the same law. As a result, the lesser penalties are forced to develop to fill the void created by this regression. To the extent that archaic forms of repression are retired from the field of penal law, new forms invade the free space which they find before them. The various modalities of detention constitute the penalties formulated last. Originally, they were at the very bottom of the penal scale, since they began by not even being punishments in the true sense but only the precondition of real repression, and since for a long time they retained an ambiguous character. For this very reason, the future was reserved for them. They were the natural and necessary substitutes for the other penalties, which were disappearing. But on the other hand, detention itself had to submit to the same law of progressive moderation. This is why, though in the beginning it coexisted with auxiliary rigors of which it was sometimes only an accessory appendage, it little by little rid itself of these latter and was reduced to its simplest form: namely, privation of freedom, now including only those gradations which result from the unequal duration of this privation.

Thus, the qualitative variations of punishment depend in part on the quantitative variations to which it was subjected in a parallel fashion. In other words, of the two laws which we have established, the first contributes to the explanation of the second. It is now time to explain it.

IV. EXPLICATION OF THE FIRST LAW

To facilitate this explication, we shall consider in isolation the two factors which we have distinguished; and since the second plays the less important role, we shall begin by setting it aside. Let us, therefore, investigate how it is that penalties grow milder as we pass from lower societies to higher societies, without for the moment concerning ourselves with the perturbations which may be due to the more or less absolute nature of the governmental power.

One might be tempted to explain this process of moderation by the parallel moderation of mores. More and more, we abhor violence; violent—that is to say, cruel—punishments should therefore inspire in us a growing repugnance. Unfortunately, this explanation turns against itself. For if, on the one hand, our greater humanity leads us away from painful punishments, it must also make the inhuman acts which these punishments repress appear more odious to us. If our more highly developed altruism is repulsed by the idea of making another suffer, then for the same reason, crimes which are contrary to these sentiments must seem more abominable to us, and, consequently, it is inevitable that we would tend to repress them more severely. This tendency, though it arises from the same source, can be neutralized only partially and weakly by the opposite tendency, which leads us to make the guilty party suffer as little as possible. For it is obvious that our sympathy must be less for the guilty party than for his victim. The refinement of mores would have to be translated into penal aggravation, at least for all crimes which harm another person. In fact, when such refinement begins to develop in a marked manner in history, it is in this way that it is manifested. In lower societies, murder and simple theft are only weakly repressed because mores are vulgar. In Rome, for a long time, violence, far from carrying penal sanction, was not even thought to impugn contracts. These crimes have been more severely punished from the day when the sympathetic sentiments of man for man were affirmed and developed. This trend would, therefore, have continued had not some other cause intervened.

Since the penalty results from the crime and expresses the way in which it affects the public conscience, we must seek the determining cause of the evolution of penal law in the evolution of crime.

Without having to enter into the details of the proofs which justify this distinction, we think that it will be conceded without difficulty that all acts reputed to be criminal by the various known societies can be divided into two fundamental categories: some are directed against collective things (whether ideal or material), of which the principal examples are public authority and its representatives—mores, traditions, and religion—the others offend only individuals (murders, thefts, violence, and frauds of all kinds). These two forms of criminality are sufficiently distinct to be designated by different words. The first could be called "religious criminality" because attacks against religion are its most essential element and because crimes against traditions or heads of state always have a more or less religious character. We might refer to the second category as "human" or "individual criminality." We also know that crimes of the first type comprise, almost to the exclusion of all others, the penal law of lower societies, but that, on the contrary, they regress to the extent that social evolution proceeds. Meanwhile, attacks against the individual (*la personne humaine*) more and more occupy this entire area. For primitive peoples, crime consists almost solely in not observing the practices of the cult, in violating the ritual taboos, in deviating from the mores of ancestors, in disobeying authority where it is strongly consolidated. On the other hand, for today's European, crime consists essentially in the disruption of some human interest.

Now, these two types of criminality differ profoundly because the collective sentiments which they offend are not of the same nature. As a result, repression cannot be the same for both.

The collective sentiments which are violated and upset by the specific criminality of lower societies seem to be collective in a twofold way. Not only do they have the collectivity as their subject and, consequently, can be found in most individual consciousnesses (*consciences particulières*), but *they have collective things as their object*. By definition, these things are outside the circle of our private interests. The ends to which we are thus attached infinitely surpass the limited horizon of each of us as an individual. It is not us personally that they concern, but, rather, the collective entity (*l'être collectif*). In consequence, the acts demanded of us for their attainment are not in accord with the inclination of our individual natures, but do them violence, since they consist in sacrifices and privations of all sorts, which man is required to impose upon himself either to please his god, to satisfy custom, or to obey authority. We have no inclination to fast, to humiliate ourselves, to forbid ourselves one or another meat, to sacrifice on the altar our favorite animals, to trouble ourselves out of respect for custom, and so forth. Consequently, in the same way that sensations come to us from the outside world, such sentiments exist within us independent of ourselves (*en nous sans nous*) and even, to some extent, despite ourselves. They become manifest to us in this way as a result of the constraint which they exert upon us. We are, therefore, forced to alienate them, to relate them to some external force as their cause, just as we do for our sensations. Besides, we are obliged to conceive of this force as a power which is not only foreign but, beyond that, superior to us, since it commands and we obey. This voice within us which speaks in such imperious tones, which enjoins us to do violence to our nature, can only emanate from a being different from ourselves, one which, moreover, dominates us. In whatever special form men have imagined it (god, ancestors, august personalities of every sort), it always partakes of something transcendent or superhuman in relation to them. That is why this part of morality is thoroughly imbued with religiosity. It is because the duties which it prescribes for us create obligations toward a personality which infinitely surpasses our own; this is the collective personality which we imagine in its abstract purity or, as most often happens, with the help of truly religious symbols.

But then, crimes which violate these sentiments and which consist in failing in these special duties can only appear to be directed against these transcendent beings, since in reality they do them harm. As a result, they appear exceptionally odious to us, for an offense is the more revolting when the offended party is higher in nature and in dignity than the offender. The more one is expected to display respect, the more a lack of respect is abominable. The same act which when directed at an equal is simply blameworthy becomes impious when it strikes at someone who is superior to us; the horror to which it leads can therefore only be appeased by violent repression. Normally, in the sole aim of pleasing his gods and maintaining regular relations with them, the believer must submit to a thousand privations. To what privations must he be subjected when he has outraged them? Even though the pity evoked by a guilty man would be fairly intense, it could not serve as an efficacious counterbalance to the indignation created by a sacrilegious act nor, consequently, perceptibly to moderate the punishment, for the two sentiments are too unequal. The sympathy which men evince for one of their peers, especially one degraded by a fault, cannot contain the effects of the reverential fear that is held for the divinity. Relative to this power, which surpasses him from so far on high, the individual appears so small that his sufferings lose their relative value and become a negligible quantity. What is an individual's suffering when it is a matter of appeasing a god?

Collective sentiments which take the individual as their object are different, for each of us is an individual. That which concerns man concerns us all, for we are all men. Thus, the sentiments which protect human dignity touch us personally. Assuredly, I do not mean that we only respect the life and property of our peers out of utilitarian calculation and in order to obtain a just reciprocity from them. If we reproach acts which are deficient in this respect, it is because they violate the sentiments of sympathy which we have for man in general, and these sentiments are without self-interest precisely because they have a general object. Therein lies the great difference which separates the moral individualism of Kant and that of the utilitarians. Both, in a sense, make the development of the individual the object of moral conduct. But for the latter, the individual in question is the perceptible, empirical individual such as each individual consciousness conceives of him. For Kant, on the contrary, it is the human personality; it is humanity in general, abstracted from the concrete and diverse forms in which it presents itself for observation. Nevertheless, as universal as it may be, such a perspective is closely related to that toward which our egoistic penchants incline us. Between man in general and the man that each of us is, there is not the same difference as between man and god. The nature of this ideal being differs only in degree from our own; it is only the model of which we are the various examples. Therefore, the sentiments which attach us to it are in part the extension of those which attach us to ourselves. This is expressed by the adage: "Do unto others as you would have them do unto you."

To explain these sentiments and the acts to which they lead us, it is not necessary to look for some transcendent origin for them. To account for the respect which we feel for humanity, there is no need to imagine that it is far more in conformity with the natural inclination of our sensibilities. Attacks which run counter to respect for humanity will not, therefore, seem directed against some superhuman being to as great an extent as the preceding ones did. We do not see in them acts against divinity, but only against humanity. No doubt, this latter ideal is not devoid of all transcendence; it is in the nature of every ideal to surpass the real and to dominate it. But this transcendence is much less marked. Though this abstract man cannot be mistaken for any of us, each of us realizes him in part. As lofty as this goal may be, it is essentially human and also to some extent immanent in us.

Consequently, the conditions of repression are no longer the same as in the first case. There is no longer the same distance between the offender and the offended; they are more nearly on an equal footing. And the more so since, in each particular case, the person whom the crime offends possesses a particular individuality, in every way identical to that of the guilty party. The moral scandal which constitutes the criminal act is, thereby, somewhat less revolting and, consequently, does not require so violent a repression. The attack of a man against a man could not incite the same indignation as the attack of a man against a god. At the same time, the feelings of pity evoked in us by him who is struck by the punishment cannot be as easily nor as completely choked off by the sentiments which he violated and which react against him, for both are of the same nature. The first are only a variety of the second. What tempers this collective rage, which is at the heart of all punishment, is the sympathy we feel for any man who suffers and the horror inspired in us by any destructive violence; but it is the same sympathy and the same horror which kindle this same rage. This time, the very cause which sets in motion the repressive apparatus also tends to impede it. The same mental state impels us to punish and to moderate the punishment. Thus, an attenuating influence could not fail to make itself felt. It might appear quite natural to sacrifice unreservedly the human dignity of the guilty party to the outraged divine majesty. There is, on the contrary, a veritable and irremediable contradiction in avenging the human dignity offended in the person of the victim by violating it in the person of the guilty party. The only way to moderate the antinomy—not to remove it, for, in a strict sense, it cannot be resolved—is to moderate the penalty as much as possible.

Since, therefore, crime is progressively reduced to attacks against persons, while the religious forms of criminality regress, it is inevitable that the average punishment should become weaker. This weakening does not arise from a moderation of mores but from the fact that religiosity, with which both penal law and the collective sentiments which were its basis were originally imprinted, progressively diminishes. At the same time, feelings of human sympathy no doubt become more lively, but this greater liveliness is not sufficient to explain the progressive moderation of penalties, since by itself it would tend to make us more severe toward all crimes of which man is victim and to heighten their repression. The real reason is that the compassion of which the guilty party is the object is no longer crushed beneath the contrary sentiments which prevent its influence from being felt.

But, we are told, if such is the case, how does it happen that the punishments attached to crimes against persons take part in the general regression? For, though they have lost less than the others, it is, nonetheless, certain that in general they are less severe than two or three centuries ago. For if it is in the nature of this sort of crime to evoke less severe punishments, the effect should have been felt all at once, as soon as the criminal character of these acts was formally recognized; the punishments which repress them should have immediately and suddenly achieved their present moderation, instead of growing progressively more mild. But the cause of this progressive moderation lies in the fact that at the moment when these attacks, long stalled on the threshold of criminal law, entered and were definitively classed therein, it was religious criminality which occupied almost the entire field. In consequence of this preponderant situation, the latter began by leading into its sphere these newly constituted offenses and by marking them with its imprint. Insofar as crime is essentially conceived of as an offense against the divinity, crimes committed by men against men are also conceived of according to this model. We believe that they, too, revolt us because they are forbidden by the gods and, therefore, outrage those gods. The ways of the mind are such that it does not even appear possible that a moral precept could have a sufficiently well-founded authority unless it borrows from that which is considered to be the sole source of all morality. Such is the origin of those theories, so widespread even today, according to which morality lacks any basis unless it is grounded in religion or, at the very least, in a rational theology—that is to say, unless the imperative category emanates from some transcendent being. But to the extent that human criminality develops and religious criminality retreats, the former more and more clearly reveals its own physiognomy and its distinctive traits such as we have described them. It liberates itself from the influences to which it was subjected and which keep it from being itself. Although even today in the minds of many, penal law and, more generally, all morality are inseparable from the idea of god, their number is diminishing, and even those who retain this archaic conception no longer link these two ideas as closely as could a Christian of earlier ages. Human morality more and more rids itself of its primitive parochial character. The regressive evolution of the punishments which repress the gravest offenses against the prescriptions of this morality occurs in the course of this development.

In a noteworthy reversal, as human criminality gains ground, it acts upon religious criminality and, so to speak, assimilates it. Although today it is attacks against persons which constitute the principal crimes, there still exist attacks against collective things (crimes against the family, against mores, against the state). However, even these collective things themselves tend more and more to lose the religiosity with which they were once marked. Once divinities, they now become human realities. We no longer hypostatize the family or the society in the form of transcendent and mystic entities; we now see in them only groups of men who coordinate their efforts in order to attain human ends. As a result, crimes directed against these collectivities partake of the nature of those which directly harm individuals, and the punishments applied to the former are also progressively moderated.

Such is the cause which led to the progressive weakening of punishments. This result is seen to have occurred mechanically. The way in which collective sentiments react against crime has changed because these sentiments have changed. New forces have come into play; their effects could not remain the same. This great transformation did not, therefore, take place with a preconceived end in view nor in the service of utilitarian considerations. But, once achieved, it quite naturally was found to be suited to useful ends. By the very fact that it necessarily resulted from the new conditions in which societies were placed, the intensity of punishments serves only to make individual consciousnesses sense the force of social constraint; moreover, it is only useful if it varies with the intensity of the constraint itself. It is fitting, therefore, that it should be moderated as collective coercion is eased, made flexible, and becomes less exclusive of free inquiry. That is the great change which occurred in the course of moral evolution. Though social discipline—of which morality, properly so called, is only the highest expression—further extends its field of action, it loses more and more of its authoritarian vigor. Because it takes on a more human character, it leaves more room for individual spontaneity; it even solicits it. There is less need, therefore, for social discipline to be violently imposed. Now, for that to occur, it is also necessary that the sanctions which assure respect for it should become less restrictive of all initiative and reflection.

We can now return to the second factor of penal evolution, which we have dispensed with until now, that is to say, the nature of the governmental organ. The preceding considerations permit us easily to explain how it acts.

In effect, the nature of absolute power necessarily has the effect of elevating its possessor above the rest of humanity, making him something superhuman. This is truer the more his power is unlimited. In fact, wherever government is absolute, he who exercises power appears to men to be a divinity. When he is not made into a special god, the power with which he is invested is at the very least seen as emanation of divine power. From then on, this religiosity cannot fail to have its usual effect on punishment. On the one hand, attacks directed against a being so obviously superior to all offenders will not be considered as ordinary crimes but as sacrileges and, for this reason, will be violently repressed. Whence derives, among all peoples subject to absolute government, the exceptional priority assigned by penal law to crimes of *lèse majesté*. On the other hand, since, in these same societies, nearly all laws are supposed to have emanated from the sovereign and to express his will, the principal violations of the law seem to be directed against him. The reprobation which these acts incite is, therefore, far more lively than if the authority with which they clashed were more dispersed, hence, more moderate. The fact that authority is so concentrated makes it more intense, therefore more perceptible to all those who offend it, and more violent in its reactions. Thus, the gravity of most crimes is heightened by several degrees; consequently, the average intensity of punishments is extraordinarily enforced.

V. Conclusion

Thus understood, the law for which we have just accounted assumes an entirely different significance.

In effect, if we go to the very heart of the matter, we now see that it expresses not only the quantitative variations through which punishment has passed, as it might have seemed at first glance, but also truly qualitative variations. If penal law is milder today than heretofore, it is not because the ancient institutions of criminal justice remained the same, little by little losing their rigor; rather, it is because they have been replaced by different institutions. The motive forces which led to the formation of the old and of the new were not of the same nature. It no longer consists of that petulance, that explosive suddenness, that indignant stupefaction incited by an outrage directed against a being whose worth is incomparably greater than that of the aggressor; it is, rather, the calmer, more reflective emotion provoked by offenses which take place among equals. Blame is not the same and does not exclude compassion; of itself, it evokes moderation. Hence, the necessity of new punishments which are in accord with this new mentality.

In this way, we avoid an error to which the superficial observation of the facts could give rise. Seeing the regularity with which repression seems to weaken as its evolution advances, one might think that this progression is destined to be pursued without end; in other words, that penal law will eventually be eliminated. However, such a consequence would contradict the true sense of our law.

The cause which has led to this regression could not produce its attenuating effects indefinitely. This cause does not consist in a sort of numbing of moral consciousness which, through the gradual loss of original vitality and sensitivity, would become more and more incapable of any energetic penal reaction. If we compare the present with the past, we find that we are not more tolerant of all crimes indiscriminantly, but only of some of them; there are others, on the contrary, toward which we show ourselves to be more severe. However, those for which we evince an ever greater indulgence happen also to be those which provoke the most violent repression. Inversely, those for which we reserve our severity evoke only moderate punishments. Consequently, to the extent that the former cease to be treated as crimes and are withdrawn from penal law to be replaced by the latter, a weakening of the average penalty must necessarily occur. But this weakening can last only as long as does this substitution. A time must come—it has nearly arrived—when the process will have been completed, when attacks against persons will fill the whole of criminal law, when even what remains of the others will be considered to be dependent on this new form of criminality. The movement of retreat will then stop. There is no reason to believe that human criminality must, in its turn, regress in the same way as the punishments which repress it. Instead, everything leads us to predict that it will develop further, that the list of acts considered criminal will grow longer and that their criminal character will be accentuated. Frauds and injustice which yesterday left the public consciousness indifferent, today arouse its revulsion. And this sensitivity will only become more lively with time. There is not a general tapering off of the entire repressive system; one particular system is giving way but is being replaced by another which, while less violent and less harsh, still has its own severities and is in no way destined to an uninterrupted decline.

Thus is explained the state of crisis in which penal law exists among all civilized peoples. We live at a time when the penal institutions of the past have either disappeared or survive only by force of habit; yet others which better respond to the new aspirations of moral consciousness have not yet been born.

11

CRIME AND SOCIAL HEALTH

[To the Editor of *La Revue philosophique*:]
I ask permission to reply briefly to the recent article by Tarde entitled "Crime and Social Health," for most of the propositions which my eminent critic attributes to me are not mine. I deem them as false as he does.[1]

1. I did not say that the increase in crime evidenced by our statistics was normal. You will not find a single sentence in my book in which this idea is expressed. So little do I accept the theory of Poletti that I have publicly refuted it in a lecture in the course on the sociology of crime which I recently delivered at Bordeaux. In a book which I am preparing on *Suicide*, will be found a refutation of the same thesis insofar as it is applicable to voluntary deaths. I hope that I have, therefore, established my first point. After this declaration, Tarde cannot place in doubt the fact that on this question he has attributed to me a sentiment which is not my own.

Tarde, moreover, seems himself to have had some scruples, for he felt the need to add a footnote to his text to demonstrate that this proposition is *"in conformity with my principles."* This method of discussion—which consists in supposing an author to have said what he did not say—was much esteemed at one time but has since been abandoned. People realized that it was too easy to draw from such a system any consequence one wished. I think that we would do better not to return to it. But it might still be asked if I must acknowledge this error simply in the name of logic. You be the judge. After

Originally published as "Crime et santé sociale," *Revue philosophique* 39 (1895): 518–23.

having stated that the existence of crime was a universal fact and, consequently, presented the criterion for normality, I felt I should raise an objection to my own line of thought. If, I asked, the facts permit us to believe that the more we advance in history, the more crime tends toward zero, without disappearing, then could we suppose that this universality and, consequently this normality, are temporary? But, strangely enough, it happens that the only information which we have available shows an increase instead of a decrease in crime. We must, therefore, discard this hypothesis, since it is without basis in fact. But just because this increase in crime prevents us from assuming that it is in decline, it does not follow that crime is normal. The question remains to be solved, and it admits of many solutions. For we are not even constrained within the dilemma which Tarde imagines. It might be that it is normal for certain crimes to advance with civilization but that the enormous increase which has occurred in our time is morbid. Finally, I am so far from absolving what is occurring that, thinking of the sad spectacle which our statistics presently offer us, I wrote the following on the very page on which the incriminated passage is to be found: "It can happen that crime itself may have abnormal forms; this is what happens when, for example, *it attains an exaggerated level. It is hardly to be doubted that this excess is of a morbid nature.*"

2. I did not say that the utility of crime consisted in preventing moral consciousness from too severely incriminating acts of minor indelicacy, as if that were a deplorable evil which must be prevented at all costs. I do not see a single word in my book which can justify such an interpretation. I simply said that, in fact, if moral consciousness became so strong that all crimes which until then had been repressed, completely disappeared, it would then be seen to tax more severely acts which it had previously judged with greater indulgence; that, consequently, crime, having disappeared in one form, would reappear in another. It follows from this, then, that there is a contradiction in conceiving of society without crime. But I did not say that this greater severity in the manner of evaluating moral acts would be evil, any more than I said it would be good. And if I did not pose the question for myself, it is because the question cannot be posed in the abstract in this way. We would still have to

know in relation to what social type we were deciding whether this increase in rigor is desirable or not. Since the primitive Roman city-state, social life was possible only if the individual personality was in large measure absorbed into the collective personality; it would have been bad for moral consciousness to have become too sensitive to offenses directed against individuals. Whereas today, if the feelings of deference and of respect which we experience for the great contemporary religions, feelings which still have legal sanctions in most of the European codes, were to exceed a certain level of intensity, we would see what would become of our free thinking. I give these examples only to show that the question is not so simple.

3. I did not say that if certain crimes became rare, the penalties which they incur would necessarily be raised. It does not follow from the fact that they would be more severely incriminated that they would be more severely punished. I spoke of incrimination, not of repression. These are two different problems, which Tarde seems to confuse. What explains why these two orders of facts do not vary directly is that very often the collective sentiment which the crime offends is also offended by the penalty. Thus, a sort of compensation is established which prevents punishments from increasing along with the intensity of blame. This is what happens in the case of all crimes which wound the sentiments of sympathy which we experience for man in general. As this sympathy becomes more lively with the advance of civilization, we become more sensitive to the least attack which the person may suffer. Consequently, light offenses, which were formerly treated with indulgence, today seem scandalous in our eyes and are punished. But, on the other hand, any repression also does violence to this same tendency which, consequently, is opposed to punishments becoming more rigorous. We have more pity for the victim, but we also have more pity for the guilty party. It even happens that for a time, and for reasons which we cannot set forth here, the guilty one benefits more from this transformation than the victim. That is how, *as far as this special case is concerned*, punishments are decreased to the degree that moral consciousness becomes, on this very point, more stringent.

4. Nowhere did I say that crime and genius were merely two different aspects of a single mental state. This entire portion of

Tarde's discussion is beyond me. I said that it was useful and even necessary that in any society the collective type not be identically repeated in every individual consciousness. Among the divergences thus produced, some are criminals, others are men of genius. But I never identified the latter with the former. It may happen that the criminal has genius, just as he may be below average. In any case, the reasons for which I said that crime is normal—has a certain incidence—are independent of the intellectual aptitudes which are attributed to the delinquent.

5. It is particularly inaccurate to say that "crime which is base and rampant, hated and despised is the only sort with which Durkheim is concerned." When I attempted to show how crime could be useful, even in a direct way, the only examples which I cited were those of Socrates and of the heretical philosophers of all epochs, precursors of free thinking; and we know that they are numerous. It is on these facts and their analogues—and the latter are themselves legion—that he would have had to base his discussion in order to attack my line of argument.

In opposition to the propositions which are inaccurately attributed to me, I would like briefly to recall those which I truly wished to establish. The reader will judge whether they have been answered.

1. First, I said that, *useful or not*, crime is normal because it is bound to the fundamental conditions of all social life. This is so because there can be no society in which the individuals do not diverge, more or less, from the collective type and because, among these divergences there are, no less necessarily, some which have a criminal character. A complete material leveling is materially impossible. I see nothing in Tarde's article which answers this argument except for the sentence: "One should not say that [the disappearance of all crime] is impossible, since one could have said the same thing about slavery in ancient times, and even now about pauperism or begging in the streets." I am unable to see the relationship between the disappearance of crime and that of slavery, slavery not being a crime. As for pauperism, we are hardly in a position to know if it is destined to disappear. A hope is not a fact. And, moreover, regarding this point also, what is the relationship with crime?

2. I then said that the existence of crime had a *generally indirect* and *sometimes direct* utility: indirect because crime cannot cease to exist unless the collective consciousness imposes itself upon individual consciousnesses with such an inescapable authority that any moral transformation would be rendered impossible; direct in that sometimes, *but only sometimes*, the criminal has been the precursor of the morality of the future.

To demolish the first part of this proposition, it would have been necessary either to prove that a fixed arrangement does not render impossible, or at least very difficult, subsequent rearrangements and that, consequently, so strongly organized and so deeply rooted a morality could yet evolve; or, to deny that there is and that there must always be a moral evolution. Instead of that, Tarde is content to enumerate the unhappy consequences of theft, murder, and blackmail. Is it necessary to say that I am aware of them and that I would not dream of contesting their existence? I did not say that crime did no harm; I said that it had the useful effects that I have restated. The harmful results which it can have do not demonstrate that this utility does not exist. It will be asked how it can be normal if it is in some respect harmful? But I have insisted precisely on establishing that it is an error to believe that a normal fact is entirely beneficial; there is nothing which is not bad in some way. Moreover, it must be recalled that the social evil caused by the crime is compensated by the penalty and that, according to the felicitous expression of Tarde—which I wish to appropriate, since it captures my thought so well—what is normal is the inseparable pairing of crime and punishment.

To destroy the second part of my proposition, it would have been necessary to prove that it is possible to innovate in moral affairs without almost inevitably becoming a criminal. How can one change morality without straying from it? It will be suggested that one can add a few new maxims without taking anything away from the old ones, but this solution would be purely verbal. The rules which are added necessarily run counter to others. A moral system is not some mathematical splendor which can grow or shrink without changing in nature. It is an organic system whose parts are integrated among themselves; the introduction of the least change throws its entire economic structure into turmoil. The great moral reformers of all times have condemned contemporary morality and have been condemned by it.

Finally, in this discussion it would have been better not to concentrate exclusively on the present forms of criminality, for the sentiments which they inspire in us all hardly permit us to speak of them objectively. Moreover, we cannot judge the role and the nature of crime in general on the basis of such special types. If we examine the past, the normality of crime no longer seems so paradoxical. For, as far as mankind's previous morality is concerned, we gain a better sense of how important it was that it not be too strongly fixed in order for it to have the potential to evolve. Given this, to deny that this necessity is imposed with equal force upon our current morality, one would have to presume that the period of moral transformations is ended. Who, then, would dare to say to any one of the developing forms that it must go no further?

3. In the third place, morality is a social function; it must, therefore, like any function, have only a limited degree of vitality. This condition is required for the maintenance of the organic equilibrium. If morality draws to itself a fraction of the vital energy which exceeds its fair share, other forms of collective activity will suffer. If our respect for human life exceeded a certain intensity, we would not tolerate even the idea of war; and yet, in the present state of international relations, we must be able to make war. Nothing is more moral than the sentiment of individual dignity; however, beyond a certain point it renders impossible military discipline, which is indispensable, and even any sort of discipline at all. Too much pity for the sufferings of animals, as in opposing the practice of vivisection, becomes an obstacle to scientific progress, and so on. The maxim *ne quid nimis*[2] is true of the moral conscience and of its authority. But since this authority is limited, it is inevitable that in certain cases it will be dominated by contrary and unknown forces and, conversely, it must sometimes be ignored in order that it not go beyond its natural limits.

Finally, if I said that crime was normal, it was through the application of a general rule which I tried to establish in order to distinguish the normal from the abnormal. The discussion of this rule should perhaps have constituted the basis of the debate, for once posited, the rest follows. Tarde touches on the question only very briefly. He raises two objections to my argument. (1) The normal type, he says, cannot be the same as the average type; for, since everyone is more or less sick, sickness would be normal. I answer: though everyone is sick, everyone has a different illness; these individual characteristics, therefore, cancel each other out within the generic type, which, itself, retains no trace of them. It will be claimed that we should find, if not a specific sickness, then at least an inclination toward sickness in general. I am willing to grant that; but let us not mince words. In what does this inclination consist? Quite simply in the fact that the average being, like any being, has only limited forces of resistance which, consequently, are ceaselessly exposed to defeat by antagonistic forces which are stronger. Why is it contradictory to say that the state of health implies only a limited vital energy? I see in that only a truism. (2) In the second place, Tarde objects, a people consisting entirely of average men with regard to their physical, intellectual, and moral characteristics, would exist at such a low level that it would not be able to maintain itself; how can we say that it would be healthy? What a strange confusion my ingenious critic has thus introduced. In the theory which I elaborated, a people comprised solely of average individuals would essentially be abnormal. For there is no society which does not include multitudes of individual anomalies, and so universal a fact is not without a reason for existing. *It is, therefore, socially normal that there be in every society psychologically abnormal individuals.* And the normality of crime is but a special case of this general proposition. This is because, as I expressly pointed out in my book, the conditions of individual health and those of social health can be quite different, and even contrary to one another. This will be conceded without difficulty if one follows me in recognizing that there is a line of profound demarcation between the social and the psychological. Moreover, and quite independent of any abstract system of thought, the facts demonstrate this opposition directly. A society can live only if it periodically renews itself, that is to say, if the older generations make room for others; it is therefore necessary that the former die. Thus, the normal state of societies implies the sickness of individuals; a certain incidence of mortality, like a certain incidence of crime, is indispensable to the collective health.

What is more—and Tarde says as much in concluding his argument—the source of the differences between us lies elsewhere. It arises, above all, from the fact that I believe in science and Tarde doesn't. For he who reduces science to an intellectual amusement, good at the very most for informing us about what is possible and impossible but unable to serve for the positive regulation of conduct, does not believe in it. If it has no other practical utility, it is not worth the trouble it costs us. If, then, he believes he has thus disarmed his adversaries, he is strangely mistaken. To be sure, science, thus understood, will no longer be able to disappoint men in their expectations, but that is because men no longer expect much of it. It will no longer be exposed to allegations of bankruptcy, but that is because it will have been forever declared to be underaged and incompetent. I do not see what science has to gain thereby, nor what we stand to gain. For what we would thus elevate above reason is sensation, instinct, passion—all the base and darker aspects of ourselves. Let us make use of them when we cannot do otherwise, to be sure. But when we see in them something other than a regrettable makeshift which must little by little yield to science, when we accord them an arbitrary preeminence, without referring the matter in all frankness to a revealed faith, we are more or less consistent mystics. And mysticism is the rule of anarchy in the practical realm because it is the rule of fantasy in the intellectual realm.

THE SCIENCE OF MORALITY

12

INTRODUCTION TO *Morality*

The word morality or ethics (*la morale*) is currently taken in two different senses.

On the one hand, it is understood to be a set of judgments which men individually or collectively bring to bear upon their own acts or those of their peers in view of attributing to them a very special value which they deem incomparable to other human values. This is moral value. Technical facility, no matter how great, has never taken the place of virtue; a dishonest act could never be compensated by a clever invention, a genial work of art, or a scientific discovery. Though we cannot state at the outset of our inquiry in what this value consists or how it is to be characterized, this incomparability of moral values suffices to establish the fact that moral judgments occupy a place apart in the realm of human judgments, and that is all that matters.

These judgments are instilled in normal adult consciences; we find them fully formed within us, though we are not usually aware of having elaborated them in any deliberate, let alone methodical and scientific way. Faced with a moral or immoral act, the individual reacts spontaneously and even unconsciously. It seems to him that this reaction springs from the depths of his nature; we praise or we blame by a sort of instinct, as if we could not do

Originally published as "Introduction à la morale," *Revue philosophique* 89 (1920): 79-97. Marcel Mauss undertook the difficult task of editing the handwritten manuscript, the introduction to an unfinished book on which Durkheim was still working at the time of his death in 1917. Mauss appended a brief note, including a summary of the book to which this piece was to serve as introduction, and notes on the few textual discontinuities. Translated here with permission of Presses Universitaires de France.

otherwise. That is why we so often imagine our moral conscience as a sort of voice which makes itself heard within us without our knowing as a rule what this voice is or whence its authority derives.

But by the term *ethics*, we also understand any methodical and systematic speculation about moral matters. Philosophers are far from having determined with precision just what this speculation consists in, what its object may be, and what method it employs.

This speculation has in part the same object as the judgments which the moral conscience renders spontaneously. In both cases, it is a matter of evaluating ways of acting, of praising or blaming, of distributing positive or negative moral values, of pointing out forms of conduct which man should follow and others from which he must turn aside. But, on two essential points, the method of evaluation is not the same.

In the first place, the judgments which philosophers have pronounced rest upon basic principles; they are coordinated and systematized. The moralist knows or believes he knows why he praises or blames. He forbids himself to obey blind instinct. He states his reasons. In a general way, these reasons are derived from a certain conception of man. Man is represented as either a thinking or a feeling being, as an individual entity or, on the contrary, as fundamentally social, as having in view general and impersonal ends or as pursuing quite particular goals. And in recommending to him one precept of action in preference to another, the moralist relies upon this conception.

These reasons, whatever they may be, are elaborated by the moralist as systematically as possible. Thus, all these speculations have or strive to have a scientific character which sets them apart from the spontaneous judgments of the average conscience.

In the second place, the rules of ordinary ethics apply to human acts; based on these rules, acts are judged to be praiseworthy or blameworthy. The doctrines of the moralists apply to the rules of moral conduct themselves; the rules are judged, accepted or rejected according to whether or not they conform to their initial principles. The moralist in no way regards himself as obliged to follow popular opinion; on the contrary, he accords himself the right to criticize it, to set it right, to reform it if there is need. He accepts it as his own only after methodical inquiry. He does not allow himself to be hindered by any of the prescriptions which men follow, however sacred they may seem. He could declare to be criminal certain practices which are held in universal respect, or proclaim to be obligatory ways of acting which are not respected at all. Kant was not in agreement with all his contemporaries; the theoreticians of socialism judge with severity the ideas which are the foundations of current conceptions of the law of property.

Every moral system, whatever it may be, has an ideal. The moral code which men follow at any given moment of their history, therefore, has its own ideal, which is incarnated in institutions, in traditions, in the precepts which usually regulate conduct. But, beyond this ideal there are always others which are in the process of formation. For the moral ideal is not unchangeable; it lives, evolves, and is transformed ceaselessly, despite the aura of respect which surrounds it. Tomorrow's will differ from today's. New ideas and aspirations spring forth and lead to modifications and even profound revolutions in the existing moral code. The role of the moralist is to prepare these necessary transformations. Since he does not allow himself to be hindered by established morality but claims the right to make a *tabula rasa* of them if his principles demand, he can do original work and move into new areas. The various currents which flow through society, attracting adherents, achieve self-awareness and deliberate expression through him. It is these very currents which give rise to moral doctrines, for it is in order to satisfy them that moral doctrines arise. Only those eras which are morally divided are inventive in the sphere of ethics. When traditional morality is uncontested and no need for renewing it is felt, reflection on matters of ethics languishes.

Moral speculation, which we first saw in its scientific aspect, now appears also to have practical objectives. It is a work of thought and reflection, but it is also an element of life. That is why we say that it is at once art and science. It tends to direct the action of both individuals and societies. But it pretends to base its guidance upon facts, upon more or less positive data. Moreover, this mixed form of speculation is not peculiar to ethics. Education and politics still have this same character just as medicine and alchemy had it in earlier times. This ambiguity is doubtless not in conformity with the exigencies of pure logic. The methodology of science is not that of art; there even exists a radical opposition between the two. Science has as its domain the past and the present, which it tries to express as faithfully as possible. Art is oriented to the future, which it seeks to anticipate and to construct in advance. But every time thought is applied to a new order of facts, it is in response to certain more or less urgent, vital necessities. When thought thus places itself in the service of action, it borrows its methods from the latter and melds them with its own. Morality, in the currently understood sense of the word, is an example of such a combination.

Indisputably, moral speculation could strip itself of all practical significance only with the greatest difficulty. The rules of ethics are above all intended to guide action. Speculation about the rules of ethics cannot, therefore, ignore the question of action. There is no science worthy of the name which does not end in art; it would otherwise be a mere game, an intellectual distraction, pure and simple erudition. This is all the more true of a form of speculation which has action itself as its object and substance. To amuse oneself in reflecting upon practical matters solely for the pleasure of so reflecting seems a little contrary to nature. A moralist who limited himself to studying ethics abstractly, without seeking to anticipate the ideal form that it is called upon to realize would, therefore, fulfill only a part of his task.

But how can and how should this practical problem be dealt with?

Here is how, up to the present time, moralists of whatever school have proceeded. They postulate as an operating principle that the complete system of moral rules is contained in a cardinal notion of which that system is merely an extrapolation. They strive to unearth this notion, and, once they believe they have discovered it, they have only to deduce from it the particular precepts which it implies and thus obtain the ideal and perfect moral system. It matters little whether this morality agrees or disagrees with that which men practice in actual fact; its function is to govern mores, to provide them with a system of regulation rather than to follow their lead. Such a morality does not concern itself with ethics as they are, but solely with ethics as they should be.

But how does one arrive at this fundamental notion? We know that, according to a school which has played a considerable role in the history of thought but which today has few representatives, the moral ideal is part of our nature. We find it completely formed within us; it is engraved deep in our consciences. To discover it, we need only look within ourselves, we need only scrutinize and analyze ourselves with care. But even assuming that this fundamental moral notion does have this origin, we can recognize it amid the other ideas which populate our minds only if we already have a representation of what is moral and what is not—that is, if we already have the notion that we are trying to discover. The problem is simply shifted, not resolved.

The moralist generally draws this basic notion from psychology. The fact that morality is the supreme rule of conduct is taken as evidence that it should naturally be contained within our concept of human nature and should be deduced from it. If one knows what man is, one knows *ipso facto* how he should behave in the principal circumstances of life. And is that not what constitutes morality? A system of ethics appears to be the simple application of the laws which psychology believes it has established.

But first of all, to conceive of ethics as applied psychology misapprehends one of its distinctive characteristics. Applied physics or chemistry, hygiene or therapy use the propositions established by the corresponding sciences to create instruments of action which they place at the disposition of mankind in order to realize the aims and attain the goals which it pursues. The engineer, for example, draws upon mechanics for the means of constructing bridges; the doctor draws upon normal or pathological biology for the means of achieving health. But none of these technical disciplines creates its ends for itself. They take these ends as given and presume that men value them. Ethics works differently. Ethics consists above all in positing ends. It dictates to man the ends that he is required to pursue, and in that way it is distinct from the applied sciences properly so called.[1]

Furthermore, how could moral objectives be deduced from psychology? The man whom psychology studies belongs to no specific era or country, is always and everywhere the same. The laws of psychology are as invariable as the laws of the physical world. The moral concept, on the contrary, varies with place and time. Rome's was different from that of Greece, and the Middle Ages' was not the same as our own. This diversity is not due to some sort of fundamental aberration which prevents man from perceiving his true destiny; it is grounded in the nature of things. The morality of a given people expresses its temperament, its mentality, and the conditions in which it exists; it is a product of its history. It is an integrative element of each civilization. Though all civilizations have a common basis, they resemble one another only in their most general characteristics. Each has its individuality and, consequently, depends only in part on human faculties. It is the same way with morality.

But the decisive objection raised by such attempts to derive morality from psychology is the following: even assuming that morality truly expresses the nature of man, it can at most correspond to a quite determinate and very particular aspect of this nature, namely, the moral aspect. The development of our speculative faculties, our aesthetics, our technical aptitudes of every sort, our physical force, and so on, has, to be sure, a human interest of the first order. But ethics does not share this interest. It is not for ethics to prescribe how to cultivate one's intellect, to condition one's body, to refine one's taste, to make one witty. Nor should it regulate all forms of action and all practical faculties, but only those which involve moral questions. It has sometimes been said of morality that it is the rule of conduct. But this expression is too general. Ethics governs only certain modalities of conduct, namely, those which have moral objectives. And which are those which share this characteristic? As important as the moral element may be in man, it does not encompass his whole being. But then, what distinguishes this element from the others? How is it to be recognized? What properties are peculiar to it? By what signs does it manifest itself? Psychology ignores these questions. It is the task of ethics to resolve them.

People generally speak of these matters as if the question resolved itself, as if everyone conceived of its solution in the same way. Don't all honest men agree on the nature of good and evil and, conse-quently, on the distinctive characteristics of what is moral? "Is there need," asks Fouillée, "for lengthy study of history, of comparative jurisprudence, of comparative religion" in order to learn "why we must not kill, steal, rape, etc.," or whence arises "fraternal affection, the respect of children ... integrity in fulfilling promises?" These seem to him to be obvious truths which are immediately apparent to the intuitive side of one's conscience. Of course, we well know that philosophers are divided on the question of how the moral alternative must be formulated and translated into concepts: thus arise the debates which have been going on for as long as philosophical thought has been applied to moral matters. And yet, despite these divisions, it is thought that ethics consists entirely in a very simple point of view, that it rests upon an elementary notion which requires no laborious, methodical, scientific research, and which could hardly provide the occasion for real discoveries. Is it not currently said that ethics belongs to everyone, that it is inherent in every conscience without having to be discovered?

But by what right do people attribute to moral life this privileged situation in the totality of what is real? For science there is no reality which is self-evident. There is none which does not first have to be treated as an unknown whose intimate nature is only progressively revealed. We begin by noting the most superficial indicators by which it manifests itself; next, for these indicators we substitute others[2] as we advance in our research. It is only when we have gone beyond the realm of sensory appearances that it becomes possible to gain insight into the more profound characteristics of the matter, those which are related to its essence, to the extent that one can use that term in a scientific way. The scientist who undertakes the study of light or electricity knows initially only what his senses perceive. He sees in it only an object of study of which he is totally ignorant; it is only when he pushes his analysis further and deeper that he manages to create for himself a different conception. Why would it be otherwise with moral reality?[3]

No doubt, as a practical matter, men take and must take moral truths to be given, as if they were axioms which need not be discussed. They are so strongly rooted in healthy consciences that they are placed beyond doubt. They serve as a basis for action, but they are, or pass for being, beyond reflection. In order that they be capable of governing conduct in an efficacious way, they must be accepted as axioms, as self-evident truths. When, in the course of history, it happens that the ideas and principles on which a morality rests no longer enjoy sufficient credibility to impose themselves with authority, when their legitimacy begins to be questioned, when their credentials are suspect, it is because that morality is in a state of disorganization and is plagued with self-doubt. For a moral code cannot endure self-doubt without losing its dominion. But we live by practical truths of this sort, though they are self-evident only in name and, in fact, respond solely to certain necessities of action. In order that we be able to move as necessary amid the objects of the perceptible world, we create for ourselves certain representations. We represent the sun as a flat disc of a few centimeters; light as a thin, impalpable, weightless body which travels through the air like an arrow; the wind as a breath, and so on. The scientist frees himself from this supposed self-evidence. He replaces these false notions, which are of practical value, with entirely different ones, elaborated according to quite different methods. Everything permits us to think that it must be the same way with moral matters. The representation which the common man creates for himself cannot conform to reality. It can respond to the exigencies of current practice, but it does not correspond to the fundamental nature of things and, consequently, cannot provide a basis for new practices.

In summary, while it is quite true that the final goal of any morality is to edify an ideal, a morality superior to that which men practice, this creative enterprise presupposes at least one notion which cannot be postulated, which we do not find inherent within ourselves, but which can only result from an entire series of research efforts, from an entire science: we are speaking of the notion of what is moral. In what can this science consist?

The notion of life can be constructed only from the science of life; the former follows from the latter and synopsizes its progress. The notion of what is moral, unless it is to be a simple matter of common sense, can only be constructed by the science of moral facts. In whatever way one conceives of the moral ideal, morality is an existing reality, as demonstrated by observation. Although, in our present state of knowledge, we still do not know in what moral facts consist, we can be certain that the word *morality*, which is found in diverse forms in all languages, connotes phenomena which are distinguished from all other human phenomena by definite and consistent characteristics.[4]

To what order of reality do they belong? That is what we cannot state at present. Are they emanations of the individual conscience or products of the collective mentality? That is what we have to pin down in the remainder of this work. But everything permits us to presume that they constitute a category of natural things. Therefore, they can—and we can even say in advance that they must—be studied by science, in whatever manner such a science must be conceived. This science must provide us with a means of analyzing them, of classifying them, of arranging them into types and species, of determining their place in the totality of other phenomena and the causes on which they depend. And it is from these descriptions, analyses, classifications, and explications that this notion of morality, which the moralists' doctrines presume and concede but do not justify, can be constructed. In a word, it is only the study of moral life which can reveal to us these distinctive properties, this essence of the moral fact, from which we think we can then deduce all the details of the moral ideal. Even assuming, as has so often been assumed, that the moral concept is entirely within us and that it is inherent in our native constitution, we can discover it only by starting with the analysis of moral facts. For it is in these facts and through them that the idea is realized; it is through them that we can discover it. To distinguish it from all the ideas which coexist with it in our consciences, we must start with those facts, with those precepts, with those practices which express it, which translate it more or less adequately. And we must then work our way back ever closer to the fundamental conception from which they originate. If, indeed, this inner source of moral life truly exists within us, it is by this means alone that we shall succeed in discovering it.

Thus, the art of ethics, namely, the construction of the moral ideal, presupposes the existence of an entire science, one which is positive and inductive and which embraces all the details of moral facts.

Furthermore, this science is far more extensive and complex than one would think from the preliminary outline just drawn. Were we to limit ourselves to what has just been said, it would involve a single problem: it would have as its sole task to determine the distinctive traits of what is moral. Once armed with this notion, the art of morality would attempt to draft a plan of the moral ideal. But, in reality, an entire science never hinges on a single problem; the questions that it poses for itself are always as numerous as the facts that it studies. And, in effect, the problem which is posed regarding morality in its totality repeats itself in various forms and in diverse conditions in connection with each of the spheres of moral life. Though the moralist needs to know what morality is in a general sense, he cannot deal with domestic morality, for example, unless he begins by determining the multiple precepts which constitute this part of morality, until he investigates the causes which have given rise to them and the ends to which they respond. Only then can he research the question of how these precepts must be modified, rectified, and made into an ideal. To be able to say what domestic morality is destined to become, one must know how the family is constituted, how it took the form that it presently assumes, what its function is in society as a whole, how the various domestic duties are related to this function, and so forth. And the same research must be undertaken with regard to professional ethics, civic morals, international morality—in a word, for every category of duties.

Moreover, it is easy to understand that the generic notion of what is moral can only be a summary or synthesis of all these particular notions and, therefore, it will be only as valuable as are these others. To conceive the essence of moral facts, it is not enough to accept a schematic and rather summary glimpse of them. No doubt, at the beginning of research, it is possible and even, as we shall see, necessary to define these facts by their external and apparent characteristics in such a way as to determine and circumscribe the object of the study. But though these initial and provisional definitions are indispensable for clearly establishing the issues with which science is concerned and for determining how they are to be recognized, they say nothing about its intimate and profound nature. The latter reveals itself only to the extent that one enters into contact with reality, that one analyzes its multiple aspects, that the study of particular facts advances. One cannot speculate upon the moral ideal with summary generalities; it is an entire world which needs to be explored. The method generally followed by the moralists needs, therefore, to undergo a grave transformation.

As we have seen, they ordinarily begin by taking a precept from established morality with the aid of poorly defined procedures which, deep down, merely express the moralist's own feelings. Then, from this precept they deduce—or think they deduce—the moral practices which they propose to recommend to their fellow men. But this precept, whatever its value, can only be the conclusion of an entire science which bears upon the details of moral rules, a conclusion which can only be provisional and which is destined perpetually to be revised to reflect the progress of the science from which it derives. But this science is only now being created; it was born yesterday. Up to the present, the only collaborators in this enterprise have been a few sociologists. There is, however, no more urgent task, for efforts to anticipate moral art have and can have no other basis than this science of acquired and actual moral facts.

We currently give to this science the title Science or Physics of Mores.[5] In my own work, the word *mores* indicates the morality which is effectively observed by men at any given moment of history, the one which has the authority of tradition, as opposed to that which the moralist conceives of as the morality of the future. But the expression is not without ambiguity and, in fact, has given rise to confusions. To be sure, the morality of an era is to be found in its mores, though in the degraded form in which it is placed within the reach of human mediocrity. For they convey the way in which the average man applies the rules of morality, and he never applies them without compromise or reticence. The motives which he obeys are mixed: some are noble and pure, but others are vulgar and base. The science which we have just outlined proposes, on the contrary, to discover moral precepts in their pure and impersonal form. It takes as its object morality itself in its ideal form, on a level far above human acts. It is not concerned with the distortions to which it is subjected in the process of incarnating current practices which can translate it only imperfectly.[6] We must ask ourselves how it can succeed. But if we are correct about its object, it would be best to give it a name which calls to mind the subject matter with which it deals. We shall therefore call it "Science of Morality" or "Science of Moral Facts," understanding thereby that it deals with moral phenomena or moral reality as it can be observed either in the present or in the past, just as physics or physiology deal with the facts they study. As for speculations about the future, they are nothing more than applied science.

This work, the first volume of which we now present, has as its aim to set forth, in its totality, the state in which this science is now found; to describe and explain, insofar as our knowledge permits, the principal facts of moral life; and to distill from these theoretical studies the practical conclusions which they imply.

But, before we approach these facts in detail, several prejudicial questions must be examined. This will be the object of this introductory volume.

These questions are the following:

1. To study moral facts, we must know where they are situated—that is, from what order of reality they spring. Obviously, these are phenomena related to the conscience. But are they related to the individual or to the collective conscience? And if they arise out of both, what part and what role belongs to each? (Book 1).

2. If, as we intend to establish, they are essentially social; if, moreover, it is their social nature which makes them of interest for scientific research, by what signs will they be recognized amid other social facts? (Book 2).

3. What is their place in the totality of collective life? (Book 3).

4. Finally, once they have been situated, localized, characterized, linked to the phenomena to which they are most directly related, it will be necessary to investigate how and according to what method science should deal with them, and how, from these scientific and theoretical studies, practical conclusions can be deduced.

SOCIOLOGY OF THE FAMILY

13

INTRODUCTION TO THE
SOCIOLOGY OF THE FAMILY

I have not come before you to deliver another opening lecture. For you, sociology is no longer a foreign discipline to which you must be introduced. However, before beginning the study of the questions with which we shall be concerned this year, it seems best to start with a first lecture in which I will set forth a general outline of our subject, the method we shall pursue in dealing with it, and the interest which it holds for your studies.

I

We devoted all last year to the initial problem of sociology. Before going ahead, we had to know what bonds unite men to one another or, in other words, what determines the formation of social aggregates. That is what we asked ourselves. Psychology was not capable of resolving this question, for it was probable *a priori* that there are different kinds of social solidarity, just as there are different kinds of societies. It was therefore necessary to proceed to a classification of societies. Although, in the present state of available information, a complete and detailed classification could only be arbitrary, as every attempt of that kind has demonstrated, we have at least been able to establish with certainty two grand social types of which all societies, past and present, are but variations. We have distinguished, on the one hand, unorganized, or what we called amor-

Originally published as "Introduction à la sociologie de la famille," *Annales de la faculté de Bordeaux* 10 (1888): 257–81. This study constitutes the opening lecture of the course in sociology (*science social*) taught in that year in the School of Letters of the University of Bordeaux.

phous, societies, which range from the primitive horde of related individuals to the city; and, on the other hand, the states, properly so called, which begin with the city and end with the great nations of the present day. The analysis of these two social types led us to the discovery of two very different forms of social solidarity. The first of these results from the similarity of consciousnesses and the community of ideas and feelings. The other, on the contrary, is a product of the differentiation of functions and the division of labor. The effect of the first is to unite minds by fusing them, by losing them, so to speak, in one another in such a way as to form a compact mass incapable of any but collective movement. Under the second, the result of the mutual dependence of specialized functions is that everyone has his own sphere of action even as he remains inseparable from everyone else. Because the latter form of solidarity reminds us of the force which holds together the organs of higher animals, we have called it *organic*, while for the former type we have reserved the label *mechanical*. This constitutes a simple definition of terms which is not wholly satisfactory but with which we shall have to be content for lack of any better. Although it might, strictly speaking, be possible to say that neither of these two types of solidarity has ever existed without the other, we find mechanical solidarity in a state of almost absolute purity in those primitive societies in which consciousnesses and even organisms resemble each other to the point of being indiscernible; in which the individual is totally absorbed by the group; in which tradition and custom rule the most minute details of private affairs. On the other hand, in the great modern societies we can best observe that higher form of solidarity, offspring of the division of labor, which maintains the independence of the parts even as it reinforces the unity of the whole. This statement permits us to determine the conditions in function of which each of these forms of solidarity varies. We have seen that there where societies are less extensive—thanks to the more intimate contact of their members, to the more complete community of life, to the nearly absolute identity of the objects of thought—the resemblances overcome the differences and, consequently, the whole transcends the parts. On the other hand, as the elements of the group become more numerous without ceasing to be in continuous relation, on this enlarged field of battle where the intensity of the struggle grows with the number of combatants, individuals can maintain themselves only if they differentiate themselves, if each chooses his own task and his own style of life. The division of labor thus becomes the primary condition of social equilibrium. The great innovation which separates contemporary societies from those of the past is the simultaneous increase of the volume and the density of societies. It is probably one of the principal factors which dominate all history. It is, in any case, the cause which explains the transformation through which social solidarity has passed.

These are the results we arrived at in last year's course. Equipped with these principles, we are now in a position to consider more specialized problems. Now that we know the general forms of sociability and their laws, we shall spend this entire year studying one specific type. I have chosen for this purpose the simplest group of all, the one whose history is most ancient: the family.

Before explaining how we shall deal with this subject, let me tell you how I would have liked us to deal with it. The exposition of what I would have liked to do will prepare you better to understand what I shall in fact do.

Of all family groups, the one which interests us above all others and which it is most important to know and understand is that which presently exists before our eyes and in the midst of which we live. We would, therefore, have taken as both theme and point of departure the family as it exists today in the great European societies. We would have described it, outlined its anatomy, and dissociated its elements. And the general results of this analysis would have been as follows. We would first have needed to distinguish between persons and goods. Then, among persons, we would have had to enumerate, aside from the spouses and the children, the general group of kin consisting of relatives in all degrees or, in a word, what remains of the ancient *gens*, the authority of which was formerly so powerful and which, even now, must often intervene in the restricted circle of the family, properly so called. Finally, there is the state, which, in certain cases, has also come to involve itself in domestic life and every day becomes a more important factor. This done, we would have investigated how these elements function, that is to say, what relations unite them one with another. The complete system of these relations, the whole of which constitutes family life, is outlined in its general form in the following table:[1]

Kin

1. Relations of the husband with his own relatives and with those of his wife.
2. Relations of the wife with her own relatives and with those of her husband.
   A. In terms of persons.
   B. In terms of goods.

(Emancipation through marriage, Dowry, Law of inheritance, Guardianship, Relation by marriage: its nature and consequences.)

3. Relations of children with the paternal and maternal kin.
   A. In terms of persons.
   B. In terms of goods.

(Family council, Trusteeship, Law of inheritance, and so on.)

The Spouses

1. Relations of future spouses to the act which creates the family (Marriage).

(Nubility, Consent, Absence of any previous marriage bonds—Monogamy. Absence of blood relatedness to a degree which is prohibited, etc.)

2. Relations of the spouses in terms of persons.

(Respective rights and obligations of the spouses. Nature of the conjugal bond: dissolubility or indissolubility, etc.)

3. Relations of the spouses in terms of goods.

(System of dowry—community or separation of goods, Gifts, Law of inheritance, etc.)

The Children

1. Relations of children with their parents in terms of persons.
(Paternal power, Emancipation, Majority, etc.)

2. Relations of children with their parents in terms of goods.
(Inheritance, Prohibition against disinheriting the child, Goods belonging to the child, Guardianship of the parents, etc.)

3. Relations of the children among themselves.

(Today, practically reduced to the law of inheritance.)

The State

1. General intervention of the state in sanctioning domestic law.

(The family as a social institution.)

2. Specific intervention in the relations between future spouses.

(Celebration of marriage.)

3. Specific intervention in the relations between spouses.

(Substitution of the courts for the husband for certain authorizations.)

4. Specific interventions in the relations between parents and children.

(Cooperation on the part of the courts in the exercise of paternal power. Guarantees to the child. Proposed law on the defaulting of paternal authority.)

5. Specific intervention in the relations with kin.

(In family councils. In requests for prohibitions, etc.)

But an analysis is not an explanation. After describing these various relations, we would have investigated the reasons for their existence. The natural sciences discover causes by experimentation. Here we obviously cannot conduct experiments in the strict sense. But, as Claude Bernard pointed out long ago, the essence of experimentation is not the production of artificial phenomena. Artifice is just a means of placing the phenomenon being studied in different circumstances and of changing their form in order that useful comparisons may be established. Indeed, if we encountered a phenomenon which is always produced in the same way and in the same conditions, it would be impossible to explain it with any assurance. For how could we know which of all the circumstances which invariably accompany it is the one on which it depends? We could only venture speculations, we could not verify them. But this is no longer true if the phenomenon, while always maintaining its basic identity, varies from one set of circumstances to another. For comparison becomes useful when we have a criterion for separating the accidental from the essential and for eliminating the former. The experimenter elicits these variations when they are not already present; but when produced naturally, mightn't we call the method of comparison *indirect* experimentation? This is the method which would permit us to explain domestic relations. It would suffice to consider each of them separately and to compare each in its present state with the forms it adopts in various types of familial society. Take, for example, the conjugal bond: we would compare the form it assumes in today's civilized nations with the form it once had in the monogamous or polygamous patriarchal family, in the patrilineal clan, in the matrilineal clan, and in all the intermediate types. Though no other institution has evolved further, it would not be difficult to recognize the identical and common foundation which lies beneath all these forms. And, having determined which of the concomitant events have not varied, we shall justifiably consider them to be the conditions which account for these fundamental characteristics. Or let us next consider the explanation of a more specific property, for example, the indissolubility of marriage. We need simply restrict the field of comparison by considering only those types in which this property is found in varying degrees. The one or several characteristics common to all these types and not found in the others and which vary with this very property would be its cause. In this way, we would obtain a truly objective explanation of the principal domestic phenomena.

The unfortunate lack which prevents us from practicing this method is obvious. It would be necessary that the various types of families be already established with certainty that we know the number of constituent elements of each as well as their interrelationships, and, finally, that we know whence they originate. Although great efforts to advance this problem have been made since the middle of the century, the results obtained, while very important in other respects, are still incomplete and in some cases in dispute. We can, therefore, neither limit ourselves to those which are definitively established nor accept without prior examination those which are still under discussion. To fulfill the program which I have just outlined, we must first establish the principal types of family, describe them, classify them into genera and species, and, finally, investigate, so far as possible, the causes which have determined their appearance and survival. It is this preparatory work which we shall undertake this year.

Do not think, however, that we shall limit ourselves to a simple classification of extinct species. This study of the past will reveal an explanation of the present which will become more complete as we advance in our research. For even the oldest forms of domestic life and those most removed from our own mores have not completely ceased to exist. They survive in part in the family of today. Because higher organisms arise out of lower ones, the former resemble and synopsize the latter. The modern family contains within itself, in abbreviated form, the entire historical development of the family. While it is perhaps incorrect to say that all the familial types are to be found in the present type, since it has not been shown that all were in direct or indirect communication with it, at least it is true for many. Considered in this light, the different species of family which were successively created appear to be the parts or elements of the contemporary family. History offers them to us in a state of natural dissociation, so to speak. It is very much easier to study them in this historical form than in the state of intimate and mutual penetration in which they exist today. Consequently, each time that we establish a familial type, we shall try to find out what it has in common with the family of today and what aspect of the latter it explains. Thus, in studying the humblest forms of domestic life in coming lectures, we shall encounter a property which has remained one of the essential characteristics of the family and which we shall be able to account for by that very fact. In order to make these comparisons easier, in the study of each particular type we shall adopt the divisions of the table which you have before your eyes, that is to say, we shall distinguish and isolate domestic relations as we have done above. Thanks to this similarity in perspective, these various monographs can more easily be compared. If, therefore, the method of explanation which we shall employ is less rigorous and less precise than that which I was sketching for you a moment ago, it will not fail to give us important results. We shall try to do, little by little in the course of our study, what we cannot yet do in a more coherent and systematic way.

Thus, we are not undertaking a work of pure erudition. As deeply as we may delve into the past, we shall never lose sight of the present. Even when we are describing the most primitive forms of the family, it will not be just to satisfy legitimate curiosity, but in order progressively to arrive at an explanation of our European family. I do not mean that we can resolve all the problems that we shall encounter. Moreover, I ask you to view this course as merely a first attempt, destined to be revised. But whatever the case, this manner of proceeding will have the great advantage of making our research more lively and of better arousing your interest. For what could be more interesting than to see the life of the modern family, so simple in appearance, resolved into a multitude of tightly intertwined elements and relationships and to follow through history the slow development in the course of which they were successively formed and combined?

II

Having introduced our subject, we shall now ask what our method will be.

I shall not take the time to demonstrate to you that the only way for us to succeed is to proceed inductively and that our inductions will have value only if they are supported by facts, a large body of facts. But gathering a great number of documents is not everything; it is also important, at the very least, properly to choose those which it is appropriate to use. There are those which must resolutely be set aside, as instructive as they may seem at first glance. Otherwise, our minds would quickly become overloaded and simultaneously carried off in the most contradictory directions. This is a rule which the theoreticians of the family have often ignored and on which it is necessary to insist.

A traveler visits some country. He comes in contact with a certain number of families in which he observes, let us suppose, a fairly large number of facts regarding conjugal devotion and filial piety. He concludes from this that the family is already quite strongly unified. Can we accept a conclusion grounded in this way? To do so would be to expose ourselves to serious errors. In effect, the degree of cohesion at which the family has arrived in a given society is an internal and general condition that extends throughout this society. The events of everyday life on which all these observations are based are, on the contrary, transitory and particularistic factors. They are generally tied to the constitution of the family, to be sure, but their relationship is too complex and too distant for us to be able in the blink of an eye to trace our way from the effect back to the cause. The interpretation which unites these two orders of phenomena risks, therefore, being entirely subjective. Because we lack the countervailing effect of any objective criterion, personal perspectives weigh on the mind of the observer with that much greater force. Thus, for a missionary imbued with Christian conceptions of marriage, the facts of polyandry will symbolize domestic anarchy and the grossest immorality. On the other hand, a mind with a revolutionary bent, especially if given to socialism, will be swept along by its passion for the weak and by its tendency to come to their defense, and will judge the varieties of families according to the way they treat women.[2] But the privileged situation of women, far from being a sure index of progress, is sometimes caused by a still rudimentary domestic organization. What is more, these isolated facts, as striking as they may seem, may be unrelated to the constitutional condition of the family. Thus, we shall encounter remarkable proofs of attachment either between spouses or between children and parents in families in which the domestic bond is still weak and loose. In such cases, it is the development of individual sensitivity which inspires these acts of solidarity; but, even if they were fairly frequent, they might very well bear no correspondence to anything in the organic type of the family, for the latter depends not on individual temperaments but on collective necessities and is imposed on everyone with the force of tradition. Here we have two categories of phenomena which arise from different causes, are independent, and hardly shed light on one another. Similarly, in certain societies, it happens that most of the inhabitants live with just one woman, though we cannot conclude from this fact that the family is monogamous. For polygamy may be tolerated by law, and though the majority may have renounced it, this may be due to quite external necessities—for example, because it is too costly to maintain several wives. In brief, then, we must seek to reconstitute the internal structure of the family, which is the only matter of scientific interest. The specific facts not only do not constitute this structure, but they do not always symbolize it with clarity and sometimes do not symbolize it at all. Note that these remarks lose none of their value if it is a native rather than a foreigner who furnishes us with the information. For example, we cannot characterize the Roman family in a scientific way either from the evaluations of Roman writers or from a few historical anecdotes, even if true.

As a general rule, therefore, we must discard these narrative accounts and descriptions. They may have literary interest, or even moral authority, but they are not sufficiently objective documents. These personal impressions are not the sort of material which science can usefully employ. There is only one way to know with precision the structure of a familial type and that is to penetrate its very nature. But where are we to discover it? We find it in those ways of acting which have been consolidated by habit or by what we call custom, law, and mores. In this case we are no longer dealing with simple incidents of private life but with regular and consistent practices, the residue of the collective experiences of a whole series of generations. For custom consists in what is common and constant in all individual conduct. It expresses in a precise way the structure of the family, or, rather, it is itself this structure. In relation to the individual events of domestic life, it is what the generic type of animal is to the details of the phenomena which are produced in individual organisms. There are, therefore, no facts more objective or more full of fertile consequences, since each of them synopsizes a multitude of facts. With their use, we no longer have to induce the general aspect of things with the help of suspect interpretations. It is given to us directly and in a concrete and tangible form. We learn more about the constitution of a family from even a very little information about customs relating to inheritance, for example, than we could from a great number of detailed sketches of the family itself.

But how can we recognize a custom? By the fact that it is a way of acting which is not only habitual but obligatory for all the members of a society. It is distinguished not by its greater or lesser frequency but by the fact that it is imperative. It does not represent merely what is done most often but what must be done. A custom is a rule which everyone is obliged to obey and which is subject to the authority of some sanction. The existence of a sanction is the distinction which keeps us from confusing custom and simple habit. Thus, we now find in our possession definite facts which are easily recognizable and analogous to those studied by the natural sciences. At the same time, we can see to what extent and under what conditions we can use these facts—the very ones whose inadequacy I was discussing just a moment ago. They cannot themselves demonstrate that a custom exists. But they can help to establish that one does not exist or that it is in the process of changing. If, in some country, specific acts freely and openly depart from a known custom, it is because that custom is undergoing modification. If these departures go so far as to contradict it, it is because that custom has disappeared or never existed. But if these facts do have some degree of authority, they do not owe it to themselves. It is their relation to custom—a collective fact of the first order—which manifests their social import and permits us to see them as something other than products of the individual's consciousness.

In the preceding, I have almost exclusively used the term *custom* because this is the expression which best designates in all its generality the whole order of phenomena about which we are speaking. Moreover, we can say that originally there were no obligatory practices other than those which custom prescribed. But with time this mass of imperative maxims—which is so extensive in primitive societies—split into two parts. In some, the rather diffuse form which custom already possessed was further escalated; these became mores, with nothing but public opinion, however vague, to serve as a sanction. Others became fixed—crystallized, so to speak—as positive law; public authority assured respect for them through specific and concrete sanctions. Since law has to an even greater degree the objective character which is the distinctive sign of custom, and since it has a sharply defined form, it constitutes a document which is generally more valuable. While we use mores only with caution because they are somewhat vague and fleeting, when they are well established they can furnish very useful information. In this way, Morgan was able to reconstruct the ideal type of exogamous clan by studying the expressions used as greetings in the daily life of members of certain families in Asia, America, and Australia.

As circumspect as we may be in the choice of our materials, we need not fear that we will not have enough; quality will be more of a problem than quantity. We shall find them either concentrated or diffused in a host of works, of which very few, I am sad to say, are written in French. Several comprehensive studies of the family have been attempted by various sociologists. Leaving aside the third part of Spencer's sociology, which is devoted in its entirety to this subject but from which there is little to retain, we have in France Dr. Letourneau's *L'Evolution du mariage et de la famille*, a work rich in documents but devoid of critical spirit or method; in Germany, Lippert's *History of the Family*[3] (*Geschichte der Familie*); and, above all, Hellwald's recent book *Die Menschliche Familie*[4] which is, I believe, the best of its kind. What is more worthwhile than these general studies are the works which ethnologists and historians have given us on particular aspects of the history of the family. They are far too numerous for me to provide a complete bibliography. I can do no more than quickly call to mind the names of the most important. On the origins and simple forms of the family we have the work of Giraud Teulon, *Les Origines du mariage et de la famille*,[5] the various books of Herman Post,[6] Waitz's *Anthropologie der Naturvoelker*, in which we find an excellent summary of all the explorer's narratives about the family among primitive peoples. On matriarchal families in particular, there are *Mutterrecht* and *Anti-quarische Briefe*[7] by Bachofen. On the exogamous family, we have the works of Lubbock,[8] MacLennon,[9] and especially Morgan[10] and Fison and Howit.[11] There is no need to remind you of the studies of the Roman family by Rossbach,[12] Fustel de Coulanges, Voigt,[13] Bernhöft, and so on. On the Aryan family in general we have a work by Hearn, *The Aryan Household*,[14] and the studies of Sumner Maine. On the Germanic family we have at our disposal an abundant literature, the principal monuments of which are the research of Friedberg,[15] Sohm,[16] and Habicht[17] on marriage, Dargun on the traces of matriarchy in Germanic law,[18] Schroeder's[19] conjugal property law, and Rive's [20] history of guardianship. On the oriental family there is a little work by Bergel on marriage among the Jews, [21] and a work by Vincenti on marriage in Islam; [22] on the domestic law of the Chinese, the brochure by Plath, [23] and so forth.

However, the rule which we have just proposed is not without its disadvantages. Law and mores express only those social changes which are already determined and consolidated; as a result, they teach us nothing about phenomena which have not yet or which will never achieve a degree of crystallization sufficient to effect structural modifications. But among those which remain in what we might call the fluid state, some are very important. You know that among higher organisms and especially in societies, the relationship between the organ and the function is in no way rigidly defined; one may change without the other. Similarly, a legal institution may far outlive the reasons which brought it into existence, remaining identical to what it was before even though the social phenomena which it relates to have changed. For example, we find in certain societies a kinship system and a set of laws of inheritance which no longer tally in any way with the true state of the family. They constitute a legacy from the past which persists by force of habit alone and which masks the present from our view. There are, therefore, certain phenomena which we risk perceiving only long after they occur or that we never perceive at all. Yet, however real this disadvantage, it should not make us renounce the cautious approach that I was recommending a moment ago, for it is far better to disregard a few facts then to make use of questionable ones. Moreover, a moment will come in this course when we shall be able to correct this imperfection in our method, namely, when we arrive at the contemporary family. In this case, we can, thanks to demography, gain insight into the phenomena of domestic life with assurance and at a stage in their development at which they have not become law. Indeed, demography manages to express, almost from one day to the next, the development of collective life. An isolated observer can never perceive more than a restricted portion of the social horizon, while demography embraces society in its entirety. It was always to be feared that the individual observer would distort reality by mixing his personal impressions with it; but statistics give us impersonal figures. Not only do these figures translate social phenomena in an authentic and objective manner, but they translate it better because they make quantitative variations perceptible and permit us to measure them. For this reason, when we are studying the contemporary European family we shall make good use not only of law and mores but also of demographic data. I shall have recourse to the works of Dr. Bertillon, which you will find in the *Dictionnaire encyclopédique des sciences médicales* and in the *Annales de démographie internationale*. I shall try at the same time to complement them with borrowings from foreign demographers.

Thus, the triple source to which we shall look for the substance of our inductions consists of law and mores, in the form in which ethnography and history give them to us, and the demography of the family. And we shall use this method to study not one or two forms of family by way of example but as great a number as possible. We shall not ignore any case from which we might obtain trustworthy information. We shall group them according to the resemblances and differences they display. In order to explain the principal characteristics of each of the genera which we shall, in this way, have constructed, we shall finally compare the conditions in which the various species comprising each were produced. This will be the most difficult part of our task and the one in the course of which we must expect inevitable failures.

I have no need to tell you that we shall approach this research with a profound sense of the complexity of the subject. But at the same time, we shall not forget that we are dealing with natural phenomena, which are, therefore, subject to laws. We shall thus strive to avoid, insofar as possible, the double danger to which any theory of the family is exposed. For it has often happened that authors who have dealt with this question have either sinned through over-simplification by trying to explain everything with a single principle or rejected any systematization under the pretext that this mass of heterogenous facts could not serve as a basis for scientific general-izations. This latter position amounts to admitting that there is a world within the world, in which the laws of causality do not apply—in other words, it postulates a miracle. We ourselves shall challenge simple explanations and linear or geometric classifications at the same time that we shall maintain that order exists in this domain of nature as in all others, though this order may be somewhat more complex. We shall attempt to discover its general outline, that is, to systematize all these facts, but without artificially combining them. We shall undertake to discover their interrelationships even as we respect the differences which separate them.

There is one other sentiment which it is no less necessary that we bring with us to this research: perfect serenity. We must rid our minds of prejudices, both optimistic and pessimistic. These questions involve us so forcefully that we cannot keep our emotions from impinging. Some will look upon the families of previous ages as models for our imitation; this is what LePlay has done with the patriarchal family. Others will try to demonstrate the superiority of the present form and to glorify ourselves in the name of the progress we have made. At the same time, they will portray the past in the most somber hues, as if they cannot show enough compassion for our unfortunate ancestors. We ourselves know that if we take in a literal sense the terms *superior* and *inferior*, they have no scientific meaning; this is an idea which I insisted upon at length last year. For science, organisms are not ranked with some above the others; they are simply different because their environment is different. There is no one way of being or of living which is the best for all and, consequently, it is not possible to classify them hierarchically according to how well or how badly they approach this unique ideal. The ideal for each of them is to live in harmony with its conditions of existence. This correspondence is encountered again and again at all levels of reality. What is good for one is, therefore, not necessarily good for another. We shall never let this principle slip from view. Today's family is neither more nor less perfect than that of yesterday; it is different because circumstances are different. It is more complex because the environment in which it exists is more complex. And that is all. The scientist will therefore study each type independently, and his only preoccupation will be with finding the relationship which exists between the constituent characteristics of each type and the circumstances which surround it. That is how we shall be able to proceed in our research with the same impartial curiosity which the naturalist or the physicist brings to his investigations.

III

All that precedes brings into focus the utility which this subject has for each of you.

One day I was speaking to a philosophy student at the university about the course I am about to present to you. He asked me if I wasn't going to end it with an essay on domestic morality. But domestic morality will not come at the end of the course because it is the framework which constitutes the course itself. For what is domestic morality if not the description and explication of the family in its most perfect form, which is to say, the form which it has most recently assumed? And from another point of view, how are we to explain the present type if we are not familiar with the others and if we don't compare it with them? This is precisely the work which we are going to undertake this year. But, you say, morality is more an art than a science and cannot be limited to explaining the present but must prefigure the future by offering us an ideal which will rouse our wills. That is fine by me. But art, when it is not purely empirical, is science put in practice. Art improves reality; but to correct reality, one must first know it. Before morality can aspire to the perfection of mores, a science of mores must be created. Otherwise, the ideal which it constructs can only be a work of poetic fantasy, an entirely subjective conception which could never occur, since it bears no relationship to facts. In a word, the methodical art of morality is possible only if the science of morality is sufficiently well advanced.

Students in philosophy cannot, therefore, remain indifferent to the efforts which we undertake in this course to establish morality as a positive science. And as a result, I feel no need to demonstrate that this course is necessary to them or that they would be making a grave error to see it as superfluous or dispensable instruction. I would even say that they have a not only scientific but also practical and strictly professional interest in taking it, for you are destined, some sooner and others later, to teach philosophy in our secondary schools. Bring back for a moment your memories of high school. Would I be exaggerating if I said that of all the parts of the curriculum there was generally none so dull or so boring to teacher and student alike as morality, and especially practical morality? Indeed, as it is often taught, it is a sort of rationalistic catechism which can hardly excite much interest because we know in advance all that it comprises. All those deductions intended to demonstrate to the young man that it is his duty to love his family and his country are of very little use from the practical point of view and are hardly the sort of thing to awaken the pupil's curiosity. Moreover, I very strongly doubt that the brand of morality which we call theoretical has much greater success. For the attempts at synthesis which it contains are so diverse and contradictory that any pupil endowed with good sense—unless he places in the words of his teacher a degree of confidence which is difficult to combine with critical spirit—will understand that he cannot, at his age, pronounce judgment on questions about which the greatest minds are so much in conflict. In addition, in order that a generalization become of interest, one must sense the facts which it is intended to summarize, must perceive that it has been in contact with them, must find their stamp upon it. But all these systems are so far from reality—are so lean, while it is so rich; are so simple, while it is so complex—that they seem to belong to another world. What relationship can there be between the legal or moral rules which govern conjugal relations, for example, and the categorical imperative or the law of utility (for I don't distinguish among all these attempts at summary explanation)?

If you wish morality to interest your pupils no less than psychology, then beef up your instruction with facts. Don't be content with rousing their minds by merely raising questions; teach them something. Make use of practical ethics—I purposely use the secondary curriculum's rather defective terminology—to show them what law and mores really are, to show them that they are not systems of thought logically connected by means of abstract maxims but organic phenomena which draw their sustenance from the very life of societies. And perform this demonstration not in a general and vague way but center it around specific and concrete facts. For example, when you explain the family, show them a few of the forms about which I shall be speaking this year and range them alongside its present form, which they believe to be the only one in the world, so that they may obtain a more accurate conception of it. Without entering into details which would only be out of place and without sticking to pure generalities, choose a few of the most characteristic relations of domestic life and speak of them with precision. Tell them, for example, a word or two about contemporary laws of inheritance and their causes, about the nature of the conjugal bond, about intervention of the state into the family and its intent. Comparisons between the present and previous state of these relations in other types of family will make these brief explanations easier. Proceed in the same way for society. Do not rest content with giving your students a general idea of the nature of social aggregates, but show them that there are different species, whose distinctive properties you can point to in order to make them understand better the principal characteristics of contemporary societies. Do you wish to speak to them about suicide? A few well-chosen statistics on the relationship of this morbid phenomenon with civil status, social conditions, and the condition of the surrounding society will take no more time and yet will be infinitely more instructive than the traditional dissertation on the legitimacy or illegitimacy of suicide, and such statistics will serve better to resolve this question. Do you wish to deal with the moral conscience? Instead of making a fresh start with the literary description of remorse and inner satisfaction, compare the modern conscience of the typical European of today with that of the savage, the unwell, or the criminal. To be sure, by following this method, theoretical morality loses the capital importance which it previously had in such courses. But by proceeding in this way you will only be following the example of the highest authority. Janet, in a philosophical abstract, went so far as to deal with practical morality before theoretical morality. I am not, therefore, advising you to adopt a subversive innovation. Indeed, I believe that in a secondary school course it is never a good idea to innovate except with moderation, and the changes which I am recommending to you can easily be accommodated to tradition. Have faith, I beg of you, in personal experience.

In order that morality, thus presented, merely manage to sustain attention, it must be more than a paraphrase of everyday experience. It must instruct students; they must find in it facts of which they were previously unaware. And it is sociology which will furnish these facts. Those of you who take this course over two or three years will take with you, I believe, an already respectable number of documents which it will later be easy to appropriate in your teaching.

But as you know, I am not addressing philosophers alone. In particular, I believe that this year's subject can be of use to other students, notably those in history. It interests them not only because of the materials we use, which are often borrowed from history, but especially because of the results at which I hope to arrive.

As I have often remarked, specific facts can only be explained by comparing them among themselves. In history, properly so called, the field of possible comparisons is very limited. Since the historian usually confines himself to the study of a single people, he can only compare the social facts which he observes among themselves. If, for example, he is concerned with an institution, there is only one way to gain insight into the conditions on which it depends, and that is to establish the variations through which it successively passed in the country under consideration and then to investigate the concomitant fact which varied at the same time that it did. But since the changes which a single institution undergoes in the course of its development cannot be very numerous, such restricted comparisons can give no more than incomplete results. Other scientists have tried another method. They have compared not the various stages of a single institution but analogous institutions selected from various societies of the same family. This is what Fustel de Coulanges did in his book *The Ancient City* and Sumner Maine in his various works. However, these comparisons can be truly fruitful only if they are broad in scope. We cannot construct theories by comparing with each other two or three facts of the same type. In order to account for the Roman family, we must compare it not only with the Greek family but with all families of the same type. And even different types of families can help clarify each other. From this point of view, the lowest species cannot be ignored. In this way, the domestic law of Australian or American tribes helps us better to understand that of the Romans. But the historian has until now remained a stranger to ethnography. He barely goes beyond the classic civilizations. Moreover, he cannot do everything; he cannot at the same time study individual societies and collate the results of these isolated studies. To sociology belongs the task of proceeding with these extensive comparisons, and that is the way in which it will prove useful to history. You will see how, through the use of this method, we shall manage to explain in a fairly satisfactory manner, I believe, certain peculiarities of the Roman family. But we will also be able to throw some light on more general facts, like paternal power, marital power, and so forth.

I know the objection which awaits me. Some say the times are not ripe for these comparisons, though they recognize the advantages they present. Some advise sociology to wait until individual histories are complete. To make sociology hinge upon such a condition would be to postpone it indefinitely. For, whatever we do, the historical sciences will always leave too great a place to conjecture and personal interpretations for us to hope to see one day a definitive understanding of the history of any period, let alone any country. Every day we see the truths which we believed to be best established placed in question once again. If nothing is less scientific than historical skepticism, can we close our eyes to these forever renewed disputes? It may seem that in speaking this way I myself diminish the worth of sociology, since it has such need of history. I mean nothing of the kind. For I believe that the advance of sociology will have precisely the effect of helping history to become more objective. What forces it to linger in the domain of probabilities and pure possibilities is precisely the dearth or insufficiency of the comparisons which it can effect. Sociology will effect them in its place. Sociology does not impose the general results at which it arrives upon the historian; it submits them to him so that he may revise them, and it puts them once again to the test of historical facts properly so called. An eminent historian once told me: "One can't be a historian if one doesn't specialize; but one can no more be a historian if one does specialize." He added that he could not very well see any way to resolve this antinomy. We must recognize that in the interest of history itself, two sciences must be established in such a way as to remain independent yet always in contact. One will describe individual societies, while the other will compare these scattered monographs. The sociologist will borrow from the historian the facts which he needs and will deal with them according to his own method. Once elaborated in this way, he will return them once again according to his own principles. Neither of these two sciences will exercise supremacy over the other. There will exist between the two a succession of actions and reactions until an equilibrium—that is, an agreement—is finally reached.

The explanations and theories which satisfy the historian's speculative curiosity have a more practical interest for the law student. They help him better to understand the nature of those legal institutions in the functioning of which he is destined to collaborate. The practice of law is, no doubt, essentially an art or matter of experience. But any art which is not mere routine is based upon some science which provides it with inspiration. For law, that science can only be sociology. It is to law what physiology is to medicine. To be sure, our science is still too young to be able to direct the evolution of facts, and no one is more skeptical of these premature attempts at application than I. Nonetheless, I feel that as of now sociology can rely upon a certain number of truths which can guide the jurist in his practice. It appears inconceivable to me that the legal art would not change with the conception we hold of society in general or with some social function in particular. Would it not make a difference in our handling of the traditional rules of paternal power or the laws of inheritance for us to know their causes? But there is only one way to discover them and that is to practice the comparative method, as we are about to attempt. Still, there is another part of the course which the law student will find even closer, if that is possible, to his interests. Everyone recognizes, I believe, that the judge's role is not to apply general rules to particular cases in a mechanical way. He must take into account the changes which occur in social life so that he may prudently and progressively accommodate legal formulas to them. It is in this way that the spirit of a law may change even though the letter remains always the same. But one can adapt law to the present state of society only if one knows what society is like; and the least common way is to know it not through subjective and vague intuition but in an authentic and precise way. Those charged with applying domestic law or with watching over its application need to know the present situation of the family, what changes have occurred, and what others are being prepared. Toward the end of this course I will attempt, as I have said, to answer a few of these questions with the help of demography.

There is no need for me to insist further, for I can only repeat to the law students what several of their teachers have already told them with greater competence than I possess. But I do insist upon stating once more that this course is addressed to this three-fold category of students because this simple remark, it seems to me, contains the most natural solution to a question which I would like to consider briefly by way of concluding.

Some have, as you know, objected that this course does not belong in the school of letters, and the law school has claimed it for its own. First, I should state that I am pleased to hear this claim. We can only be proud to see a law school, whose spirit of wisdom and circumspection is well known, quite ready to open its doors to this newly created science. For sociology, this amounts to a sign of approbation which I could hardly have hoped would come so soon. But does it follow that we should dispossess the school of letters of this course of instruction with which it has only recently been endowed, at least as an experiment?

In defense of this point of view, some have said that these schools live solely on the psychological plane and that they ceased to be in their element once they began to consider the social world. That is, gentlemen, to extend beyond all reason the domain of psychology. In reality, the entity which psychology studies is only an abstraction. We cannot examine psychology in its entirety without running across something which is not psychology itself, namely, the society which not only surrounds but also penetrates it and which cannot be separated from it. And that is the unique object of study which is conceded to be our domain! But aren't historical facts essentially social, and can't we say that our faculties are almost totally schools of historical sciences? It is not just the history of political institutions that is taught you here but also the history of ideas, of literature, and of languages. Finally, do we need to recall that morality has remained a philosophical matter and that it arises out of social science? I won't even mention religion, since everyone already abandons its study to us. If, then, we wish to speak in a strict sense, it would not be difficult to show that it is here that the social sciences have their center of gravity.

But I do not intend to defend this extreme solution. I simply feel that this instruction is not out of place in a school of letters, since it speaks to the needs of many students in this curriculum. Moreover, I recognize that it would be no more out of place in a school of law, since everyone concedes that it is useful to law students. I am not, therefore, claiming that we shall be the exclusive benefactors of sociology. On the contrary, I hope that similar courses will be established elsewhere, for science stands only to gain by having the same problems studied from various points of view. I ask only that we be treated with the same liberalism in return.

Having said all this, I must confess that the question does not excite my passionate interest. The social sciences are quite recent and are only in the process of being organized. We cannot, therefore. expect them to conform exactly to the old administrative frameworks which the Middle Ages left us as a legacy. Any arrangement will necessarily be a compromise incapable of satisfying everyone. But what does it matter? Do law students feel as out of place here as we do when we visit them? Try as I may, I cannot get excited about this minor constitutional problem. The essential in all things is not to force a fixed course upon life but simply to encourage it to come forth on its own. Let it flow freely there where it exists; it will know how best to fix its own course. The important thing is not that this class take place here or there, but that it be produced at all and that it survive. In Germany, the study of political economy is tied, for reasons that we cannot fathom, to the school of philosophy; yet you know what role the German economic school of thought has played. Therefore, I conclude by expressing the wish that this debate not be prolonged. I am not saying that it was useless to undertake it, but I do not believe that it would be good to have it continue indefinitely, and I address this plea to the friends of sociology in particular. Too much insistence would end by convincing the skeptics that sociology (*la science social*) would change its basic nature just be changing the place it called home. That would not be to its credit, nor is it the opinion of any party. Whatever progress we have made, we are not yet so numerous in France as to believe that the future of the political and moral sciences should consist in following the model of their elders, the natural sciences. We are not, I am saying, numerous enough for it to be wise for us to divide our forces at this point in time. Let us not become overconcerned with details of organization which the future will resolve on its own. Let us proceed as quickly as possible and, since we have essentially the same end in view, let us unite our efforts and work in common.

14

THE CONJUGAL FAMILY

By "conjugal family" I mean the family as it evolved among societies descended from Germanic society or among the most civilized peoples of modern Europe.[1] I shall describe its most essential characteristics as they emerged from a lengthy evolution and were laid down in our system of civil law.

The conjugal family is the result of a contraction of the paternal family.[2] The latter consists of the father, the mother, and all generations descended from them except for daughters and their descendants. The conjugal family includes only the husband, the wife, and unmarried children who are not of age. There exist among the members of the group thus constituted kinship relations which are quite characteristic, which exist only among them and only within the limits over which paternal power extends. The father is required to feed the child and see to his education until he comes of age. In return, the child is placed under the father's domination. He disposes over neither his person nor his fortune, which is the father's to enjoy. He has no civil responsibility; that reverts to the father. But when the child attains majority as far as marriage is concerned—for despite attaining the civil majority of twenty-one years, he remains his father's ward as regards marriage—or as soon as the child is legitimately married, whenever that occurs, all these relationships come to an end. The child thenceforth has his own personality, his separate interests, and is responsible for himself. He can, to be sure, continue to live under his father's roof, but his presence is only a material or purely moral fact and has none of the legal consequences

Originally published in *Revue philosophique* 90:1–14.

which it had in the paternal family.[3] Moreover, he usually ceases to live there even before he attains majority. In any case, once the child is married, the rule is that he must start a separate household. To be sure, he maintains his ties with his parents; he owes them food in case of illness and, conversely, he has a right to a certain portion of the family fortune, since he cannot (in the French legal system) be totally disinherited. These are the only legal obligations which survive (from the earlier forms of the family), and even the second seems destined to disappear. There is nothing left that recalls this state of perpetual dependence which was the basis of the paternal family and of the patriarchal family. Since its only permanent elements are the husband and the wife, since all the children sooner or later leave the paternal household, I propose to call it the *conjugal family*.[4]

What is new about the internal organization of this family is that the old familial communism has been shaken apart to an extent that we have never before encountered. Until this type of family developed, communism had been the basis of all domestic societies, with the possible exception of the patriarchal family. In the latter, the preponderant position of the father had compressed the communitarian character of the family association.[5] But this character has not completely disappeared. To be precise, paternal power results from a transformation of erstwhile communism. It is communism based no longer on the family itself, living in an indivisible manner, but on the person of the father. Moreover, in it domestic society forms a whole, the parts of which no longer have any distinct individuality.[6] This is no longer true of conjugal society. Each of the constituent members has his own individuality and sphere of action. Even the underaged child has his own, though it is subordinated to that of his father as a result of its more limited development. The child can have his own fortune. While it is true that until he is eighteen, the father disposes of it, even this right of usufruct is not without certain obligations toward the child (see article 385, *Code Civil*). The minor can even possess goods which are not subject to this control, namely, those which he has acquired through his own work and those he has received on the condition that his parents not benefit from them (article 387, *Code Civil*). Finally, in the realm of personal relationships, the disciplinary rights of the father over the person of the minor are narrowly limited. All that remains of the former communism is the right of the parents of a child under age sixteen to the use of his possessions and the right, limited moreover, which the descendant has over the goods of his ancestry as a result of restrictions applied to the right of testament.[7]

But what is even newer and more distinctive about this type of family is the ever increasing intervention of the state into the internal life of the family. One can say that the state has become a factor in domestic life. It is the intermediary which exercises the right of correcting the father when he exceeds certain limits. It is the state which, in the person of the magistrate, presides over family councils, which takes the orphaned minor under its protection when no guardian is named, which adjudicates and sometimes calls for the suspension of an adult's civil rights. A recent law even authorizes the court, in certain cases, to declare the forfeiture of paternal power. But there is one fact which, better than any other, demonstrates how great a transformation the family is subjected to in these conditions. The conjugal family could have arisen neither from the patriarchal family nor from the paternal family, nor even from a combination of the two types of family, without the intervention of this new factor, the state.[8] Up to this point, kinship relations could always be broken off, either by the relative . . .[9] who wanted to leave his family or by the father on whom he depended. The first case is that of the agnatic family, and also that of the paternal family;[10] the second case occurs only in the patriarchal family. With the conjugal family, kinship relations became altogether indissoluble. The state, by taking them under its warranty, has withdrawn from individuals the right to break them.

This is the central zone of the modern family.[11] But this central zone is surrounded by other secondary zones which complete it. Here as elsewhere, these secondary zones are nothing but the previous forms of the family, which go back, so to speak, one degree of consanguinity.[12] There is first the group formed by ancestors and descendants: grandfather, father, mother, brothers, sisters, and ancestors—that is to say, the old paternal family, displaced from the first rank and relegated to the second. The group thus constituted has preserved a fairly distinct character in our law. When a man dies without leaving an heir, his fortune is divided among his parents and his brothers and sisters or their descendants. Finally, beyond the paternal family, we find the cognatic family[13]—that is, the group of all the collaterals aside from those just mentioned, but diminished and weakened still further than it was in the paternal family. In the latter, the collaterals, even to the sixth and seventh degrees and sometimes even more distantly, still had very important domestic duties and rights. We noted a few examples in the last lecture.[14] Thenceforth, their role in the family is practically nil. Almost all that remains is a contingent right of inheritance, a right which can be reduced to nothing as a result of the freedom to leave a will should there be neither descendants nor ancestors. For the first time, no more than traces of the clan remain. (The individuality of the two secondary zones seems no longer to be as distinct as in the previous types.)[15]

Now that we are familiar with the last type of family to be formed, we can look back over the terrain covered and make explicit the results which this long evolution reveals.

The law of contraction or progressive emergence has been thoroughly verified. We have more and more restricted groups which tend to absorb the whole of family life emerged from primitive groups in the most regular manner.[16] Not only does the regularity of this evolution result from the preceding, but it is easy to see that it is linked to the most fundamental conditions of historical development. In effect, the study of the patriarchal family has shown us that the family must necessarily contract as the social milieu, with which every individual is in direct relationship, extends further.[17] For the more it is restricted, the better it can prevent particular divergences from appearing; consequently, only those divergences that are common to a sufficiently large number of individuals to have a mass effect and thus overcome the collective resistance can become manifest. In such conditions, only large domestic societies are able to disengage themselves from political society. On the contrary, to the extent that the milieu becomes more vast, it leaves more free play to private divergences and, consequently, those which are common to a smaller number of individuals cease to be contained, can come into being and affirm themselves. At the same time, by virtue of a general law already observed in biology, differences among individuals multiply by the simple fact that the milieu is more extensive. Now, if there is one fact which dominates history, it is the progressive extension of the social milieu into which each of us is integrated. The village organization was succeeded by that of the city; the milieu formed by the city with the surrounding villages placed in a state of dependence was succeeded by nation states, which embraced various cities; nations of limited volume, like the Germanic peoples, were succeeded by the vast societies of today. At the same time, the various parts of these societies placed themselves more and more closely in contact as a result of the proliferation and increased rapidity of communication, and so on.[18]

At the same time that the volume contracts, the constitution of the family changes.

The great change which occurred from this point of view was the progressive disruption of familial communism. In the beginning, it extended to all kinship relations; all the relatives lived in common, possessed in common. But as soon as a first dissociation occurred in the heart of originally amorphous masses, as soon as the secondary zones appeared, communism withdrew and concentrated itself exclusively in the primary or central zone. When the agnatic family emerged from the clan, communism ceased to be the basis of the agnatic family. Finally, little by little, it was confined to the primary circle of relatedness. In the patriarchal family, the father of the family was liberated from it, since he freely and personally controlled the family property. In the paternal family, it was more marked, because the familial types belonged to a lower species.[19] However, the members of the family could have title to personal wealth even though they could not dispose of or administer it personally. Finally, in the conjugal family, only vestiges of this right remained: this development was, therefore, linked to the same causes as the preceding one. The same causes which had the effect of progressively restricting the family circle also allowed the personalities of the family members to come forth more and more. The more the social milieu extended, the less, we are saying, the development of private divergences was contained. But, among these divergences, there were some which were specific to the individual, to each member of the family, and these continually became more numerous and more important as the field of social relations became more vast. Therefore, wherever they encountered weak resistance, it was inevitable that they reproduce themselves outside, that they be accentuated, consolidated, and, as they were the property of the individual personality, they necessarily tended to develop. Each individual increasingly assumed his own character, his personal manner of thinking and feeling. In these circumstances, communism became more and more impossible because it, on the contrary, presupposed the identity and fusion of all consciousnesses within a single common consciousness which embraced them. We can be certain that this disappearance of communism which characterizes our domestic law not only is not a transient, chance event but, on the contrary, that it will become ever more pronounced—unless, by some unforeseen and nearly incomprehensible miracle, the fundamental conditions which have dominated social evolution since its beginning do not remain the same.

Does domestic solidarity emerge weakened or reinforced by these changes? It is very difficult to respond to this question. In one sense, it is stronger, since the bonds of relatedness are today indissoluble; but in another, the obligations to which it gives rise are less numerous and less important. What is certain is that it is transformed. It depends on two factors: persons and things. We retain solidarity with our family because we feel solidarity with the persons who compose it; but we also retain solidarity with it because we cannot do without certain things and because, under a system of familial communism, it is the family which possesses them. The result of the breakdown of communism is that things cease, to an ever greater extent, to act as a cement for domestic society. Domestic solidarity becomes entirely a matter of persons. We are attached to our family only because we are attached to the person of our father, our mother, our wife, or our children. It was quite different formerly, when the links which derived from things took precedence over those which derived from persons, when the whole familial organization had as its primary object to keep the domestic property within the family, and when all personal considerations appeared secondary to these considerations.

That is how the family has tended to develop. But if this is an accurate description, if things possessed in common cease to be a factor in domestic life, then the right of inheritance no longer has any reason to exist. It is nothing but familial communism being continued under a system of private property. If, therefore, communism goes away, disappears from all the zones of the family, how can the right of inheritance maintain itself? In fact, it regresses in the most regular manner. At first it belongs in an imprescriptible manner to all relatives, even the most distant collaterals. But soon the right of testament appears and paralyzes it as far as the secondary zones are concerned. The right of collaterals to inherit from the deceased only comes into play if the deceased has not created any obstacle, and the power which the individual exercises in this regard becomes more extensive every day. Finally, the right to leave a will penetrates even the central zone, enters into the group formed by the parents and children. The father can disinherit his children either totally[20] or partially. There is no doubt that this regression is destined to continue. I mean that not only will the right of testament become absolute, but that a day will come when a man will no longer be permitted, even through a will, to leave his fortune to his descendants; that, since the French Revolution, he is not permitted to leave them his offices and honors. For conveying one's estate in a will is but the final and most diminished form of hereditary transmission. As of the present, there are valuable commodities of the greatest importance which can no longer be transmitted by any hereditary means; [these are, to be precise,] offices and honors.[21] At present, there is a whole category of workers who can no longer transmit to their children the fruits of their labor, namely, those whose work brings only honor and respect rather than wealth. It is certain that this rule will tend to be generalized more and more and that hereditary transmission will tend to become more and more distinct.

From still another point of view, the change becomes more and more necessary. As long as riches are transmitted hereditarily, there are some who are rich and some who are poor by birth. The moral conditions of our social life are such that societies can be maintained only if the external inequalities with which individuals are faced are leveled to an ever greater degree. This does not mean that men must become more equal among themselves—on the contrary, their internal inequality continually increases—but that there should be no social inequalities other than those which derive from the personal worth of each individual, and this inequality must not be exaggerated or reduced through some external cause. But hereditary wealth is one of these causes. It gives to some advantages which do not derive from their own merit but which confer upon them this superiority over others. This injustice, which seems more and more intolerable to us, becomes increasingly incompatible with the conditions of existence of our societies. Everything converges, therefore, in proving that the right of inheritance, even in the form of a will, is destined progressively to disappear.

But, as necessary as this transformation may be, it will hardly be easy. Without doubt, the rule of hereditary transmission of property has its cause in the ancient familial communism, and the latter is in the process of disappearing. But, in the course of this development, we have become so used to this rule and it has been so closely linked to our entire organization that, were it to be abolished without being replaced, the vital source of social life would run dry. In effect, we are so well conditioned, so accustomed to it, that the prospect of hereditarily transmitting the fruits of our labor has become the preeminent force behind our activity. If we pursued purely personal ends, we would be far less encouraged to work, for our work makes sense only because it serves something other than ourselves. The individual is not an end sufficient unto himself. When he looks for his purpose within himself, he falls into a state of moral misery which leads him to suicide.[22] What binds us to our work is the fact that it is our means of enriching the domestic patrimony, of increasing the well-being of our children. If this prospect were withdrawn, this extremely powerful and moral stimulant would be taken away as well. The problem is not, therefore, as simple as it first appeared. If it is to be possible for the ideal which we have just outlined to be realized, this driving force, which we risk losing, must be replaced, little by little, by another. We must be stimulated to work by something other than personal or domestic interest. On the other hand, social interest is too distant from us, too vaguely glimpsed, too impersonal for it to serve as an effective motive force. We must, therefore, be integrated into some group outside the family, one more limited than political society and closer to us. It is to this group that the very rights which the family is no longer capable of exercising will be transferred.

What can this group be? Will matrimonial society do? We have, indeed, seen it grow in the most regular fashion; it has been consolidated and become more and more coherent. The importance it assumes in the conjugal family marks the apogee of this development. Not only has marriage become almost completely indissoluble in this type of family, not only has monogamy become just about complete, but it presents two new characteristics which demonstrate the force it has assumed with time.

In the first place, it has completely ceased to be a personal contract and become a public act. A [magistrate] presides over the contracting of the marriage. Not only does the ceremony have this public character, but if the constituent formalities are not accurately fulfilled, the marriage is not valid. And we know that no legal act assumes solemn forms unless it assumes great importance.

If, from another point of view, we pass from the external conditions of marriage to the organization of matrimonial relationships, they present us with a peculiarity without parallel in the history of the family. This is the appearance of the system of community property between spouses, whether this community is all-encompassing or limited to acquisitions. Indeed, community is the rule of matrimonial society. It can be qualified, but it exists with full legitimacy if there are no contrary conventions. Thus, while communism was retreating from domestic society, it appeared in matrimonial society.[23] Is not the latter destined to replace the former in the function we have been discussing, and isn't conjugal love the force capable of producing the same effects as love of the family?

Not at all. For conjugal society, taken by itself, is too ephemeral for that. It does not provide us with sufficiently vast perspectives. In order that we be bound to our work, we must feel that it will survive us, that some portion of it will remain after us, that even when we are no longer around, it will serve persons whom we love. We quite naturally have this feeling when we are working for our family, since it continues to exist after us. But conjugal society, on the contrary, dissolves with death in every generation. The spouses do not survive one another very long. As a result, they cannot be for one another an object sufficient to tear them from the search for fleeting sensations. That is why marriage alone does not have an influence on suicide comparable to that of the family.[24]

There seems to be only one group close enough to the individual for him to adhere tightly to it, yet durable enough for him to aspire to its perspective. That is the occupational group. In my view, only it can succeed the family in the economic and moral functions, which the family is becoming more and more incapable of fulfilling. To extricate ourselves from the state of crisis which we are passing through, the suppression of the rule of hereditary transmission is not enough. Men must gradually be bound to professional life and must establish strong groups of this kind. Professional duty must assume the same role in men's hearts which domestic duty has hitherto played. This is the moral level already attained by the entire elite which we have discussed, and this proves that this transformation is not impracticable.[25] (Moreover, this change will not be accomplished in an absolute manner, and there will long remain a great many vestiges of the old laws. Parents will always be encouraged to work by the desire to feed and raise their families, but this driving force would not, by itself, be sufficient to)[26] [disperse and eliminate the family. On the contrary, the occupational group is, in its essence, a perpetual entity.]

A few words on the secondary effect of marriage. In the paternal family, free union is maintained alongside marriage; but in the conjugal family, the former is almost wholly rejected. [It no longer gives rise to any legal regulation.] The more the family is organized, the more the marriage has tended to be the sole condition of kinship.

[The] causes [of this fact are as follows.] Marriage establishes the family [and, at the same time], derives from it. Therefore, any sexual union which is not contracted in the matrimonial form disturbs the familial duty and the familial bond and, from the day when the state itself has intervened in family life, disturbs the public order. From another point of view, this reaction is necessary. There is no moral society in which the members do not have obligations toward one another. When these obligations attain a certain degree of importance, they take on a legal character. Free union is a conjugal society in which these obligations do not exist. It is, therefore, an immoral society. And that is why children raised in such conditions present such great numbers of moral flaws. It is because they have not been raised in a moral environment. The child can have a moral education only if he lives in a society all the members of which have a sense of their obligations toward one another, for without this there is no morality. Also, [to the extent that the legislator and morality itself are concerned with this problem] the tendency is not to make free unions of all marriages, but to make marriages, of at least an inferior sort, of all unions, even free ones.

These are the general conclusions which can be drawn from this course. The family has developed by becoming concentrated and personalized. The family continues to contract, and, at the same time, relations continue to assume an exclusively personal character as a result of the progressive disappearance of domestic communism. While the family loses ground, marriage, on the contrary, becomes stronger.

15

DIVORCE BY MUTUAL CONSENT

Certain men of letters have made a fad of the question of divorce by mutual consent. Lawyers and statesmen have followed suit, and the movement has been propagated with uncommon rapidity. Public opinion, which only yesterday was little concerned with the problem, now seems ready to pronounce itself without hesitation in favor of the most drastic and revolutionary solution as if it were self-evident. Anyone who tries to resist so universal a current risks passing for a reactionary. Yet, to whatever extent one can know oneself, I do not feel that I am a reactionary. There is no institution, even among those which pass for being the most sacred, which I consider to be above question. I believe that the moral world is just as properly the object of the disputes of men as the physical. Our conception of the fatherland or our conception of the family are destined to evolve; indeed, they are already evolving before our eyes. This is, however, no reason to yield to the whims for change which arise overnight. Despite the sort of unanimity with which the idea of Paul and Victor Margueritte was received (at least outside Catholic circles proper), despite the authority of the defenders it has encountered both in Parliament and in the courts, the reform which they have proposed causes me an uneasiness, the reasons for which I would like to state.

I do not propose, in the present context, to deal with the problem in all its scope. I would simply like to consider one of its aspects which seems to have been rather generally misunderstood. It is especially in the interest of the parents—and also, people say, somewhat in the interest of the children—that the right of the

Originally published in *Revue bleue* 5 (1906): 549-54.

spouses to separate is demanded when their union has become intolerable. It is above all to liberate them from a bond which ties them to one another in common misery and to put an end to their sufferings. But there is another point of view from which the question must be examined: there is the interest of the institution of matrimony itself, which the system of divorce cannot fail to affect. Most assuredly, nothing is further from our intent than to place in question the principle of divorce. It would seem indisputable that in certain conditions spouses must be allowed to escape from their marriage. And yet divorce must not be extended in such a way that it contradicts and destroys the principle on which the state of marriage reposes; for then, under pretext of remedying individual evils, it would constitute of itself a grave social malady whose repercussions the individual would bear.

Yet there are indeed reasons to fear that divorce by mutual consent would have a very dangerous influence on marriage and its normal functioning.

I

If there exists any well-established statistical law, it is that which Bertillon pronounced in 1882 in the following terms: in all Europe the number of suicides varies with the number of divorces.[1]

This law is verified when we compare either the various countries of Europe one with another, or the various provinces of a single country. Switzerland is, on this score, particularly instructive. There we find cantons of all religions and of all nationalities, and we know that the inclination to commit suicide varies according to religious persuasion and national origin. Now, in Switzerland, there is one influence which dominates that of religion and nationality, namely, divorce. Whether we consider Protestant cantons, Catholic cantons, or mixed cantons, whether the population is French, German, or Italian—wherever divorce is frequent, suicide is frequent; wherever divorce is rare, suicide is rare; and the same parallelism recurs over the entire extent of the intermediary range.

Of course, it is not the suicides of divorced persons which thus swell the numbers of voluntary deaths. To be sure, the divorced kill themselves more often than married people—about three or four times more often. But their number is too small for their contribution to the suicide-mortality to be very significant. Even taking things at their worst, there might be fifty to one hundred suicides per year among divorced persons in France. What is this figure compared to the eight or nine thousand suicides that our statistics annually register? It is like a drop of water in a river, and it is not the insignificant variation in this miniscule drop which can cause variations in the level of the river.

Bertillon, when he discovered and formulated his law, believed he could give a very simple explanation of it. According to him, there are more divorces in countries which have more irregular, unbalanced individuals or ones with badly formed and poorly adjusted characters, for irregular and unstable persons make poor spouses, and this same temperament also predisposes one to suicide. This would quite naturally explain the correlation between these two phenomena. But, aside from the fact that it is completely arbitrary to impute to Switzerland, for example, fifteen times more disbalanced persons than to Italy and six times more than to France just because divorces are fifteen times more frequent there than in the first of those two countries and six times more than in the second, this very simplistic theory of Bertillon appears completely untenable in the light of the new findings which I published in *Suicide.* [2]

Instead of comparing global figures of suicides in countries where divorce is frequent with the global figures corresponding to countries where divorce is less frequent, I have separated that special portion of the total number of voluntary deaths which is due to each category of marital status: the unmarried, the married, the widowed. It happens that the increase in suicides which is observed where divorce is frequent is due principally to married people. Thus, in France, divorce and suicide are far more frequent in Paris than in the provinces. But this aggravation of the suicide rate is almost nonexistent among the unmarried; it occurs almost exclusively among the married and, moreover, in every age category, as tables 1 and 2 show.

Except during the years of great struggles—that is, between

Table 1. Number of suicides per million unmarried men of each age (1889-1891)

Age (in years)	In the provinces	In Paris	Number of times more frequent in Paris
20-30[3]	579	986	1.5
30-40	590	869	1.4
40-50	976	985	1.08
50-60	1445	1367	0.9
60-70	1790	1500	0.8
70-80	2000	1783	0.8

Table 2. Number of suicides per million married men of each age

Age (in years)	In the provinces	In Paris	Number of times more frequent in Paris
25-30[4]	103	298	2.9
30-40	202	436	2.1
40-50	295	808	2.9
50-60	470	1152	2.4
60-70	582	1559	2.6
70-80	664	1741	2.6

twenty and forty years of age—unmarried persons do not kill themselves either more or less in Paris than in the provinces. And, moreover, even when the unmarried Parisian's tendency to suicide is most aggravated in relation to that of the unmarried provincial, it is quite weakly so (1.5). But, on the other hand, in every age category, married Parisians commit suicide from two and a half to three times more often than married provincials.

The widowed, it is true, also contribute to this increase: their tendency to suicide is about two and half times stronger in Paris than in the provinces. The augmentation is also far stronger among them than it is among the unmarried. But this fact is only a specific case of a more general law which I established in that same book and which can be stated thusly: *The tendency to suicide among the widowed varies with that of the married.*[5] When the married commit suicide infrequently, the widowed commit suicide infrequently; when the inverse takes place on the one side, it also occurs on the other. And, indeed, we can easily see that marriage conditions the spouses into a certain moral constitution which affects their inclination to suicide in a determinate manner, and which, while somewhat weakened by the crisis of widowhood, manages to survive the dissolution of marriage. There exists a whole set of ideas, habits—in a word, dispositions—which continue to produce their effect when the cause from which they arose has ceased to exist.

If, therefore, the higher number of suicides in countries where divorce is common arises almost exclusively from the fact that married people kill themselves more there than elsewhere, Bertillon's hypothesis becomes inadmissable; for it is impossible to assume that there would be more unstable and unbalanced persons among the married than among the unmarried. But since the observed augmentation is a fact peculiar to the married, there is no doubt, because the practice of divorce strongly affects the moral constitution which the state of marriage determines. For there is no question that marriage creates in the spouses a moral constitution sui generis, which in the widower survives the dissolution of the conjugal bond and which is certainly related to the tendency toward suicide.

And, in effect, we know that marriage in and of itself, without even having its effect reinforced by the presence of children, confers upon the spouses a relative immunity against suicide; the married man, even if the marriage is childless, kills himself one and a half times less than the bachelor or, in more concise terms, he has, in relation to the latter, a coefficient of preservation of 1.5. When there are children, this coefficient rises to 3 or higher. In the work mentioned above, I have assembled a certain number of facts which demonstrate that *the coefficient of preservation of the spouses varies inversely with the number of divorces*: it rises when divorce is rare; it falls in the opposite case. Between the years 1889 and 1891, in the provinces, where divorce is less common, the coefficient of preservation for married men between 25 and 80 years of age varied between 3.54 and 3.01; in Paris during the same period it never exceeded 2.01 for any age category, and it attained this figure only once (for men of 25 to 30 years of age); for those between 40 and 80 years of age it was barely greater than unity (1.21 was the maximum). It even fell below unity for those between 60 and 70 years of age; that is to say that at that age married men killed themselves more often than bachelors. Finally, the average coefficient of preservation for men between 25 and 80 years of age in the provinces was 3.15 and in Paris 1.49 or two and a half times weaker.

We begin to perceive that the extensive practice of divorce never occurs without grave moral disadvantages which should cause reflection among those who demand a reform whose inevitable effect would be to facilitate it still more and to make it a more integral part of our mores.

II

It is true that the preceding facts apply solely to men. Divorce does not appear unfavorable to married women. To be sure, they kill themselves more in Paris than in the provinces. But unmarried women also kill themselves more and the aggravation is appreciably the same in the two categories of marital status as tables 3 and 4 prove.

The augmentation is a little stronger—a very little, moreover—for unmarried over married women until the age of fifty, but the inverse

Table 3. Number of suicides per million unmarried women of each age (1889-1891)

Age (in years)	In the provinces	In Paris	Number of times more frequent in Paris
20–30[6]	217	524	2.4
30–40	101	281	2.7
40–50	147	357	2.4
50–60	178	456	2.5
60–70	163	515	3.1
70–80	200	326	1.6

Table 4. Number of suicides per million married women of each age

Age (in years)	In the provinces	In Paris	Number of times more frequent in Paris
20–30[7]	116	167	1.4
30–40	74	156	2.0
40–50	95	217	2.2
50–60	136	353	2.6
60–70	142	471	3.3
70–80	191	677	3.5

relationship holds above that age. These two contrary divergences compensate each other, and the average augmentation is 2.4 for unmarried and 2.5 for married women.

In my book *Suicide*, I went so far as to say (pp. 266 ff.) that the effect of divorce was to increase somewhat the immunity of wives. And, in effect, between 1889 and 1891, the coefficient of preservation of married women relative to unmarried members of the same sex was, on the average, a little higher in Paris than in the provinces: it was 1.79 instead of 1.49. But in taking up this question once again with respect to the present work, I perceived that the advantage enjoyed by married Parisian women is purely apparent and arises not from the fact that the married woman is in better moral conditions in Paris than in the provinces and, consequently, kills herself less often there, but from the fact that unmarried women of about 20 to 35 years of age are in more unfavorable moral conditions there and kill themselves more often. Indeed, while bachelors do not commit suicide much more often in the capital than in the provinces, there is, on the contrary, the just-mentioned augmentation among unmarried females, the level of which varies between 2.4 and 3.1, except at a single period when it falls to 1.6. We have no difficulty explaining these special dangers to which the unmarried woman, while still young, is exposed in Paris, and which predispose her *more strongly* to suicide.

The result is that wives *appear* to be more protected in the provinces relative to unmarried women; but it is not because the moral constitution of the married woman is more resistant there. It is quite simply because in Paris a greater number of unmarried women (as a result of the conditions in which they live, or of the inherent weakness of their moral temperament, or for both reasons at once) are strongly disposed toward suicide. In consequence, all that can reasonably be said about the preventative influence that the state of marriage exerts directly on suicide is that it should not be appreciably different in Paris than in the provinces.[8] It does not seem that the practice of divorce affects feminine suicide in an appreciable way.

Moreover, this fact should hold no surprise; it is a specific case of a more general law, which can be formulated as follows: the state of marriage has only a weak effect on the moral constitution of women. This lack of effectiveness of conjugal society is particularly evident as far as suicide is concerned. When there are no children, married women seem to kill themselves somewhat more than unmarried women of the same age.

When the wife is, at the same time, a mother, she is protected better but still much more weakly than the husband.[9] Since, therefore, marriage, in a general way, has only a slightly beneficial effect on her, it is quite natural that divorce has no very pronounced harmful effect on her. She stands somewhat beyond the moral effects of marriage. Just as she benefits from it only a little, she suffers by it only a little. But we must also be careful not to use the fact that divorce does not increase her tendency to suicide to conclude that it is inoffensive; it is inoffensive only to the extent that the marriage is inoperative.

III

We have therefore established that marriage is capable of exercising a moral influence, especially on the male sex, which benefits the individuals themselves; for it integrates them more with life while, contrary to everything one might foresee *a priori*, they detach themselves more when it is easier for them to break the conjugal bonds. Now this fortunate influence makes itself felt to an ever diminished extent as divorce is more widely practiced. This is because marriage, by subjecting the passions to regulation, gives the man a moral posture which increases his forces of resistance. By assigning a definite, determinate, and, in principle, invariable object to his desires, it prevents them from wearing themselves out in the pursuit of ends which are always new and always changing, which grow boring as soon as they are achieved and which leave only exhaustion and disenchantment in their wake. It prevents the heart from becoming excited and tormenting itself vainly in the search for impossible or deceptive happiness; it makes easier that peace of mind, that inner balance, which are the essential conditions of moral health and happiness. But it only produces these effects because it implies a respected form of regulation which creates social bonds among individuals.

On the other hand, to the extent that these bonds are fragile, that they can be broken at will, marriage ceases to be itself and, consequently, can no longer have the same virtue. Regulation from which one can withdraw whenever one has a notion is no longer regulation. A restraint from which one can so easily liberate oneself is no longer a restraint which can moderate desires and, in moderating them, appease them.

There is no need to demonstrate that by instituting divorce by mutual consent we would add a new and easy avenue to those which the spouses already have available for withdrawing from the conjugal state. And a very easy avenue, since the role of the judge would be reduced to making sure that the will of the parties is indeed real and powerful! In this regard, divorce by mutual consent constitutes a type of divorce sui generis, one which is totally distinct from the others: when divorce takes place for determinate causes, the magistrate must examine whether the spouses are justified *by law* in desiring it; if mutual consent suffices, the existence of consent becomes the equivalent of the right to divorce, and the rupture of the conjugal bond takes place *ipso facto*, by the very fact that the interested parties desire it. In the one case, divorce is accorded only if it is just; in the other, it is obligatorily accorded by the sole fact that it is requested. To the extent, therefore, that we are justified in predicting the future from the past—and we have seen that the relation which links the level of divorce with the level of suicides is without any known exception—this new broadening of divorce must surely have the effect of increasing the suicide mortality. Marriage will be, more even than today, prevented from playing its role as a restraint, from exercising the moderating and salutary effect which is its principal reason for existing; and thus a measure, the goal of which is to lessen the moral miseries of spouses, will have the result of demoralizing them and detaching them further from life.

Such is the eventual cost of the reform which is in the process of seducing public opinion; it is difficult to ignore its importance.

To avoid these considerable risks, we must at the very least be able to invoke singularly grave reasons to justify this reform. Let us briefly review what these are alleged to be.

It has been said that marriage, being a contract, must be able to be annulled by the simple agreement of the parties. This ignores the fact that any contract potentially affects third parties; in this case, the contracting parties find themselves, at a given moment, engaged in relations which no longer depend on their wills, but on interested third parties. This is what happens in marriage. Marriage, of itself, modifies the material and moral economy of two families: the relations among persons and the relations of things to persons are not the same after as they were before. And thus, even when there are no children, marriage has repercussions which extend beyond the spouses. However, these repercussions are, in sum, secondary. But this is no longer the case from the moment that children are born. From then on, the character of the marriage completely changes its aspect. The conjugal couple then ceases to be an end in itself and become a means in view of an end which is superior to it: this end is the family which it has established and for which it thenceforth assumes responsibility. Each spouse becomes a functionary of domestic society charged, as such, with the task of assuring for his own part its proper functioning. Neither husbands nor wives can any longer liberate themselves from this duty at their whim just because their marriages do not procure or no longer procure for them the satisfaction that they expected of it.

They are obligated to someone other than themselves. It happens, to be sure, that in the interest of domestic order and of the children it may be better to dissolve the conjugal society than to let it endure without advantage to anyone; for, if it is not or is no longer capable of fulfilling its functions, there is no reason to maintain it despite everything. But to resolve this question, it is not enough just to consider the mutual sentiments of the parents and their material or moral well-being. Higher and more serious interests are at stake, ones which are beyond the competence of the spouses and which only a judge can evaluate. Moreover, it is inadmissable that the marriage could be held together by their will alone.

But, some will say, when the spouses no longer want to live together, is separation not better for the children, too? To be sure, the rupture between the parents can be such that any harmony between them is impossible; this removes from their association any moral utility. But aside from these extreme and probably infrequent cases, how many simply mediocre marriages make life more bearable and gentler for the partners—marriages in which the spouses do not have for one another all the sympathy which might be hoped for, yet in which, nonetheless, each has sufficient feeling for his duty usefully to fulfill his function, while this attachment to the common task brings them together in mutual tolerance. But for them to remain attached to their functions in this way it is also necessary that they feel that it is their strict duty. And how could they have this feeling if the law—interpreter of public conscience—encourages them, on the contrary, to discard it by permitting them to do so as soon as they have the desire? Where will they draw the moral force necessary to bear with courage an existence whose joys can be no more than rather austere if public authority solemnly proclaims that they have the right to free themselves of it whenever they please? Thus, divorce by mutual consent can only take the resiliency out of domestic life and disorganize a greater number of families without, however, resulting in an increase of happiness or a diminution of unhappiness for the average spouses.

But there remains one final argument which many consider decisive. It is useless, they say, to prohibit divorce by mutual consent because, in practice, the prohibition is easy to get around. Two spouses who want to obtain a divorce can easily give their request a legal pretext before which the judge is obliged to yield: the husband feigns adultery, the wife resigns herself to submitting to the serious mistreatment which the law requires, and so on. But, assuming that these collusions between spouses who are forgetful of their duties are effectively difficult to foil, is that a reason to smooth their way still more? Just because it is relatively easy to circumvent the law, is that a reason to abrogate it and to declare lawful that which is not? There are many thieves, swindlers, and blackmailers of every kind who live on the margin of the law; we would not dream, however, of consecrating swindling or blackmail in law. There is something worse than the judge's powerlessness to enforce respect for the law and that is the compliance of the legislator who sets up as law that which is the very violation of the law. We do not sufficiently take into account the public demoralization which results from these legislative lapses. Such an abdication of the public conscience can only weaken individual consciences where, from that point on, the idea of divorce germinates and develops without difficulty and without meeting any resistance. The necessity of resorting to the pitiful subterfuges mentioned above is, at the very least, a moral obstacle which reminds the interested parties of the fraudulent and immoral character of their act; and that may suffice to dissuade those among them who retain some sense of their own dignity. If, therefore, divorce by mutual consent, *at least where there are children*, were judged to be contrary to the very idea of marriage and the family, we could not resign ourselves to recognizing it and legally sanctioning it.

Moreover, is it quite certain that the judge would at that point be disarmed? Is there not often a great deal of complacency in the way in which he lets himself be fooled? Many frauds could be established if there were a clearer sense that it is a veritable duty not to be made an accomplice; if, when there is no spouse cited as defendant, the proceedings were conducted more seriously; if certain magistrates did not take part in a certain dilettantism and a sort of rivalry to rule on an unbelievable number of cases in one sitting.[10] In any case, if the judge truly does not have sufficient weapons in hand to enforce respect for the law, it does not appear impossible to furnish him with new ones. It would be sufficient to define a little more exactly the notions of cruelty and wrong which the magistracy has so abused: a word uttered in a moment of anger or a violent movement which escapes in a momentary outburst does not suffice to prove that a man and a woman cannot live together and raise their children together. The abandonment of the conjugal domicile *when there are children* could for good reason be considered a misdemeanor; and if this misdemeanor were punished with some severity, as is only just, people would be less tempted to feign it. Moreover, would not any feigning, agreed upon to deceive justice, constitute a criminal act which should be punished?

But I would not wish further to stress these considerations, since I feel that I am incompetant to treat the problem in its purely legal aspect. All the reasons which have been given to justify divorce by mutual consent vanish just as easily once one properly understands what a pressing necessity there is not to weaken in people's minds the feeling that conjugal and domestic relations cannot be abandoned at the will of individuals; that in their own interest these are duties from which the individuals cannot be freed for simple reasons of personal convenience: for man can be happy and can satisfy his desires in a normal way only if he is regulated, contained, moderated, and disciplined. This is why conjugal discipline cannot be weakened without also affecting the happiness of the spouses. Let us not, therefore, be troubled by the dramatic nature of certain specific incidents, real or imaginary, which cannot be placed above this imperious necessity. Nothing is more plausible than that the rule of matrimony, like any rule, can sometimes be harsh in the way in which it is applied to individuals; yet this is not a reason to weaken it. The individuals themselves would be the first to suffer for it.

Let us not hide the fact that, unfortunately, this notion of rules and of their utility is far from being widespread and popular. Public opinion still sees all regulation as an evil to which one must sometimes be resigned but which one must attempt to reduce to a minimum. Moreover, it is strongly to be feared that this new assault upon marriage will achieve its ends. And yet the experience of the revolutionary period should serve as a lesson to us. At that time divorce was broadened without limit. The result was that the very principle of the institution has remained in disrepute, and in the opinion of outstanding thinkers, for more than half a century.

Notes

A NOTE ON THE TRANSLATIONS

1. For a more discursive treatment of Durkheim's use of this term, see Harry Alpert, *Emile Durkheim and His Sociology* (New York: Russell and Russell, 1961), pp. 163ff.; also, Terry N. Clark, "Emile Durkheim and the Institutionalization of Sociology in the French University System," *Archives Européenes de sociologie* 9 (1968): 51ff. For Durkheim's own discussion, see part 2 of "Sociology and the Social Sciences," chapter 2, this volume.

2. For a discussion of the concept's broader import, see Steven Lukes, *Emile Durkheim, His Life and Work: A Historical and Critical Study* (Harper and Row: New York, 1972), p. 4ff.

3. As Bohannan has pointed out, in either language the concept of "consciousness" involves a further ambiguity which is superimposed upon the difficulty of French-English translation, namely, that it may refer to any of the following: subjective awareness, the cognitive instruments whereby that awareness is achieved, or the objects to which that awareness is applied. See Paul Bohannan, *"Conscience Collective* and Culture," in Emile Durkheim et al., *Essays on Sociology and Philosophy,* edited by Kurt H. Wolff (Harper and Row: New York, 1960), pp. 77-96.

INTRODUCTION

1. Harry Alpert, *Emile Durkheim and His Sociology* (New York: Russell and Russell, 1961).

2. Célestin Bouglé, "Quelques Souvenirs," part of a hommage to Durkheim which appeared as Célestin Bouglé et al., "L'Oeuvre sociologique d'Emile Durkheim," *Europe: Revue mensuelle* 22 (1930): 281-304. The play on words is lost in English. The French word *chaire* means at once rostrum, pulpit, and academic chair. It is curious to note in this transference of religious sentiments rejected in childhood a distinct parallel to Weber, who declared himself to be "tonedeaf" in religious matters, while similarly devoting much of his academic work to their explication. In both cases, the proselytical impulse had been ruthlessly secularized. Bouglé continues the passage cited with this qualification: "But this preacher wanted above all to be an expositor; he hoped to convince on the strength of the facts."

Georges Davy has also stressed the quality of Durkheim's scholarship as vocation in "Emile Durkheim: L'Homme," *Revue de metaphysique et de morale* 26 (1919): 181-98; 27 (1920): 71-112.

3. Steven Lukes, *Emile Durkheim, His Life and Work: A Historical and Critical Study* (New York: Harper and Row, 1972), p. 299. The committee's decision was unanimous despite the fact that it included such arch-critics as Paul Genet, who had once solicitously warned Durkheim that the study of sociology led to madness. See Raymond Lenoir, "Lettre à R. M.," in Célestin Bouglé et al., "L'Oeuvre sociologique d'Emile Durkheim," p. 294.

4. Terry N. Clark, "Emile Durkheim and the Institutionalization of Sociology in the French University System," *Archives Européenes de sociologie* 9 (1968): 54. A brief summary of the substance of this course on "Social Solidarity" will be found in the opening lecture of the course on "The Family" which Durkheim offered in the following year. See "Introduction to the Sociology of the Family," chap. 5, this volume.

5. See "Opening Lecture," chap. 1, this volume.

6. Ibid., p. 65. Robert K. Merton cites Durkheim as inspirator of his more explicit formulation of this doctrine, referring specifically to "Two Laws of Penal Evolution." See *Social Theory and Social Structure* (Glencoe, Ill.: Free Press of Glencoe, 1968), p. 115ff.

7. Of Durkheim's three categories, social physiology is most fully elaborated into the following subdivisions: the sociology of religion, the sociology of morality, the sociology of law, economic sociology, linguistic sociology, and aesthetic sociology. Not surprisingly, these categories correspond almost exactly to those used to organize material in *L'Année sociologique*. A reworking of Terry Clark's classification and coding of articles which appeared in the twelve volumes of that journal reveals the relative importance which Durkheim, as editor in chief, attributed to each:

Social Morphology	4
Social Physiology	
Religious Sociology	26
Juridical and Moral Sociology	25
Criminal Sociology	1
Economic Sociology	29
General Sociology	11

See Terry N. Clark, "The Structure and Functions of a Research Institute: The *Année sociologique*," *Archives Européenes de sociologie* 9 (1968): 76-77.

8. If, for present purposes, we emphasize the points of continuity between this article and *Suicide* itself, it should be noted that Durkheim introduced a number of significant changes in his reasoning in the later piece. These are discussed in detail in an excellent article by Philippe Besnard, "Durkheim et les femmes ou le *Suicide* inachevé," *Revue française de Sociologie* 14 (1973): 27-61.

9. Having shown that the suicide rate in Catholic countries tended to be lower than that of Protestant countries, it remained for him to prove that the obvious conclusion was the correct one. It was possible and even plausible, after all, that the higher rate of suicide in Protestant countries resulted largely from an increased propensity to self-destruction on the part of a Catholic minority oppressed by life in a predominantly Protestant social environment. He looked, therefore, at second-order political divisions—for example, the constituent states of the German federation—and noted that the relation was reproduced in these more homogeneous units.

In point of fact, Selvin has shown that, while under specifiable conditions this technique can set limits upon the extent of ecological fallacy, these conditions are not met in the study of a low frequency phenomenon such as suicide. See Hanan C. Selvin, "Durkheim's *Suicide*: Further Thoughts on a Methodological Classic," in *Emile Durkheim*, edited by Robert A. Nisbet (Englewood Cliffs, N.J.: Prentice-Hall, 1965), pp. 113-36.

10. Robert N. Bellah sought to correct this misapprehension in "Durkheim and History," in *Emile Durkheim*, edited by Robert A. Nisbet (Englewood Cliffs, N.J.: Prentice-Hall, 1965), pp. 153-76.

11. See, for example, "Introduction to the Sociology of the Family," chap. 13, this volume.

12. "Sociology and Social Sciences," p. 85, this volume.

13. Ibid., p. 261. In this statement, and also in his remarks concerning "social morphology," Durkheim's position bears a remarkable resemblance to that of the European school of historians known collectively as *les Annalistes*, from the title of the journal, *Annales: Economies, societés, civilisations,* which served as their focal point. See, for example, Fernand Braudel, "History and the Social Sciences," in *Economy and Society in Early Modern Europe; Essays from Annales,* edited by Peter Burke (New York: Harper and Row, 1972), pp. 11-42.

This convergence is no accident. Durkheim had a direct and significant impact on the thought of Henri Berr, the philosopher-historian around whom the founding circle of the *Annales* first gathered. A generation of "synthetic historians," among them Lucien Fevre and Marc Bloch, were avid readers of *L'Année sociologique*. In this connection, see Lukes, *Emile Durkheim, His Life and Work*, p. 394 and Fernand Braudel, "Personal Testimony," *Journal of Modern History* 44 (December, 1972): 448-67.

14. "Divorce by Mutual Consent," pp. 247-48, this volume. Durkheim's most concise statement of this principle is found in *Moral Education* (New York: The Free Press, 1973), p. 42. "The totality of moral regulations really forms about each person an imaginary wall, at the foot of which a multitude of human passions simply die without being able to go further. For the same reason—that they are contained—it becomes possible to satisfy them. But if at any point this barrier weakens, human forces—until now restrained—pour tumultously through the open breach; once loosed, they find no limits where they can or must stop. Unfortunately, they can only devote themselves to the pursuit of an end that always eludes them."

15. See chap. 5, this volume.

16. See pp. 121-22, this volume. I do not wish to imply that Durkheim selected these terms directly in response to Tönnies, but only in response to the type of argument which Tönnies, like other German scholars before him, was advancing. It should be pointed out that in a reply to Durkheim's review, Tönnies asserts that it was never his intention to make the argument Durkheim attributes to him. In any case, Durkheim's terminology was already fixed in 1886 or 1887.

17. See "Course in Sociology: Opening Lecture," especially part 1, below.

18. In his early descriptions of societies based on mechanical solidarity, Durkheim often relies on a rather indecorous simile which likens their aggregation of individual, familial, or clanic units to the arrangement of the segments of a worm (whence "segmental"). In *The Division of Labor*, he describes the consequences of this form of social organization in the following terms: "When society is made up of segments, whatever is produced in one of the segments has as little chance of re-echoing in the

others as the segmental organization is strong. The cellular system naturally lends itself to the localization of social events and their consequences . . . This is no longer true when society is made up of a system of organs. According to their mutual dependence, what strikes one strikes the others, and thus every change, even slightly significant, takes on a general interest." (p. 233) It is interesting to note the strong substantive parallel of Durkheim's argument with the following depiction of simple rural societies in which Karl Marx employs the only slightly more elegant potato metaphor:

The small-holding peasants form a vast mass, the members of which live in similar conditions, but without entering into manifold relations with one another. Their mode of production isolates them from one another, instead of bringing them into mutual intercourse. The isolation is increased by France's bad means of communication and by the poverty of the peasants. Their field of production, the small holding, admits of no division of labor in its cultivation, no application of science, and, therefore, no multiplicity of development, no diversity of talents, no wealth of social relationships. Each individual peasant family is almost self-sufficient; it itself directly produces the major part of its consumption, and thus acquires its means of life more through exchange with nature than in intercourse with society. The small holding, the peasant and his family; alongside them another small holding, another peasant and another family. A few score of these make up a village, and a few score of villages make up a Department. In this way, the great mass of the French nation is formed by simple addition of homologous magnitudes, much as potatoes in a sack form a sackful of potatoes.

See Karl Marx, "The Eighteenth Brumaire of Louis Bonaparte," in *The Marx-Engels Reader*, edited by Robert C. Tucker (New York: W. W. Norton, 1972), p. 515.

19. "Introduction to the Sociology of the Family," p. 206, this volume.

20. "Course in Sociology: Opening Lecture," p. 53, this volume. See also "Introduction to the Sociology of the Family," p. 211, this volume. For more equivocal statements of his principles, see "Two Laws of Penal Evolution," p. 263n.3 below, and *The Rules of the Sociological Method* (New York: Free Press, 1964), chap. 4.

21. *The Division of Labor*, pp. 141-42 n. 21.

22. Emile Durkheim, "Individualism and the Intellectuals," in *Emile Durkheim on Morality and Society*, edited by Robert N. Bellah (Chicago: University of Chicago Press, 1973), pp. 43-57.

23. Throughout this section, I have relied heavily on the excellent paper by Fred Dubow, "Nation-Building and the Imposition of Criminal Law," presented at the 1974 meeting of the American Sociological Society in Montreal, Canada.

24. Actually, it would be more correct to say that while the weakness of *The Division of Labor* thesis was pointed out some time ago—for example, in Robert K. Merton, "Durkheim's *Division of Labor in Society*," *American Journal of Sociology* 40 (1934): 319-28—only in the recent past has the issue generated the heated debates now much in evidence in specialized journals.

25. Durkheim hints at the argument of "Two Laws" in *The Division of Labor* (cf. p. 220 ff.), but this insight is never systematically elaborated.

26. "Two Laws of Penal Evolution," p. 157, this volume. For a criticism of this assumption, see Steven Spitzer, "Punishment and Social Organization: A Study of Durkheim's Theory of Penal Evolution," *Law and Society Review* 9 (1975): 613-37. This article includes an empirical investigation of these questions, based on a more systematic sample drawn from *The Human Relations Area File*.

27. See p. 172, this volume.

28. See Dubow, "Nation Building," p. 2.

29. Some of these variations can be noted in the work of A. S. Diamond, who makes use of a finely graded classification of penal systems according to the level of material culture. See *Primitive Law Past and Present* (London: Methuen, 1971), especially part 2.

30. Here we are speaking of the differentiated and more or less centralized state's right to existence, not of the legitimacy of its particular ideology or policies.

31. See "Deuxième lettre de M. Durkheim," *La Revue néoscholastique* 14 (1907): 613. This letter was written in response to criticisms directed at Durkheim by Simon Deploige in his article "La Genèse du système de M. Durkheim," *La Revue néoscholastique* 14 (1907): 329 ff. Durkheim's assertion that his ideas underwent a radical transformation appears overdrawn, in light of evidence to be presented below. He was undoubtedly motivated to state this position in such unequivocal terms by his desire to counter Deploige's interpretation of the origin and orientation of his theory. It was in this same exchange that Durkheim vehemently denied the influence of various German thinkers, in particular Schaeffle and Wundt, who had, in fact, figured prominently in his intellectual formation. While this attempt to rewrite the history of his own theoretical background is understandable in view of the growing antagonism between France and Germany in the first decade of this century, it would be naive to accept it at face value.

A suggestive, if only loosely documented interpretation of this shift in emphasis is offered in an unpublished dissertation by Bernard Lacroix. Making liberal use of psychoanalytic insights regarding the oedipal conflict, the author notes that the change roughly coincides with the death of Durkheim's father. See Bernard Lacroix, *Emile Durkheim et la question du politique: Essais sur la logique du développement interne d'une construction théorique.* Doctoral thesis: University of Paris, Department of Political Science, 1976.

32. *The Division of Labor*, p. 179. Another such anticipation will be found in *Suicide*, p. 387. See also the discussion in Lukes, *Emile Durkheim, His Life and Work*, pp. 230-32.

33. Durkheim's treatment of these issues can also be found in part 1 of *Moral Education*.

34. He directs this sort of objection at political economy in particular in "Sociology and the Social Sciences."

35. Cf. "Introduction to *Morality*," and "Introduction to the Sociology of the Family," chaps. 12 and 13, this volume.

36. Despite Mauss' claim that Durkheim intended to "recast his whole theory" and Davy's conviction that this book would have "replaced his existing publications on morality," I find nothing in the outline of the book's prospective contents which represents a significant departure from arguments Durkheim had made many times before.

37. "Review of Gaston Richard," p. 136, this volume. See also the "Review of Antonio Labriola," p. 128, where Durkheim cautions the reader against confusing economic materialism with the objective (that is, scientific) conception of history.

38. It seems worth noting that Durkheim's sensitivity on this point could only have been heightened by the tendency on the part of the public to confuse the terms "sociology" and "socialism." An instance where this confusion struck very close to home is documented in the report by M. Perreur available among the papers held in the Durkheim archives of the Maison des Sciences de l'Homme in Paris. In his

account of Durkheim's doctoral defense, which led him to characterize Durkheim as "one of the most distinguished doctors, perhaps the most distinguished whom I have yet seen," Perreur inserts the following aside: "This word 'sociology' is of ill repute, no doubt because it is too closely related with the term 'socialism' which encompasses so many enormities, so much rhetoric and violent nonsense . . ."

39. "Review of Labriola," chap. 6, this volume.

40. See the "Review of Richard," p. 132, this volume. Those who consider this a parochial opinion should remember that Durkheim was most concerned with the narrowly sociological, rather than political or economic merit of socialist theory, and in this area lay Saint-Simon's special value. Furthermore, it could be argued that Durkheim was no more fulsome in this regard than Marx was miserly in adamantly refusing to acknowledge the great debt which socialism in general and his own work in particular owed the founder of the French school.

41. "Review of Antonio Labriola," p. 127, this volume.

42. Of course, the opposite criticism was also advanced, as in Sorel's review, "Les théories de M. Durkheim," *Le Devenir social* 1 (1895): 1-26. But while Sorel's main objection was to the idealism of the book, Durkheim proved more sensitive to the mere note, appended in conclusion, that with Durkheim sociology had proceeded as far as it could go without the help of socialism.

43. "Review of Antonio Labriola," p. 128, this volume. Note that Durkheim had been critical of the liberal economists and utilitarians for much the same reason. He believed that in narrowly focusing on the economic sphere they had missed the full breadth, complexity, and coherence of social life. See "Course in Sociology: Opening Lecture," chap. 1, this volume.

44. "Review of Antonio Labriola," p. 130, this volume. The parallel with arguments advanced by Max Weber in *The Protestant Ethic and the Spirit of Capitalism* is striking, and even more so when we recall that, like Weber, Durkheim turned increasingly to the study of religion as a means of demonstrating the importance of non-material aspects of social life. These substantive parallels and the inter-connections between Weber and Durkheim become more complex and charged with irony when we also consider the review which Durkheim published of Marianne Weber's book on the status of women. In it, Marianne Weber seeks to broaden Engels' conception of family development and the role of women in much the same direction that Max Weber had attempted to expand upon Marx' materialist thesis regarding the origins of capitalism, by stressing the significance of non-economic factors. In his review, Durkheim chides Marianne Weber for refusing to acknowledge the real and efficacious causal role of economic forces in the determination of the status of women, believing that her overly defensive reaction to *The Origins of the Family, Private Property, and the State* served only to heighten the saliency of a work Durkheim considered overrated. See "Review of Marianne Weber," chap. 8, this volume.

45. "Review of Antonio Labriola," pp. 128-29, this volume. He is equally slighting in his review of Richard:

> To be able to make judgements on the sum of our social institutions as categorical as those of the socialists, we would need to know a little better what these institutions are, the causes which have given rise to them, the needs to which they respond, and the relationships which they maintain with one another. But that would require all sorts of research which has, of necessity, barely begun. To speak with precision, socialism cannot, therefore, be scientific. It can only make use of

certain incomplete and fragmentary scientific data in the service of a cause which it supports for reasons which are foreign to science because they go beyond its scope. Think, for example, of how much observation, how many statistical, historical, and ethnographic comparisons are assumed in the least of the theories of *Capital*! Yet not only had Marx not accomplished them in his time, but, for the most part, they still remain to be done.
See "Review of Gaston Richard," pp. 136-37, this volume.

46. Review of Labriola, pp. 129-30, this volume.

47. Max Weber, *The Protestant Ethic and the Spirit of Capitalism* (New York: Scribners, 1958), p. 183.

48. "Review of Albert Schaeffle," p. 94, this volume.

49. Ibid., pp. 96 ff. Schaeffle's idea, though rudimentary, clearly anticipates Parsons' use of the term "medium of exchange."

50. This argument from *The Division of Labor*, book 2, chap. 2, is much more succinctly summarized in a passage from "Introduction to the Sociology of the Family," chap. 13, this volume.

51. Because of its saliency in the sociological literature, the role of social interaction in Durkheim's theory of the determination of suicide rates will not be elaborated here. In *Suicide*, we find numerous extensions of the logic employed in *The Division of Labor*, in particular the claim that the "mental sets" of whole peoples are "related to the way in which the social elements are grouped and organized." See *Suicide* (Glencoe, Ill.: Free Press, 1951), p. 387. In point of fact, it was precisely in the period which stretched from 1895, the year in which *The Rules of the Sociological Method* was published, to 1897, when *Suicide* first appeared, that Durkheim seems to have systematized this strategy of studying the patterns of concentration of social interaction and to have proposed the differentiated subfield of social morphology which will be discussed below.

52. "Two Laws of Penal Evolution," pp. 154-55, this volume.

53. Ibid., pp. 166-67.

54. Ibid., p. 168.

55. *L'Evolution pédagogique en France: Des origines à la Renaissance*, vol. 1 (Paris: Felix Alcan, 1938), pp. 90-91.

56. "Review of Lucien Levy-Bruhl and Emile Durkheim," chap. 9, this volume. In posing the terms of his argument, Durkheim reiterates the differences which separate economic materialism from his own structural approach:

... it is necessary to avoid seeing in this theory of religion a simple restatement of historical materialism: that would be misunderstanding our thought to an extreme degree. In showing that religion is something essentially social, we do not mean to say that it confines itself to translating into another language the material forms of society and its immediate vital necessities. It is true that we take it as evident that social life depends on its material foundations and bears its mark, just as the mental life of an individual depends upon his nervous system and in fact his whole organism. But collective consciousness is something more than a mere epiphenomenon of its morphological basis, just as individual consciousness is something more than a simple efflorescence of the nervous system.

See *The Elementary Forms of the Religious Life* (Free Press: New York, 1965), p. 471.

57. *The Elementary Forms*, p. 241.

58. "Note on Social Morphology," p. 88, this volume.

59. See part 2 of "Sociology and the Social Sciences," chap. 2, this volume.

60. In this pragmatic orientation to the merits of structural analysis, it might be argued, Durkheim differs little in essentials from Marx in the preface to "A Contribution to a Critique of Political Economy" or in "These on Feuerbach," where the superiority of economic materialism is justified in terms of its "scientific precision" but where material factors are accorded no final determining role. Marx's exposition of his methodology in those articles is free of the "vulgar" economic determinism which others later imposed upon it. Without denying the equally significant differences which separate their positions, it is even reasonable to contend that on this basic point the convergence was a natural and necessary consequence of their common assumptions concerning the systemic character of society and the need for a group unit of analysis. In this same vein, it is interesting to note how Arthur Stinchcombe has assimilated the Marxist and structural-functionalist approaches in *Constructing Social Theories* (New York: Harcourt, Brace and World, 1968), chap. 3.

61. In *Suicide* Durkheim raised this search for a just equilibrium to the level of an explanatory framework. The categories of altruistic and fatalistic suicide, though left relatively undeveloped, were carefully inserted in order to complement the more typically modern egoistic and anomic types. A continuum of levels of social regulation was thus defined, permitting Durkheim to argue that *any* excessive state of regulation, whether in the direction of too much or too little social constraint, was harmful.

62. "Crime and Social Health," chap. 11, this volume.

1. COURSE IN SOCIOLOGY: OPENING LECTURE

1. *Cours de philosophie positive*, 4:234. (E. D.)

2. SOCIOLOGY AND THE SOCIAL SCIENCES

1. The word, formed by the coupling of one Latin and one Greek root, has a hybrid quality which purists have often reproached. But despite this unfortunate derivation, it has today won acceptance in all European languages. (E. D.)

2. In the *Tableau des progrès de l'esprit humain*. (E. D.)

3. The principal works of Saint-Simon concerning sociology are: *Mémoire sur la science de l'homme*, 1813; *L'Industrie*, 1816-1817; *L'Organisateur*, 1819; *Du Système industriel*, 1821-1822; *Cathéchisme des industriels*, 1822-1824; *De la Physiologie appliquée aux améliorations sociales*. (E. D.)

4. People object that sociological determinism cannot be reconciled with free will. But if the existence of freedom truly implies the negation of any determinate law, it is an insurmountable obstacle not only for the social sciences but for all sciences. For, since human volitions are always bound to some external movements, it renders determinism just as unintelligible outside of us as within. However, no one, even among the partisans of free will, any longer disputes the possibility of physical and natural sciences. Why would it be otherwise with sociology? (E. D.)

5. See in particular his book *L'Imitation*. (E. D.)

6. The nature of societies doubtless depends in part on the nature of man in general; but the direct, immediate explanation of social facts is to be found in the nature of the society, for, otherwise, social life would not have varied more than the constituent attributes of humanity. (E. D.)

7. See his *Principles of Sociology.* (E. D.)

8. A few examples are to be found in my *Rules of the Sociological Method.* (E. D.)

9. This is the law according to which humanity has successively passed through and must necessarily pass through three stages: first, the theological age; then the metaphysical age; and finally, the age of positive science. (E. D.)

10. What the Germans call *Anthropogeographie* is not unrelated to what we call social morphology. (See the works of Ratzel in Germany and of Vidal de la Blache in France). (E. D.)

11. See Meillet's works, especially the memoire which appeared in *L'Année sociologique,* volume 9, under the title *"Comment les mots changent de sens"* (E. D.)

12. The form of kinship which is established exclusively or essentially through women is called uterine; agnatic kinship is that which is essentially or exclusively established through men. (E. D.)

13. We do not intend to explain here what we think the future relationships of sociology and history will be; we are convinced that they are destined to become ever more intimate and that a day will come when the historical spirit and the sociological spirit will differ only in nuances. In effect, the sociologist can proceed in his comparisons and inductions only on the condition of knowing well and from close up the particular facts which he relies upon, just like the historian; and, on the other hand, the concrete reality which the historian studies can be most directly clarified by the results of sociological inductions. If, then, in what precedes we have differentiated history and sociology, it was not in order to raise an impassable barrier between these two disciplines, since they are, on the contrary, called upon to become more and more closely integrated; it was only in order to characterize as exactly as possible what the sociological perspective possesses in its own right. (E. D.)

14. Durkheim published a study of precisely this sort on the subject of divorce in 1906. See "Divorce by Mutual Consent," chapter 15 in this volume. (M. T.)

15. One must not confuse morals and morality. Morals (*la moralité*) are assessed according to the way in which morality (la morale) is applied. The same kind of question could be posed concerning religion. (E. D.)

3. NOTE ON SOCIAL MORPHOLOGY

1. Here Durkheim refers to his review of Friedrich Ratzel's book, *Politische Geographie,* which immediately followed this explanatory note. (M. T.)

4. REVIEW OF ALBERT SCHAEFFLE

1. See Espinas, *Sociétés animales,* p. 139 and *Revue philosophique* (October, 1882), p. 351. (E. D.)

2. Fouillée, *Science sociale,* p. 76 and passim. (E.D.)

3. The complete work comprises three volumes. The second studies social life. The last two are devoted to a special analysis of each of the social factors. (E. D.)

4. *Bau und Leben,* pp. 8 and 10. (E. D.)

5. Ibid., p. 396. (E. D.)

6. *Bau und Leben,* p. 63. (E. D.)

7. Ibid., p. 7; see also the last chapter of the book. (E. D.)

8. *Sociétés animales,* p. 133 and ff.; see also *Revue philosophique* (October, 1882), p. 353. (E. D.)

9. *Bau und Leben*, p. 84. (E. D.)
10. Ibid., p. 12; on the same subject, see pp. 8, 9ff., 17, 51, 594, etc. (E. D.)
11. *Bau und Leben*, pp. 419, 426. (E. D.)
12. June 15, 1884. (E. D.)
13. Renan: "Qu'est-ce qu'une nation?", Conference at the Sorbonne, March 11, 1882. (E. D.)

5. REVIEW OF FERDINAND TÖNNIES

1. Ferdinand Tönnies, *Gemeinschaft und Gesellschaft* (Leipzig, 1887), p. 26. (E. D.)
2. Ibid., p. 32. (E. D.)
3. Ibid., pp. 46, 47. (E. D.)

6. REVIEW OF ANTONIO LABRIOLA

1. All quotations are from Labriola's book. Page references, where indicated, are from the edition published by Giard et Brière (Paris: n.d.); in this case, p. 149. (M. T.)
2. Ibid., p. 239. (E. D.)
3. Ibid., p. 223. (E. D.)
4. Ibid., p. 237. (E. D.)
5. Ibid., p. 238. (E. D.)
6. Although orthodox economics has its own materialism. (E. D.)

7. REVIEW OF GASTON RICHARD

1. In his use of the term "corporation," Durkheim, through Richard, refers to the medieval economic institution, not the modern, and not to the form of occupational group he proposed in the preface to the second edition of *The Division of Labor* as an organizational device for the regeneration of the collective consciousness. (M. T.)

8. REVIEW OF MARIANNE WEBER

1. Durkheim refers to the edition published by Mohr (Tubingen, 1907). (M. T.)
2. In case of disagreement over the way to raise children, the author asks that daughters be entrusted to the mother's guidance, sons to the father's. (E. D.)
3. The author attributes the consideration which the Roman matron enjoyed to the institution of *justae nuptiae sine manu*, but this historical assertion seems to us quite difficult to justify. (E. D.)

9. REVIEW OF LUCIEN LEVY-BRUHL AND EMILE DURKHEIM

1. Page references to Levy-Bruhl's book are from the edition published by Felix Alcan (Paris, 1919), in this case, p. 77. (M. T.)
2. Ibid., pp. 151–204, pp. 204–57, 261–21. (E. D.)
3. Durkheim, *Les Formes élémentaires de la vie religieuse* (Felix Alcan: Paris, 1912), pp. 12 ff., 205 ff., 290, 386, 518. (E. D.)
4. Ibid., pp. 616–27. (E. D.)
5. Ibid., p. 628. (E. D.)
6. Ibid., pp. 329ff. (E. D.)

10. Two Laws of Penal Evolution

1. Here and throughout this paper, where the French term *répressif* has been translated by its English cognate, it should be understood to retain its original meaning of "crime-repressive" or "penal." (M. T.)

2. See our *Rules of the Sociological Method* [New York: Free Press, 1964], chapter 4. (E. D.)

3. This is why it does not seem to us very scientific to classify societies according to their level of civilization, as Spencer and even Steinmetz did. For, in that case, one must place *one and the same society* in several species according to the political forms which is has successively assumed or according to the levels of civilization through which it has progressively passed. What would we say of a zoologist who fragmented an animal into several species in this way? Yet a society, even more than an organism, has a definite personality, identical to itself in certain respects from the beginning of its existence; consequently, a classification which ignores this fundamental unity gravely distorts reality. One can quite well classify social conditions in that way but not societies. When thus detached from the permanent substratum which links them one to another, these social conditions lack any solid foundation. It is, therefore, the analysis of this substratum and not of the changing life which it supports, which alone can furnish the basis for a rational classification. (E. D.)

4. *Rules of the Sociological Method*, p. 135. (E. D.)

5. Thonissen, *Etudes sur l'histoire du droit criminel des peuples anciens*, chap. 1, p. 142. (E. D.)

6. Ibid., p. 69. (E. D.)

7. Ibid., chapter 1, pp. 60 and 65. (E. D.)

8. Ibid., chap. 1, p. 160. (E. D.)

9. Ibid., chap. 8, p. 281. (E. D.)

10. V. Benzinger, *Hebraeische archaeologie*, pp. 292-203 [sic], p. 71 and 41. (E.D.)

11. Benzinger, *Hebraeische archaeologie*, p. 333; Thonissen, *Etudes*, chap. 2, p. 28. (E. D.)

12. *Deuteronomy* 25:11-22. (E. D.)

13. *Numbers* 35:31. (E. D.)

14. This is explained in a passage in *Deuteronomy* 25:1-2. (E. D.)

16. Benzinger, *Hebraeische archaeologie*, p. 312. (E.D.)

17. See Hermann, *Griech. Antiq.*, II (1) Abtheil, pp. 124-25. (E. D.) Durkheim may refer to Karl Friedrich Hermann's *Lehrbruch der griechischen Antiquitaten*, which had been published in a new edition in 1889. (M. T.)

18. Hermann, *Griech. Antiq.*, pp. 126-27. (E. D.)

19. *C. Midias*, 105, Cf. Plato, *Republic*, II, 362. (E. D.)

20. C. Agoratos, 56, 67, 68; and Demosthenes, *Discours sur l'ambassade*, sec. 137. (E. D.)

21. *Accusation d'empoisonnement*, p. 20. (E. D.)

22. *C. Agoratos*, 54; and Plutarque, *Phocion*, 34. (E. D.)

23. Thonissen, *Etudes*, p. 100. (E. D.)

24. Walter, *Histoire de la procédure civile et du droit criminel chez les Romains*, p. 821; and Rein, *Criminalrecht der Roemer*, p. 55. (E. D.)

25. Livy, 1.28. (E. D.)

26. *Pro Rabirio perduellionis reo*, p. 3. (E. D.)

27. *Coutume de Beauvoisis*, chapter 30, no. 2. (E. D.)

28. *Etablissements de Saint Louis*, book 1, chapters 4 and 11. (E. D.)

29. See du Boys, *Histoire du droit criminel des peuples modernes*, 2:231. (E. D.)

30. The relative mildness of penal law was even more accentuated in the democratically governed parts of the society, namely, in the free communes. "In the free towns," du Boys says [2:370], "as in the communes properly so called, we find a tendency to change punishments to fines and to use shame rather than pain or corrective punishment as a means of repression. Thus, at Mont-Chabrier, he who stole two *sols* had to carry two *sols* around his neck and thus to run all day and all night; moreover, he was fined seven *sols*." Kohler makes a similar remark with respect to the Italian cities. (*Das Strafrecht der Italienischen Statuten rom 12-16. Jahrhundert.*) (E. D.)

31. See du Boys, *Histoire du droit criminel*, 5:234, 237 ff. (E. D.)

32. Ibid., 6:62-81. (E. D.)

33. Ibid., 9:288. (E. D.)

34. *Second Chronicles* 16:10, 18:26; *Jeremiah* 27:15, 16. (E. D.) The reference to Jeremiah is incorrect. Durkheim *may* have been referring to Jeremiah 38:6, 7, 9, etc. This error is not an isolated instance. Durkheim, like many French scholars of his day, was exceedingly casual about citations, as the reader will have noticed. (M. T.)

35. "For all those who shall not observe the law of god and the law of the king, may they forthwith be punished and condemned either to death, banishment . . . , or imprisonment." (*Ezra* 7:26). (E. D.)

36. Post, *Bausteine f. eine allgemeine Rechtsw.*, 1:219. (E. D.)

37. *Discours contre Timocrate*, sec. 151. (E. D.)

38. *Apologie*, p. 37. (E. D.)

39. *The Laws*, VIII, p. 874; IX, p. 864, 880. (E. D.)

40. Hermann, *Griech. Antiq., Rechtsalterthuemer*, p. 126. (E. D.)

41. *Criminalrecht der Roemer*, p. 914. (E. D.)

42. Du Boys, *Histoire du droit criminel*, 5:88-89. (E. D.)

43. Ibid., 6:60. (E. D.)

44. See the article "Carcer" in the *Dictionnaire* by Saglio. (E. D.)

45. Walter, *Histoire*, sec. 856. (E. D.)

46. *Jeremiah* 20:2. (E. D.)

47. Ibid., 32:2. (E. D.)

48. Ibid., 37:15. (E. D.)

49. See the article "Carcer," already cited. (E. D.)

50. See Schaffroth, *Geschicte d. Bernischen Gefaengnisswesens.* (E. D.)

51. See Stroobant, *Notes sur le système pénal des villes flamandes.* (E. D.)

52. Abbé Laffitte, *Le Dahomé* (Tours, 1873), p. 81 (E. D.)

53. Bancroft, *The Native Races of the Pacific States* . . . , 2:453. (E. D.)

54. See Thonissen, *Etudes*, p. 118. (E. D.)

55. Schaffroth, *Geschichte des Bernischen Gefaengnisswesens.* (E. D.)

56. See Letourneau, *Evolution juridique*, p. 199. (E. D.)

11. CRIME AND SOCIAL HEALTH

1. See the February, 1895 edition of *La Revue philosophique.* (E. D.)

2. "Nothing in excess." (M. T.)

12. INTRODUCTION TO *Morality*

1. Two versions of the next conceptual section survive. I have included both first and second drafts, following the example of Marcel Mauss. While the later version is more complete and, no doubt, the one which Durkheim intended to publish, it varies little in substance from the original; for this reason, and because Durkheim failed to provide transitions from and to the main body of the manuscript, I have left the first draft in place and included the second draft herewith. (M. T.)

Some will say that the aim of these practices is to actualize the nature of man and that, seen in this way, they are only practical corollaries and applications of psychology. But first, they are imposed in an imperative fashion, and this obligatory nature, as we shall see, is inherent and essential to them and could not be explained if they truly had their origin in human nature. For if they were no more than an expression or extension of human nature, they would not be imposed upon man. They are, indeed, imposed because they translate something other than man, because they convey another order of reality, because they are in some sense more than human. They are related to another world, one which requires another science.

But what is more, when it is said of morality that it expresses the nature or the goals of man, we understand that man has a definite and unchangeable nature which is always and everywhere identical. It is this invariable entity, which belongs to no specific time or country, which psychology studies. But in point of fact, man, the living being, cannot be encapsulated in any definite, concise formulation. Life—all life—is rich with an infinite number of potential forms of all sorts, some of which are presently actualized in response to specific exigencies and stimuli in the environment, but many of which lie dormant, provisionally unused, merely possible. Perhaps tomorrow when new circumstances arise, they will awaken to existence. All life is change and is refractory to static states. A living being is not made for a unique end; it can lend itself to very different ends and adapt itself to multiple situations. It is always premature to say that it is made for a unique type of existence and to fix for it in advance a limited mode of existence which it cannot change. Such fixity is the negation of life. One cannot say of it once and for all: this is what it is and it cannot become anything else.

This is particularly true of human nature. History is not merely the natural framework of human life; man is a product of history. If we remove him from the historical context, if we try to conceive of him outside time, fixed and immobile, we distort his nature. This immobile man is man no longer. These are not simply secondary aspects or accessory characteristics of his nature which are placed in relief in the course of time; they are profound and essential qualities, fundamental ways of thinking and acting. Primitive man does not have the same representation of time, space, force, causes, and so on, as contemporary man. The concepts which are the basis of his mental life have changed at various moments of history. The concept of personality which is the basis of our present moral life appeared late in this development. The Romans had it only in a veiled and restricted form. The way in which man situates himself in this world, the way in which he conceives of his relationships with other beings and with his peers varies according to conditions of time and place. The moral ideal always depends narrowly upon the precise conception which men create of themselves and of their place in the universe. It cannot, therefore, be deduced from the abstract laws of psychology which are invariable.

Furthermore, is it not a recognized historical truth that morality is one of the essential elements of civilization, and do we not know that civilization is an essentially changing thing? Though it is related to the generic constitution of man in its most general attributes, nonetheless civilization presents the most diverse forms and modalities. Consequently, it must depend on certain causes which are themselves variable and cannot be related directly and uniquely to the general nature of human faculties.

[Durkheim wrote these words in the margin: "Man exists in a general sense. But this is not all of man. Man is always alike, identical to himself, and always different." (M. M.)]

Finally, even assuming that morality were merely an expression of man's nature, it could correspond only to a very determinate aspect of it, namely, his moral nature. The development of the speculative and aesthetic faculties, of technical aptitudes of every sort, of physical force, and so on, has, to be sure, a human interest of the first order; but it does not concern morality. The latter's task is not to prescribe how to cultivate one's intellect, to condition one's body, to refine one's taste or to sharpen one's wit; nor should it regulate all forces of action and all practical faculties, but only those which involve moral questions. But how are we to recognize those which share this characteristic? That is what we need to know. As important as the moral element may be in man, it does not encompass his whole being. But then, what distinguishes this element from the others? How is it to be recognized? By what signs does it manifest itself? So long as we have not answered these questions, we cannot deduce morality from human nature even if the moral ideal truly were entirely contained within it. For we do not know in what man's moral nature consists or what makes him a moral being.

People generally speak of these matters as if the question resolved itself; as if there were no question to begin with; as if the solution followed of itself; as if everyone conceived of it in the same way. Don't all honest men agree on the nature of good and evil and, consequently, on the distinctive characteristics of what is moral? (Quote from Fouillée). [Here Durkheim refers to the quote used in the first draft; see pp. 196-97. (M. T.)] To be sure, it is known that philosophers disagree over the way in which morality should be formulated, translated into concepts, and characterized, and debates on such questions have been going on as long as philosophical thought has been applied to moral matters. And yet, despite these divisions, which demonstrate and testify to the fact that there exists a reality which is not itself manifest, all thinkers agree in the belief that morality consists entirely in a very simple perspective based on an elementary and obvious notion which could under no circumstances result from methodical and laborious—that is, properly scientific—research; it is simply self-evident. Though it may pose problems because men fail to perceive this self-evident entity in the same way, still it neither results from nor occasions problems of itself. The whole trick is properly to grasp this self-evident entity, not to confuse it with another, and to formulate it in an appropriate manner. Yet everyone recognizes that it can only be postulated.

But what are we to think of a supposedly self-evident truth on the nature of which people are in disagreement and on the expression of which men are in conflict? By what right is it presumed that a self-evident truth, namely, moral reality, reveals itself to the observer all on its own? For the scientist, there is no reality which is self-evident; there is none which in the initial stages of research is not and must not be treated as an unknown quantity. In order to discover its nature, we first make use of the external signs which are its most obvious manifestations. We then substitute others in place of these external and perceptible signs as our research progresses. But it is only when we have gone beyond the realm of sensory appearances that it is possible to discover the profound characteristics of the thing itself, those which comprise its essence, insofar as that word can be used in scientific terminology. The scientist who undertakes the study of light or electricity knows only what his senses perceive; he sees in them an object of study. It is only when he pushes the analysis further—both further and deeper—that he arrives at a different conception of it. Why would it be otherwise with moral reality? We are told that it depends on the nature of man. But the nature of man is a complex thing. What does it say about man? Does it concern the individual or the collective being? And what aspect of one or the other does it translate? If we wish to place ourselves in the state of mind which the scientific method demands, we must tell ourselves that, at this point in our inquiry, we know nothing and can know nothing. We are totally ignorant of what makes man a moral being, of the causes which have given rise to the diverse states of mind, ideas, and sentiments which constitute morality. Why does man present this gestalt, this quite specific state of mind and of will which animals do not know or know only in an indirect and purely analogous form? To what do these states and attitudes correspond in reality? What is there in the milieu in which the human being lives which determines and accounts for them? (E. D.)

2. At this point there occurs another discontinuity in the manuscript, which has been resolved by suppressing a few words and picking up the remainder of this paragraph further down the page. (M. T.)

3. Here ends the material which would have been replaced by the revised draft included in footnote 1. (M. T.)

4. Durkheim wrote these words in the margin: "They are precepts of a certain type, the singular properties of which are recognized by all." (M. M.)

5. The expression which we used in teaching was "Physics or Science of Mores and of Law." Explication of the two words. (E. D.)

6. Durkheim wrote these words in the margin: "Opposition between mores and morality." (M. M.)

13. INTRODUCTION TO THE SOCIOLOGY OF THE FAMILY

1. This table is, of course, only provisional, and we present it only in order to clarify our ideas. We shall be able to provide something a little more definite only at the conclusion of the course.

Moreover, you will note that all the above examples are borrowed from law and not from mores. This is because the determination of contemporary domestic mores constitutes a problem which will come up in good time but which we cannot presume, in our first lecture, to have been resolved. (E. D.)

2. See Letourneau, *Evolution du mariage et de la famille.* (E. D.)

3. (Stuttgart, 1884), 259 pages. (E. D.)

4. (Leipzig, 1888), 597 pages. We can only mention in passing the book by Wilcken, *Over de verwandschaft en het Huwelijks en Erfrecht by de volken van het maleische Ras*, which I have not been able to read. I know of it only through Hellwald, who gives it the highest praise. (E. D.)

5. (Geneva and Paris, 1884), 325 pages. (E. D.)

6. Notably *Geschlects genossenschaft der Urzeit* (Oldenburg, 1875), 122 pages. (E. D.)

7. (Stuttgart, 1861); (Strassburg, 1880), 278 pages. (E. D.)

8. *Origines de la civilisation.* (E. D.)

9. *Studies in Ancient History* (London, 1886), 387 pages. (E. D.)

10. *Ancient Society* (London, 1877), 560 pages. (E. D.)

11. *Kamilaroi and Kurnai* (Melbourne, 1880), 372 pages. (E. D.) Durkheim has misspelled the name of A. Howitt. (M. T.)

12. *Untersuchungen über die roemische Ehe* (Stuttgart, 1853). (E. D.)

13. In his *XII Tafeln, passim.* (E. D.)

14. (London, 1879), 494 pages. (E. D.)

15. *Das Recht der Eheschliesung* (Leipzig, 1863). (E. D.)

16. *Trauung und Verlobung* (Weimar, 1876). (E. D.)

17. *Die altdeutsche Verlobung in ihren Verhoeltnisse zu dem Mundium* (Jena, 1879). (E. D.)

18. *Mutterrecht und Raubehe und ihre Reste im Germanischen Recht und Leben* (Breslau, 1883). (E. D.)

19. *Geschichte des ehelichen Güterrechts in Deutschland,* 1863-1874. (E. D.)

20. *Geschichte der deutschen Vermundschaft Braunschweig,* 1866-1875. (E. D.) The correct reference is *Geschichte des deutschen Vormundschaft.* Braunschweig, 1862-75. (M. T.)

21. *Die Ehe verhoeltnisse der alten Iuden* (Leipzig, 1881). (E. D.)

22. *Die Ehe im Islam* (Vienna, 1876). (E. D.)

23. *Uber die hoeusliche Verhoeltnisse der alten Chinesen* (1863). (E. D.)

14. The Conjugal Family

1. This article is based on a fragmentary manuscript and notes taken by Marcel Mauss and other students in Durkheim's 1892 course on the family. Despite meticulous editorial work, the process of reconstruction has produced a text less fluid and concise than was Durkheim's norm. This version appeared with the following introduction by Mauss.

This is the seventeenth and last lecture in the course on the family which Durkheim offered at Bordeaux in 1892. It was delivered on April 2nd of that year.

It had long been Durkheim's intention to publish the whole of his research on the family. However, shortly before the war, at the time when he was undertaking the publication of his book *Morality,* he hesitated. He intended to include only its substance, which had become his course on domestic morality and which comprised the second part of his course on morality. The war settled the question. Long before his death, Durkheim had definitively renounced this project, which all those who took the course would have liked to have seen completed. He recommended that we publish only his "Domestic Morality."

"The Family" surely could not have appeared in the definitive form of a vast treatise except at the cost of a lengthy work of verification and elaboration. The history of domestic law, especially in primitive societies, had made immense progress since 1892.

On the other hand, in reviewing this course, a great many sections still seemed so accurate and profound after more than a quarter of a century that we thought it our duty to have the greatest possible audience profit from it.

This concluding lecture is quite brief and, in Durkheim's thought, would have called for many complements. Starting with the earliest volumes of *L'Année sociologique*, a quantity of data which facilitate the elaboration of this question can be found under the rubric of "Domestic Organization," which Durkheim was in charge of until the end. (M. M.)

2. The preceding lecture dealt with the paternal family. That is the name which Durkheim gave to the domestic institutions of the Germanic peoples and which he sharply distinguished from those of the Roman patriarchal family. The principal difference consisted in the absolute and excessive concentration of power in the Roman case as the *patria potestas* of the *pater familias*; the rights of children, the wife, and especially those relatives in the maternal line were, on the contrary, characteristics of the paternal family. (M. M.)

3. Collective responsibility, and so forth. (M. M.)

4. Today sociologists would, of course, refer to the "nuclear family." (M. T.)

5. Here Durkheim alludes to the right of testament and to the right of alienation. (M. M.)

6. Durkheim had abundantly demonstrated the fact that the patriarchal family, in particular the Roman version, consisted in a concentration of the rights of the former group of undivided agnates in the person of the *pater familias*. (M. M.)

7. In French law. But we must not forget that Durkheim proposed, in the first sentence of this lecture, to explain in particular the family of the *Code Civil* in 1892. (M. M.)

8. I have added these two clauses on the basis of old notes taken in this course, and of the context. In the manuscript, the sentence is merely written in the margin. (M. M.)

9. "Himself" (?) Illegible but unimportant word. (M. M.)

10. Here Durkheim alludes to one of his preceding lectures in which he opposed emancipation, under barbarian law, to expulsion from the patriarchal family, in Greece and Rome, as means of breaking the bonds of agnatic relationship. (M. M.)

11. The word *zone* is used by Durkheim to designate more or less proximate circles of relatedness; it is part of his general nomenclature and rather self-evident. (M. M.)

12. Just as the phratry exists beside the clan; the clan beside the uterine or masculine or agnatic family; the agnatic family beside the patriarchal family, and so on. (M. M.)

13. In analyzing the Germanic paternal family in a preceding lecture, Durkheim had shown that, for the first time in the history of domestic institutions, both maternal and paternal lineages had been placed on an equal footing. The paternal uncle and the maternal uncle, the nephews on the mother's side and the father's side have the same rights. "This is why," he said, "I propose that we call the collateral family thus constituted the cognatic family." He quoted from Heusler: "The *Sippe* is absolutely cognatic. Thus, the *parantèle* (Latin translation of the word *Sippe*) of the Salic Law designates the parents descended from both sides, *parentes tam de patre quam de matre* (title 42) . . . etc. . . ." (*Institutionem des Deutschen Privatrechts*, 2: 172). Cf. *L'Année sociologique*, 8:429. (M. M.)

14. Here Durkheim recalls the elements of his demonstration of the extension of relatedness in the female line: the matter of penal responsibility in the case of *Wergeld* (*Salic Law*, title 88); the matter of the prospective husband's redemption of

the widow's right to remarry from the latter's uterine nephew or even, in the absence of various other degrees, from the son of the maternal cousin (*Salic Law*, title 44); and the other traces of the maternal family, properly speaking. (M. M.)

15. This sentence is in parentheses in the text and can be ignored by those not familiar with Durkheim's nomenclature or with the importance which he attached to the study of what he called the secondary zones. We need only explain that he meant that while, until now, there were always distinct traces of the extended family and distinct traces of the clan alongside the restricted family; with the modern conjugal family, on the contrary, there are no longer any distinct traces of the cognatic family, now conceived of as derived from conjugal relatedness—that is, from the simple original couple. (M. M.)

16. It is impossible to summarize in a footnote the whole of Durkheim's theory or especially his proofs: of the progressive contraction of the politico-domestic group; of the transition from the amorphous, exogamous clan, that vast group of relatives, to the differentiated clan or families in the proper sense of the word, whether matrilineal or patrilineal; from there to the undivided family of agnates; to the patriarchal, paternal, and maternal families; to the conjugal family. The phenomenon of the reduction in the number of members of the family and of the concentration of the familial bonds is, according to him, the dominant phenomenon in the history of familial institutions. See Durkheim's review of Grosse's *"Formen der Familie,"* in *L'Année sociologique* 1:326ff. (M. M.)

17. Here Durkheim alludes to his deduction from the patriarchal family, both Roman and Chinese, which he interpreted as a feudal concentration of a group of agnates under a head of family. Granet, in his *Polygynie Sororale* (1920), has admirably illuminated the matter with excellent Chinese texts. (M. M.)

18. The conclusion seems to be missing, both here and in my course notes. It is obviously the following: "The familial group is thus enabled to contract, up to the extreme limit." (M. M.)

19. Durkheim demonstrated in an earlier lecture that the Germanic paternal family does not presuppose the undivided agnatic family, but came directly from the matrilineal family and retained numerous traces of it. (M. M.)

20. Here, according to my old course notes, Durkheim indicated that Anglo-Saxon law already admitted this absolute right of testament. (M. M.)

21. According to my notes, at this point in the lecture Durkheim added certain important considerations on the defunct character of literary, industrial, and commercial property (the rights of authors, the right to trademarks and patents), which fall in the public domain and which the owner cannot transmit beyond a certain term. He returned to this subject later in this lecture. (M. M.)

22. By this time, Durkheim had already given a first course on suicide. Here we recognize the ideas which he published in 1896 in his book on this subject. (M. M.)

23. Here Durkheim mentioned to us the various rights of the surviving marital partner: the right of usufruct in French law and the right of inheritance *ab intestat* in Anglo-Saxon law. (M. M.)

24. See *Suicide*. (M. M.)

25. The manuscript contains no trace of the development which Durkheim gave to this idea. Thanks to my notes, I can fairly well reconstruct it as follows: "[Do civil servants, soldiers, and scholars who give the state a poorly recompensed life of labor have in view the prospect of hereditary transmission? Do authors, artists, scholars, engineers, and inventors, whose work so quickly falls within the public domain and

whose literary, artistic, and industrial property is so eminently uninheritable, have in view the prospect of transmitting it to their children as perpetual property? Why do they work? Is their work not as effective as or more effective than that of anyone else? One can, therefore, work without having as one's sole aim to endow one's children with a legacy.]" (M. M.)

26. Durkheim himself added the parentheses in the manuscript. He did, however, speak these sentences, the last few of which I have been able to complete. He no doubt intended to delete them in a subsequent draft. (M. M.)

15. DIVORCE BY MUTUAL CONSENT

1. *Annales de démographie internationale* (September, 1882). (E. D.)

2. To be precise, we must add that Bertillon also invokes the greater aptitude for resignation that Catholicism develops in its adherents, especially among women; this would dispose them to patiently suffer. But the law applies equally to Protestant countries. (E. D.)

3. In the first figure in both columns of this table and in tables 3 and 4, Durkheim commits an error in transposing the data from table 22 of the English language edition of *Suicide*. As pointed out by Philippe Besnard, he constitutes the category for individuals 20 to 30 years of age by *adding*, rather than averaging, the rates for the two original categories of individuals 20 to 25, and 25 to 30 years of age. (Moreover, in the case of unmarried men residing in Paris he adds them incorrectly; the figure 986 should read 1086.) The result is a rate so anomolously high that one wonders that Durkheim did not realize his error. Because he is consistent in miscalculating the rate for both Paris and the provinces, the coefficient of preservation remains essentially unchanged, and as Durkheim does not refer to the absolute rates, the error does not have serious repercussions. See Philippe Besnard, "Durkheim et les femmes où le *Suicide* inachevé," *Revue française de sociologie* 14 (1973): 58. (M. T.)

4. We do not mention the suicides of married persons under twenty-five years of age because the figures are too small (one per year per million); one cannot, therefore, draw reliable conclusions. (E. D.)

5. See the facts which demonstrate this law in *Suicide* [(Glencoe, Ill.: Free Press, 1951), p. 132 ff.]. (E. D.)

6. See n.3 (M. T.)

7. Ibid.

8. The preceeding figures even show that the married woman commits suicide more often in Paris than in the provinces. But nothing permits us to think that this augmentation can be traced to the state of conjugal society in Paris, for there are many other causes in the Parisian milieu which could explain it. (E. D.)

9. See *Suicide*, p. 188, and the explication of this phenomenon, p. 215. (E. D.)

10. One hears of 159 and even of 242 judgments of divorce rendered in a single sitting. See Valinsi, *L'Application de la loi de divorce en France*, p. 102. (E. D.)

Index

272